I HEAR THEIR VOICES

A VETERINARY MEMOIR

Irving Pudalov

I HEAR THEIR VOICES

A VETERINARY MEMOIR

IRVING PUDALOV

COGENT PUBLISHING

Cogent Publishing, a division of The Whitson Group, Inc.
3 Miller Road
Putnam Valley, NY 10579
Email: CogentPub@aol.com

Copyright © 2000 by Irving Pudalov, DVM

All rights reserved. No part of this book may be reproduced, stored in or introduced into an information storage and retrieval system, or transmitted, in any form or by any means (electronic, mechanical, photocopying, recording or otherwise), without the prior permission in writing from both the copyright owner and the publisher of this book.

Published by Cogent Publishing, a division of The Whitson Group, Inc., 3 Miller Road, Putnam Valley, NY 10579.

Manufactured in the United States of America.

Library of Congress Cataloging-in-Publication Data is available on request.

ISBN 0-925776-05-X
10 9 8 7 6 5 4 3 2 1

To Mary, whose participation and inspiration made this memoir possible.

PROLOGUE

It was 5:00 a.m., ten below zero and the cold was seeping into my bones. All my liquid medications had frozen solid and would have to be thawed out in a milk pail of warm water. I recoiled at the thought of having to handle my obstetrical instruments, knowing they would glue to my hands—a sensation much worse than scratching your fingernail on a blackboard. Now I understood why Eskimos rub noses rather than kiss.

The morning cold had permeated the car and my body. My car's chronic bronchitis was worse than ever. Its persistent cough and expectoration suggested a deep-seated problem. I hand-choked the engine to prevent a stall as it bucked along the road. The car heater would scarcely heat and I cussed at its impotence. In spite of all my clothing, I convulsively shuddered.

I had been awakened by Tom Henzel. He had been trying to help a first-calf heifer calve without success.

"She's too small and the calf's too big," he explained. "I need you badly. Dress warm, Doc. My face and ears about froze walking to the house to make this call. The wind blew right through me."

His voice reminded me of my mother once again advising me to dress warmly. There were many calls to be made but a calving had priority, and delivering a live, healthy animal was always an upbeat thing for me.

The frozen, rutted country road caused my front wheels to grope wildly for a pathway, while my cold hands struggled with a willful steering wheel to maintain control. Cottony patches of fog weaved through hibernating fields of corn stubble. Occasionally, the fog meandered across the road obscuring my vision. I crept along listening for the gravel crunch of my tires to indicate I was still on the road. I emerged from a shroud of fog to be greeted by the glimmer of sunrise gilding the landscape. It was a wondrous scene, but my pleasure was dispelled by uncontrollable shivering. My fingers were tingling with cold, and all I could think of was the warmth they would enjoy inside the uterus of the calving heifer.

You might think I was experiencing severe distress alone on the prairie, bitterly cold, cursing my existence, but nothing could be more untrue. This was the environment I wanted to live and work in. With its teeming abundance of crops and animals, it was a granary that could feed untold millions. There was no need for hunger, no need for malnutrition and its accompanying devastation of human life. The earth was fair and there was food for all.

To live and work in this environment was stimulating and gratifying. I was a part of its remarkable capacity to raise livestock. Being available to treat farm animals day and night, seven days a week, might sound like a fierce sentence to endure, but I found that it nurtured me. I still miss those moments of quiet exultation, that elusive sense of accomplishment. It was something I had done on a wintry sub-zero night or on a glorious May day as oat shoots popped from the soil. Sure somebody else might have done it, but it was I who was called. I was there to minister to that sick animal.

The sense of achievement, the physical hardships and a loving wife made the late '40s and '50s a most memorable part of my life. Everyday was an adventure, and as I relive my experiences in my memoirs, I still feel the spirit of that life within my soul.

EARLY DAYS

The overworked dray horse, succumbing to the summer heat, lay flat out on sizzling black asphalt. As I watched its final agonal moments I suddenly felt that the poor animal only needed some water. I commandeered my mother's mop bucket, filled it with cold water and rushed back to the horse. Flies, the vultures of our neighborhood, had descended upon his heaving body, probing his eyes and nostrils. I tried to raise the animal's head so it could drink, but the sheer weight of it was more than a ten year old could handle. There were plenty of bystanders but no one offered to help. Unable to get the animal to drink, I poured the water over the horse's body hoping to cool him down.

"Get away from that horse," I heard a voice say.

I turned to see a policeman standing behind me holding a gun.

I remember pleading with the policeman not to shoot the animal. I was convinced all it needed was some water to be able to stand.

"Get away from that horse, boy."

I began to sob, "All he needs is water."

"God damn it, move," his voice boomed. "If you don't get out of the way, I'll take you to the lockup."

I did not budge, but continued to kneel over the animal. My friend, Dave, thought I was praying.

"God, save him," I murmured. I was startled to feel Dave's hand laid gently on my shoulder.

"Come on, Puddy, (my nickname at that time) let's go. I'll buy you a Charlotte Russe. My treat—I got the money, too."

I turned to see Dave tugging at my arm. A small crowd had gathered and I half expected my mother to come charging through to berate me for confronting a policeman. I let Dave lead me away. I could not face my mother's anger, or the strong recriminations of my father when she told him what had happened.

I heard the policeman's voice, "Stand back, everybody, stand back."

The shot imploded within me. I began to tremble and sob uncontrollably. The poor animal had been shot in the head and was spasmodically quivering. With the passage of considerable steamy manure, his death throes were over. His tongue lolled from the side of his mouth and became peppered with grime. Flies were already feasting on the red blood that crawled on the black asphalt.

"Move on. The show is over. And I mean you too, boy," the policeman said.

Our neighbor, Abe Newman, appeared with two empty buckets. He proceeded to fill them with manure.

"Fertilizer for my garden," he said. "You can't believe how this stuff makes things grow."

I looked on in amazement as he carried his two buckets of horse manure from the street. I had seen people gather manure from the streets, but never realized they were taking it for purposes other than keeping the streets clean.

A garbage truck came that afternoon to remove the horse from the street. Everybody said the animal would end up as glue. I had no idea how that animal could be reduced to a jar of glue and explanations were hard to come by.

The nonchalance of the onlookers was most disturbing. There were no expressions of regret—only a sideshow curiosity. For myself, the effect was a mind-altering experience. I wondered if one could dispose of an animal without at least trying to help in some way. Perhaps he only needed some water to revive. When I discussed it with my father, he said, "It's only a horse." I could not dismiss it so easily.

We lived in a tiny apartment on the top floor of a brownstone, having moved from a cold water flat whose only heat came from a coal-burning stove. Hot water was obtained from a kettle that lived on that stove. The brownstone introduced me to the unbelievable luxury of hot water coming out of a faucet and the warm caress of central heating in winter.

I was playing hopscotch in front of our brownstone waiting for my mother to take me to buy a pair of shoes. My shoes had been repeatedly repaired and were now ready to be secretly reclaimed for part of a slingshot I was making. My father said he had never seen anyone abuse shoes the way I did. I must admit that the clamps on my Union Hardware roller skates did chew up the soles, but I was sure he would confiscate my skates if I told him about it.

I remember my father to be a very harried man in those days. Each day he would return from the garment district, his face set and glum.

"Another failure," he would tell my mother. "The man's out of business and he owes me money. There's no way I can collect. The man has to support his family."

He was not an unloving father, but demonstrations of affection were rare indeed. I never saw him embrace or kiss my mother. In fact she would always address him by his last name. We were not the type of family that greeted each other with hugs and kisses. All my overt affection was reserved for animals.

Other than a shot glass of Canadian Club, two on a very good day in the garment district, my father never drank. He had an aversion to saloons, considering them alien, hostile places, not to mention expensive. When my father reached for his shot glass, I immediately disappeared from his view. He always insisted that I have a drink with him.

"Just a sip. You don't want to be a sissy, do you?"

What perverse pleasure he had, seeing me gag on the whiskey, still mystifies me. Yet, I never for one minute felt that he didn't love us.

During that period of my life, I was only peripherally aware of the Wall Street crash of 1929 and its subsequent depression. With eight million unemployed, the bread lines threading through the streets of New York were more of a curiosity than a reality to me. I know my father gave my mother considerably less household money, but I never heard a murmur of complaint. Our needs continued to be met as they always had been. I was never aware of what sacrifices my parents made to provide us with food, shelter and clothing. They must have been considerable.

One day while I was absorbed in a game of hopscotch, a small dog on a leash came lunging down the street pulling a little girl behind him.

"Stop pulling, Buster," she yelled. "You're going to choke yourself."

Buster paused, gulped some air, and continued onward. Before I knew it,

Buster and I were on a collision course. As he lunged forward, my knee collided with his head and I heard him yipe. The next yipe came from me. He bit me inside my thigh, tearing my knickers. At that moment, the crisis in my life was not the bite, but the obviously torn knickers. It took but a moment for my mother to materialize and another for her to see my torn knickers greedily blotting blood.

"How did this happen?" she demanded, her voice icy and contained. Undoubtedly she was deciding how best to repair the damage to my knickers.

"I was bitten by that little dog down the street," I blurted out.

Suddenly her face contorted with fear and horror. She grasped me by the shoulders.

"My God, do you know what you have done?"

"I tore my knickers," I responded blithely.

Then she vigorously slapped a part of my anatomy I thought to be inviolate—my face. I began to sob uncontrollably, not that her slap hurt me, but because I felt she had violated an unspoken agreement. Abruptly she grasped my arm and we started to walk. There was an urgency in her manner, and I was afraid to ask where we were going. "Walk faster. We have to hurry."

"Where are we going, Mama?"

"We're going to the hospital. Stop talking and walk faster."

I had trouble keeping up with her, and was being half dragged along. Mama had always been a fast walker.

"Why are we going to the hospital, Mama?"

"Because you're a stupid boy to have let yourself get bitten by a sick dog. Now you'll get sick if we don't hurry."

"But Mama, the dog is not sick."

"Then why did he bite you?"

"We bumped into each other while I was playing. I might have stepped on his foot."

"Dogs are not supposed to bite little boys. My little dog, Tubby, would never bite—only sick dogs bite."

This was the first I heard that she had a dog named Tubby.

"In American we called him Tubby, because he was such a nice fat little dog," she said.

There's a lot I didn't know about Mama and I found the revelation exciting. Maybe she'll let me get a little dog. I'd even call him Tubby, just to please her. I was momentarily a happy boy.

Suddenly there loomed before us a building of monstrous proportions. It dwarfed and shadowed the neighboring brownstones. Carved in stone were the words, "Beth Moses"—The House of Moses. Was this a synagogue we were going to? I immediately felt better. We entered through the wide front doors and reality struck when we were confronted by a nurse whose personality seemed as starched as her white uniform. My mother informed her that I had been bitten by a dog.

"Dog bite you, boy? Come with me quickly."

She led us down corridor after corridor and finally into a room with an eye-watering acrid odor. A young man approached.

"Where were you bitten, young fella?"

I pointed to my torn knickers.

"Take off your pants," he ordered.

My mother helped me off with my knickers. My B.V.D.s hung limply, encircling my body. They were torn and blood stained as well. The doctor examined my wound.

"Hmm, I see you had some bleeding. That's good. You did good."

I appreciated his friendliness and was glad my bleeding pleased him. Meanwhile my mother sat on the edge of a white enameled stool, clutching my knickers to her chest. Her face was ashen... maybe her thoughts were rooted in some horrible memory.

A nurse entered carrying a tray containing a glass-stoppered jar, a syringe and some cotton swabs. If all they were worried about was that small wound certainly a little Mercurochrome would have sufficed. A firm hand on my shoulder forced me to sit down. The doctor examined my bite wound more carefully and turned to the nurse.

"I see it is a fairly deep wound, and we will have to swab it with phenol."

The word "deep" immediately alerted me to the fact that I was about to experience pain. And as if to confirm my expectations, the doctor turned to me and said, "Now this will hurt a bit, but I know you are a brave little boy."

The nurse held my leg tightly as the doctor proceeded to swab the solution into my wound. My gasp of pain was mirrored in my mother's face. Then it was over. The acid had blanched my wound giving it a frosty appearance. My mother came over to hug and kiss me. I had never known her to be so demonstrably affectionate.

Suddenly my right eye began to hurt, and blink after blink and, rub upon rub would not dislodge the irritant. The doctor had left and the nurse remained to question us about the whereabouts of the dog. My eye was so painful I could hardly answer her questions. The nurse totally ignored my discomfort, choosing to focus exclusively on her note pad.

"Nurse, would you be so kind as to look at my little boy's eye? It's hurting him a lot."

"I'm very busy and won't have time to look at his eye just now."

"But it'll only take a minute," My mother was pleading.

"You people are more trouble than everybody else," the nurse said, still looking down at her note pad.

My mother flushed—her lips pinched together. She said nothing, but once again her memories of the old country flared in her mind. She swallowed hard and said, "Nurse, will you please look at his eye?"

"Didn't you hear me before? When I have time," the nurse replied, and abruptly left the room.

My mother was truly disturbed by this crisis upon crisis. She looked intently at my bloodshot eye and ordered me to stand against the wall. Quickly she steadied my head with one hand, placed the fingers of her other hand against my eyelids to keep them open, and leaned toward me. I felt her lips against my eyelids and suddenly her tongue darted out. I felt its tip, soft and spongy, wiggle inside my eye, and then it was over. Somehow her tongue had displaced whatever was in my eye and I immediately felt better. I looked at my mother in amazement. Her face had flushed and it seemed that this intimate contact caused her some embarrassment.

We waited in the room for almost an hour not knowing whether or not to leave. Finally the nurse returned, and with a voice that hissed and scratched at us like a straw broom on the tile floor she swept us out of the room.

Sometimes a traumatic event produces a life-long fear, but I was fortunate to react otherwise. After all, I decided it was just as much my fault as the dog's. I became increasingly curious about the dogs, cats and horses that populated our streets and alleys. I yearned for a pet, but was forbidden even to go near one. My father was outraged when I dared broach the possibility of having a pet.

"You almost died because of a dog bite. Look at the gray hair you've given your mother," he said.

I looked toward her and thought I detected a wisp of a smile. I knew she would never openly disagree with her husband. Meanwhile I began to fantasize about animals. I saw them in cloud formations, in the shadows of evening, and in my day and night dreams.

My romance with animals reached a high intensity when I became a reader. They were truly alive in books that abounded in the public library.

Despite the fact that my only contacts with animals were with the dead horse and the dog that bit me, I made my choice of what I thought to be the ultimate profession—veterinary medicine. My exposure to animals continued to be rare indeed. Even a trip to the zoo was frowned upon, but my life within books continued to enthrall.

Once I'd made my decision to become a veterinarian all my energies were focused toward that goal. I talked to my grade advisors and my best friend, but quickly found that they had minimal knowledge of my chosen field. Fearing some adverse repercussions, I never mentioned it to my family.

My mother constantly encouraged me to become a teacher.

"When you're a teacher, you're set for life. Good money, time off—a nice, easy clean job," she said.

"Become a doctor," my father would say. "You'll be powerful and important—you'll control lives. But I don't know if you're smart enough to become a doctor. Everybody takes advantage of you. You don't have a mind of your own. If things don't work out, maybe you should become a lawyer. Lawyers are not as smart as doctors."

I listened to all their advice, but my mind was made up. When the moment of truth arrived and I told them I was going to veterinary school, my father angrily announced, "Jews don't go to such schools. Jews don't become pig doctors, it's a sin. I'm against it. What am I going to tell the business people on 38th street... that my oldest son is a pig doctor?"

His reaction was entirely predictable and I listened to his criticisms day after day, but I was fortified by years of dreams. My longings were sustained by occasional barks or yowls in the night, and the clippity-clops of horse-drawn milk wagons in the morning. My life was devoid of animals; they were a mirage within my mind.

My motivation to become a veterinarian was reinforced during my passage through high school and college. Over my parents' objections I was accepted into veterinary school just as World War II broke out. To speed graduation of veterinarians, summer holidays were eliminated, and since my financial survival depended on my working through the summers, this produced my first financial crisis. Being twenty one years of age, I could not burden my family with my support, nor were they capable of it. My parents were living marginally with two other children to care for.

Desperate for funds, I worked as a waiter Friday night through Sunday. In addition, I cleaned and restocked biochemistry labs early mornings before classes, became a Gallup poll-taker and sold school rings. My passage through veterinary school was less auspicious than I would have liked, but the animals I worked with made every day a joyous event.

The goal was in sight and I persevered.

Finally I was ceremoniously awarded a Doctor of Veterinary Medicine degree and turned loose on an unsuspecting animal population. I had a reasonable amount of erudition but minimum skills. I was more of an emotional than a functional veterinarian. There was so much to learn—a never-ending process.

For individuals to practice veterinary medicine, each state required a licensing exam—usually given twice a year. I knew that the State of Illinois was having an exam two days after I graduated in December, and since Illinois was one of my target states to practice, I journeyed to Chicago to take the exam. Illinois was the "Prairie State," blessed with fertility and diverse livestock, but above all with industrious and dedicated farmers. To practice amidst such munificence was the realization of my quest. The blast of icy air that greeted me when I got off the train was just a taste of the weather I was to endure for years to come.

Now began a waiting game. First—to see if I passed the exam and obtained a license to practice. Second—to await my induction into the army, and that could take months insofar as there had just been a recent call up. I checked into an immense Y.M.C.A. hotel in Chicago and was given a large closet that contained a narrow bed, a skinny chair and a miniature chest of drawers—furniture more suitable for a large doll house—and no maid service. A common bathroom was very yonder down the hall. For the penurious person that I was, the dollar-a-day charge, paid in advance, suited me fine. With an adequate meal at the Y priced forty to fifty cents, plus two dollars every other week from my mother, I could survive for three to four months, providing I reduced the cost of any dalliance to a Dutch treat. If I failed to gain employment, my next recourse would be the Salvation Army. I heard they took pity on down-and-out veterinarians, probably sending them to the Congo for missionary work.

I confess that I was not distressed by my circumstances. I was responsible for only myself. My D.V.M. degree was my main asset, and I felt something would soon be forthcoming. However, I was lonely and thought back to my younger days when I held at bay a lovely girl because she wanted to get married. She would not wait, wanted to support and care for me, but I would have none of it. It seemed unnatural for a woman to support a man no matter how much they loved each other. She decided I was a lost cause and married another. Suppose I had married her? How would we have managed under my present circumstances?

My veterinary journal listed an ad by the City of Chicago for a meat inspector at the stockyards. I thought this might be okay until I was inducted, plus it would give me some economic solvency. My D.V.M. degree qualified me and I was employed immediately.

My job was to inspect cattle before their slaughter and inspect their viscera and meat afterwards. My days were a living hell. My nights were nightmares of bellowing, screaming, stampeding animals on their way to slaughter. When I awoke, my pajamas were soaked in sweat. I was horrified that I had to go back once again to the killing floor.

It was not long before I began to doubt myself... doubt my profession.

Above all I wanted to practice large animal medicine—cows, horses, pigs. How naive I was not to consider the ultimate destiny of most of my patient... I was to be their pied piper, leading them to slaughter. Was this the work I really wanted to do? Perhaps mother knew best when she said I should be a teacher.

Amid the odor of death and entrails and the ear-splitting cacophony of the butchering, I withdrew within myself to consider my future. In only two weeks, the mystique of veterinary medicine, which I had nurtured for a lifetime, had all but dissipated. I continued to do my job with increasing revulsion, trying to gain comfort with the thought that this was the way of all flesh—it was an evolutionary imperative.

Man had always eaten the flesh of animals, so why did I find their slaughter so horrifying? Perhaps it was the merciless brutality that I saw on the killing floor or the clamoring aura of death that invaded my mind like some virulent organism.

It was during my third week that I found myself staring out at the corrals, pens, chutes, ramps, roads and rails that make up the stockyards. Freight cars and cattle trucks were arriving continuously, unloading cattle, hogs and sheep for their eventual conversion into edibility. I watched them being electrically prodded, poked at with sticks, screamed at by stockyard men, hustled into holding areas.

At the end of my third week, I gave notice that I was leaving. A week later I was liberated, but what I had seen would forever remain imprisoned in my mind. For a week I sat brooding in my little room listening to music from a radio purchased from a fellow resident, trying to regain my equanimity. I began to love my tiny room—couldn't wait to get back to it. Its snugness and silence encouraged me to reflect and meditate and reaffirm my love of all creatures.

Once again I achieved peace of mind to renew my quest—to heal and nurture animals to the best of my ability.

It was with a brave heart that I accepted a position with a dairy co-op in Minnesota to develop a mastitis disease control program among their members.

I must confess that I did not really know how qualified I was for this job.

Young, inexperienced, and only academically knowledgeable, I plunged into what was the bane of dairy farmers around the world—mastitis. The arrangement included a car and, fortunately, a small furnished apartment. I organized a diagnostic laboratory, lectured farmers and traveled the frozen roads of Minnesota to problem farms.

One day I returned to my apartment happy to be alive. I had skidded off the road in a snow storm, but fortunately minimal damage was done to the car or myself because of a thick cushion of snow that rimmed the road. Awaiting me in my mail was a notice of induction. Drop everything. Uncle Sam wants me.

My service in the Army was uneventful. My skills were in no great demand, and I was placed in a casual battalion with other professionals to await assignment.

The sheer boredom of doing nothing month on end sent me to the base library where I spent many pleasurable hours. Poking through some army memoranda, I came across a listing of various types of honorable discharges available to qualified soldiers. A discharge in The Interest of National Health and Safety seemed to fit my situation.

Marking time indefinitely—being totally unproductive when I could be working in my profession was frustrating. I documented the need for large animal veterinarians in Illinois, describing shortages that existed. While I was not an Illinois resident, I did have a license to practice veterinary medicine in that state. I submitted my request for discharge to the commanding officer of my battalion. It was necessary to follow the chain of command when submitting such applications.

"How did you come up with this hog wash?" the battalion commander asked.

"There was an army memorandum on this type of discharge," I explained.

"When you speak to me, address me as Sir or Major, soldier."

"Yes, Sir."

"You're one of those smart-ass doctors in the casual battalion. You're lucky I don't deal with your training schedule. You guys have quite a racket. I'll pass your request to the base commander. It should give him a good laugh. Dismissed."

I saluted and said, "Thank you, Sir." I about-faced and left.

Well it didn't look too encouraging. Although I was vaguely aware of Senator Scott Lucas of Illinois, I dashed off a letter to him explaining my situation. Imagine my surprise when three weeks later, I received a letter from the Senator. It contained one sentence.

"I shall direct inquiries in your behalf." Scott Lucas, Senator from Illinois.

The reply was meaningless and I promptly forgot it.

Expecting to spend the remainder of the war in this country club with German P.O.W.'s doing all the chores, I was shocked to receive an assignment. My orders, containing a train ticket, an upper Pullman berth and meal tickets, instructed me to report to the Army General Hospital in Topeka, Kansas. I was ordered to carry a gas mask on my person at all times. I immediately packed it in my duffel bag. When M.P.'s boarded the train, they requested to see my orders.

"Where's your gas mask?" they immediately inquired.

"In my duffel bag at the ready," I answered.

Their serious demeanor suggested that I was about to spend sixty days in the stockade followed by a dishonorable discharge. Further conversation revealed to them that I was a veterinarian. An animated discussion about dogs and their problems followed. Fortunately I knew just a little more about dogs than they did. The gas mask was forgotten, and we separated on rather friendly terms.

The Army General Hospital was on one floor. There was not an up or down step in the whole facility, making it a wheelchair-friendly place. Soldiers in wheelchairs were racing about with impunity. From its main corridor, long extensions right-angled outward to make up the wards. I was told that I would be quartered in Ward 14. It had been emptied of wounded soldiers two weeks ago, and was available for my use. I found the setup curious but learned not to ask too many questions in the army. The answers were always forthcoming, usually in a short period of time.

I was taken to Colonel Winters, the commanding officer and advised that I was assigned to inspect food for the hospital. Our conversation finally got down to a discussion of dogs, especially his. I had not even been to my new quarters, and here I was detained by a long-winded account of his dog.

Finally I set out to find Ward 14 and where and when we ate. I passed the hospital cafeteria and discovered I could eat there any time I wanted. After a considerable hike, I found a wide doorway with a sign indicating that I had arrived at Ward 14. I entered to find sixty empty hospital beds, thirty on each side, separated by a wide corridor. "Pick any bed you like. This ward will be your private quarters," I was told. "You have the option of sleeping in any bed you wish."

There are some of us who find that making beds is an insurmountable challenge to our sense of order. Sheets do not seem to have straight lines, blankets are forever rumpled, and pillows that defy energetic plumping. Unfortunately, I did not have German P.O.W.'s to make my bed as I had in the casual battalion. I considered sleeping in a different bed each night for sixty days and see if I could contrive to have some nurses make up the beds for another sixty days. What a horror it would be for somebody to enter this ward and find sixty unmade beds. Perhaps a single unmade bed in the far corner of the ward would escape notice.

I had barely unpacked my duffel bag when a nurse summoned me to return to Colonel Winters' office on the double.

The Colonel had a male Springer Spaniel named Sarge, that he used for hunting. It was his pride and joy. In spite of the considerable efforts of a local veterinarian, a chronic infection in both ears could not be resolved.

"His ears stink so badly I can't stay in the same room with him," the Colonel said. "How about you taking a look at him, Doctor?"

Taking that to be an order rather than a request, I replied, "Of course, Sir. You must understand that I have no medicines or even an otoscope to make an examination of Sarge.

"Hell man, you're in a hospital. Tell me what you need and I'll have everything at your disposal."

I suddenly deeply regretted not having claimed total ignorance regarding ear infections in dogs. "Large animals that's my specialty," I should have said. But it was too late now. I had committed myself.

The next morning, I was escorted to a large examination room to find the Colonel amiably chatting with two nurses, while Sarge explored the room with his nose. Everyone seemed oblivious to the nauseating odor that pervaded the room. Sarge's ears really stank. I made no mention of some urine dripping down the side of a cabinet that Sarge had christened.

"Good morning, Doctor," the Colonel said.

"Morning, Colonel," I replied.

"These are Nurses Kelly and Anderson. They will assist you in any way you wish. And this is Sarge, your patient," he proudly announced.

Sarge, upon hearing his name, approached to give me a sniff. I was thankful he seemed to be a friendly dog. This was no place to do battle with a difficult animal. I was about to lift him onto the table when the Colonel touched my shoulder.

"Let the nurses do that. That's their job."

After several clumsy attempts, they finally got him on the table. The Colonel looked displeased with their efforts, but made no comment.

I made a quick examination of Sarge. The long hanging ears were badly matted and I could scarcely see the ear canal. The odor meanwhile had blanched the faces of my assistants.

"Do you think we could get an electric animal hair clipper so I can clean this up?" I said to them.

They looked at me blankly.

The Colonel interceded, "We have an animal lab here. Just a moment while I make a call."

He picked up the phone, "This is Colonel Winters. I'm in exam room 7 and I need an electric animal clipper, pronto. You'll have it here in five minutes? Good."

He turned to me and said, "Five minutes."

Three minutes later a brand new Oster clipper was in my hands. I proceeded to clip laboriously the matted hair from Sarge's ears. I ended up with a ridiculously looking dog, but there was no comment from his master. The nurses had carefully disposed of every speck of hair and the odor had dissipated to a significant extent.

"Colonel, before I clean the insides of Sarge's ears, I would like to make a microscopic examination of some of the material in the ear canals. Can I get the use of a microscope?"

"Seems I signed a requisition order two months ago for fifteen Bausch and Lomb microscopes. Let me make a call."

I interrupted to request some slides and mineral oil as well. Still on the phone, he turned toward me and held up five fingers. Four fingers later, a spanking new microscope arrived with several hundred slides and a gallon of mineral oil. Maybe there's really something to say for this military life. I placed a couple of drops of mineral oil on a slide, mixed it with a specimen from the ear canal and proceeded to examine it microscopically at 100 magnification.

Holy smoke, the Gods were smiling on me today. There they were—ear mites. How lucky could I be? I had made a diagnosis and there was an effective treatment.

"Colonel, take a look."

"They look like little crabs. How are we going to get rid of those little suckers?"

"There are several good mite killers on the market and I'll place an order immediately," I explained. "After I irrigate the ears with an antiseptic solution, I will put some mineral oil in the ear canals. It plugs their breathing mechanism and should slow them down until we get the mite medication."

"Well Colonel, I'll be leaving now. I'm already late."

"Wait a minute. I'm the boss here, and I say you'll spend the day with me. We'll have a great lunch and spend our time talking dogs."

This guy was regular army and the thought of spending a day with him was about as appealing as a sore throat.

"Colonel, I have a large shipment of perishables awaiting my inspection. How about a rain check?"

Obviously disappointed, the Colonel said, "Return to duty, but see me as soon as Sarge's medicine arrives."

"Thank you, Sir," I said as I made a hasty exit.

Days went by and never have I enjoyed such anonymity while in the army. No one entered my quarters—no one seemed to be aware that I even existed. The nights had a morphined silence, but at times I swear I could hear the stirrings and moans of wounded, tormented men who had lain in these beds. I heard that men had died here. Whose ghost was I sleeping with tonight?

I slept well, but some nights I would awaken to hear rustling sheets and unintelligible whispers. Maybe I was really resented. Perhaps they were saying I was an interloper—only the wounded shall sleep in these beds. My misgivings persisted until one night I was awakened by what I shall never know. In the dim light I rose, walked down the corridor scrutinizing each bed like a sentry on guard duty. When all was seen to be in order, I returned to my bed to fall immediately into a deep sleep.

I got that wake-up call and did my sentry duty every night at exactly 3:00 a.m. Somewhere within me there was this inner compulsion to make my rounds. I could not resist it nor did I want to.

Three months later still in Topeka, Kansas, I was in a warehouse inspecting food for the army hospital when somebody grabbed me by the arm and said "Where the hell have you been hiding? We promised Senator Lucas that you'd be out of the Army as of tomorrow. I have orders to get you on a train to Camp Crowder, Missouri for your separation. Let's move or we'll miss the train. I have all your stuff in my car."

I was whisked to the train. At Camp Crowder I was met by a car and taken to the separation center. By evening I was wearing a ruptured duck and honorably discharged. It was an abrupt, overwhelming experience—possibly undeserving especially when I was given precedence over the many veterans awaiting discharge. The scenario was unplanned, unanticipated. I had innocently put into motion what I thought would be a non happening.

I wrote the Senator to thank him for his efforts on my behalf. I was resolved to do everything in my power to justify my release from the Army.

I returned to Chicago and back to the YMCA. Rooms were now a dollar-fifty a day, meals seventy five cents—a substantial increase from my previous stay. My objective was to find work with a large animal practitioner and gain the experience I desperately needed.

A former classmate contacted me to ask if I would join him in taking horses overseas to Europe for the United Nations Relief and Rehabilitation Administration (U.N.R.R.A.). I would net an enormous fifty dollars a day all expenses paid. I urgently needed a car for large animal practice and this temporary job would provide the necessary money.

I reported to Savannah, Georgia, to screen horses and cattle arriving from western states for overseas shipment on Liberty ships. Their condition was deplorable—most suffering from a variety of respiratory diseases, parasitism and malnutrition. They must have been the culls of any rancher asked to sell an animal to U.N.R.R.A. For a week, we attempted to treat them for their problems—a week, incidentally, in which I learned to throw a lariat with reasonable accuracy. We were finally forced to load them into the hold of the ship, sick or not, four to a stall. Eight hundred horses and one hundred cows were loaded for a three week voyage to Greece. Our Liberty ship and its suffering cargo were to drift along at ten knots per hour, whimsically rolling and pitching to the never ending swells of the South Atlantic.

To assist in the care and feeding of the animals, thirty-five inexperienced young men actually volunteered for the job. I later discovered they were Quakers, conscientious objectors involved in an overseas aid project. They were truly remarkable young men—dedicated, reliable and intensely devout. Except for the first two or three days when they were pitifully seasick, I could not ask for a finer crew.

The ship's hold contained several decks that could only be reached by ladder. In less than a week, in spite of considerable apprehension, we were all scrambling up and down those ladders with packs on our backs like monkeys in a tree. Ventilation in the holds was totally inadequate, in a ship designed for cargo not livestock.

One afternoon as I was busily playing chess with the Captain, who frequently insisted that the Swedes and Jews would eventually control the world, a young Swede, Ernest, one of my Quaker volunteers, rushed into the Captain's cabin.

"Doctor, in hold three, way down at the bottom, there's blood pouring out of a horse. Better come quick."

"C'mon, make your move. No bloody horse is going to interrupt this game," the Captain growled.

"Sorry, Captain, I'll be right back." I thought he was getting a little tipsy anyway. Come to think of it, he was always tipsy. I hated to think of how he could handle the English Channel with its intricate lacing of minefields. That might be my next trip. I wondered whether this Captain had the sobriety to make those precise maneuvers.

I grabbed my kit and rushed out of the cabin, clambered down to the bottom of hold three, with Ernest close behind.

"Where is he, Ernest?"

I need not have asked. A rivulet of blood had found its way down the corridor and I followed it upstream to a horse that was nonchalantly eating its oats. Blood was pouring from his neck and it was obvious that a major vessel had broken—probably the jugular vein. Many of these horses had swollen necks, some with major abscesses. I was told that ranchers had given these horses injections of a sulfa drug that was supposed to go I.V., obviously missing their mark and producing an explosive tissue reaction.

"Ernest, put a twitch on his nose while I see what I can find out."

The three other horses in the stall continued to eat their oats, totally undisturbed by our efforts. I reached into the area where the bleeding was most pronounced. The entire anatomy of the neck had been disintegrated by massive infection. My fingers explored the area where I thought the jugular vein would be—nothing. My hand and arm were soaked with blood. Fortunately, the horse endured the examination without protest. I started separating tissue, exploring deeper and higher. My hand was finally able to grasp a three-quarter inch rope-like structure that I thought to be the jugular vein. I squeezed it as tight as I could and the bleeding subsided almost immediately. What do I do now?

Ernest was controlling the horse and was of no help, and I was reluctant to release my grip on the jugular to get some forceps to clamp the severed vessel—I might not find it again so easily. I tugged on the jugular vein hoping to exteriorate it. Much to my amazement, it came away from its furrow. The abscess had destroyed all supporting tissue and had transected the lower portion of the jugular. I had ten to twelve inches of jugular vein out of the neck—enough to twist it into a knot. It would be non-functional, but the other jugular vein would make up the difference.

I went back to my kit, retrieved a forceps, clamped the vessel and sutured it closed. An attempt to debride the necrotic tissue was extremely difficult. For now, I would settle for some drainage and antibiotic therapy.

"Okay Ernest, release the twitch and let's get cleaned up.
"I don't believe what I just saw, Doc."
"Neither do I, Ernest."
The horse immediately proceeded to eat his oats.

As we approached Gibraltar, the temperature in the holds rose to over one hundred degrees Fahrenheit, and ammonia fumes from the urine of the horses became so intense our eyes burned and teared each time we entered. Any horse falling in its stall was immediately trampled to death. We could only look on in despair. The manure piled up behind the horses—we had no way of removing it. Their rear ends were elevated two or three feet when we reached our destination, the Aegean port of Volos in Greece.

We lost seventy horses on this voyage, hoisting them out of the hold with a Rube Goldberg arrangement of block and tackles, pulleys and a power winch. The horse hung by its neck high above the deck of the ship to be dropped into the sea as the ship rolled to one side. That is burial at sea for a horse. The ship's crew were not as deeply disturbed as my Quaker volunteers. I soon learned that each member of the crew received a dollar for every animal buried at sea. Most of the horses died as a result of infectious disease and heat exhaustion. Of the one hundred cows, ten had calved, giving us a total of one hundred and ten. We had no losses among the cows because they were grouped in well ventilated corrals, giving them an area to lie down and an opportunity for my Quaker cowboys to remove manure and provide fresh bedding.

Unfortunately, Greece has only fifteen percent arable land and little capacity to feed and care for these relatively huge work horses. I'm sure they ended up as food rather than working animals on farms as intended.

For myself, it was an intensive exposure to horses and cows and I signed up for several other trips. All in all, I accumulated three thousand dollars and was a wealthy man.

I returned to Chicago, purchased a new Ford no less, and began my search for a job with a large animal practitioner.

I answered an ad from my veterinary journal placed by a large animal practitioner who was looking for an assistant veterinarian. This was the opportunity I was looking for. My new Ford took me to a farm town in northern Illinois where I met a vet of about fifty-five years of age. Tom Swingley was a short, lean man with an unwrinkled, but deeply lined face. He looked strong and tough, was recently widowed and had an active practice.

"Glad to see you have a car. I couldn't use you if you didn't," was his first greeting. "That is your car, isn't it?"

"Yes, and that's all I got in the world," I replied.

"Can't pay you much, but you're here to learn. Right?"

"Right," I responded.

"I'll give you room and board, and some car expenses, and if you're real useful around the house, I'll kick in a few dollars here and there."

I soon found out what he meant by "real useful around the house." He obviously did no housekeeping, laundry, or dishes. What did he want me for? Certainly not as an assistant. He needed a housekeeper, but I was cheaper.

"Ready to go to work, Doctor?"

"I'm ready," I replied.

I'll give it a try I thought. If things don't work out, I'll get in my Ford and take off.

"First thing you do is wash those dishes. Second thing you do is get that washing machine going. Then we'll eat. You'll find I'm a damn good cook."

We developed a tacit understanding—he would cook, and I would wash dishes and do laundry. And that I did for the eight months I spent with him.

It turned out to be one of the most intense learning experiences I ever had. We made calls morning till night, often seven days a week. Sometimes I accompanied him and other times I went on my own. That man made a functional veterinarian out of me—and a superb dishwasher.

One of the things he absolutely refused to handle were small animals. Being the only vet in town, there were numerous requests for his services, but he always responded with some degree of disdain. One night after I had done the dishes and put some laundry in the washing machine, there was a timid knock at the door. I opened the door to be greeted by a middle-aged lady.

"Is Tom Swingley here?" she asked. Behind her on a leash was an elderly dog.

"Just a minute, I'll get him." "Tom," I called, "someone to see you."

"Who the hell is calling at this hour," he answered back in disgust. "Why it's you, Rose. Is there something wrong?" His whole demeanor had changed from unpleasant to friendly.

"Tom, Ralph's face is all swole' up and there's a big sore on his cheek. He's in so much pain that I hadda bring him over. I know you don't treat dogs, but could ya make an exception? For old times sake."

Tom's smile froze on his face. "Rose, I know we were once sweethearts, but I don't treat dogs—period."

Then, as if a ray of light had penetrated his brain, he said, "Maybe my assistant will look at him."

"Oh, that would be wonderful," she said looking at me imploringly.

"Okay, bring him into the kitchen," I said.

Ralph, meanwhile, refused to enter the house, obviously sensing some disaster. Finally, I picked him up and carried him into the kitchen and placed him on the kitchen table. I turned to see Tom giving me a disgusted look. I examined the dog and immediately discovered the problem.

"He has a terrible toothache, Rose. One of his premolars is badly infected and will have to come out. The infection has eaten through the sinus and out the face, as you can see. It's not an easy extraction."

"Can you do it?" I heard Tom ask.

"I could try if I had some dental instruments," I replied.

"Hell, I got lots of them. Just a minute, I'll be right back."

Tom returned with a long leather case which he unrolled on the floor. Sure enough, he had some forceps, two feet long for extracting the teeth of horses and cows, an assortment of floats for grinding teeth, a variety of large chisels, plus rusty instruments I could not identify.

"Will you stop horsing around (no pun intended). This is a dog, not a horse."

He was taken back a bit by my remarks, but said, "What do you need?"

"I need a dental forceps like they use on people, some elevators to loosen the tooth, possibly a small chisel and mallet."

"Okay, I'll be right back," and off he went out of the house and down the street. Ten minutes later, he was back with all I had requested and more. Apparently, he had a cousin who was a dentist, practicing nearby. I wished he had brought his cousin along as well.

"I'll stay with Rose in the living room while you pull the tooth—and close the door."

"Tom, at least hold the dog while I give him some I.V. Nembutal," I said.

Expecting some resistance, he readily agreed. With the dog under anesthesia, he joined Rose in the living room.

This was a tough tooth to remove. It had three deep roots extending into the maxillary sinus. Most of the tooth had been worn away and it was a matter of literally digging it out. Twenty minutes later, the tooth was out, three roots and all. I was quite pleased with myself. The anesthetic had worked well and there had not been a whimper out of Ralph.

When I looked a little closer at Ralph, I saw to my horror that he was not breathing.

"Tom, come quick," I yelled. "Ralph is not breathing."

Tom bolted into the room. The door was open and I heard Rose's piercing wail, "Ralph is dead, Ralph is dead." It was maddening. Meanwhile I started artificial respiration, stopping to assure myself that Ralph had a heartbeat. Tom had disappeared, but was back in a minute with a pint bottle and a wad of cotton. He poured some liquid from the bottle onto the cotton and pressed it to the dog's nose and mouth. I could smell the aromatic spirits of ammonia. It was but a minute for Ralph to begin spasmodically breathing.

"You can come in Rose, Ralph will be okay," I heard Tom say.

Rose entered the kitchen and for the first time I noticed that she was a comely woman, slender and well dressed. She stood looking at Ralph, still not sure whether he was dead or alive.

"C'mon Rose, give him a hug. He's just sleeping it off," Tom said gently. "I'll take him home for you.

Tom cradled the dog in his arms and they were off.

The next morning, apparently in a very good mood, he motioned for me to sit down.

"I liked the way you handled Rose and that dog last night. Would you like to handle any of the small animal cases that might come in?" he said with one of his rare smiles.

"Sure," I said, "but I'll need some small animal medication and some instruments."

"Okay," Tom said. "Order whatever you need and I'll put the word out that we now have a vet willing to treat dogs and cats. The big news for a money-hungry guy like you is that all fees will be yours. One more thing, you must never use the kitchen table, only the work bench in the basement. Cover for me this afternoon."

Where did he get off calling me "money hungry?" He hardly ever paid me.

"Where will you be, Tom, in case I need you?"

Tom blushed and said "I'll be with Rose."

Two months later, after an elaborate dinner, he announced that he was going to marry Rose and move into her house... probably retire very soon. Would I be interested in taking over his practice at no charge, provided I bought his house? It was a fabulous offer. I knew his clients and the highly productive countryside. I had achieved my goal, and yet I hesitated to consummate a deal. Although Tom was a very competent veterinarian, he was not exactly a role model. The house had become a gloomy place to return to at night, and I had found myself inexorably assuming some of his mannerisms and attitudes. This was no life for a young man, and while my eight months with this vet had been very rewarding, it was time to move on. Filling his shoes would be more like joining him in a prison from which he was soon to be released. I had to escape before it was too late.

With Tom's permission, I brought his proposition to the attention of a soon-to-be-married classmate. He immediately came out to replace me. I had roomed with him briefly while in college, and knew that he was willing to make beds but hated to do dishes. I foresaw some insoluble conflicts arising, but fortunately Tom would be leaving.

I packed everything I owned in my Gladstone suitcase and once again was adrift, but this time I felt confident, employable... even entrepreneurial. There's nothing like money in your pocket. My small animal practice had been very profitable. A trip to see my family was most rejuvenating. I was able to bestow some of my largesse on my protesting parents, a second-hand bike for my brother and perfume for my sister; I was soon off again—Don Quixote in search of his quest.

Again I gravitated to Chicago, but this time I found the "Y" too stifling.

I answered an ad to share an apartment, and that's how I met Miltie. He had rented a subterranean two-bedroom apartment where the light of day entered only by your imagination. It was dark, dank, and cheap. Miltie's girlfriend had given it some decor and I gave it some curtains for its non-existent windows.

My plan was to literally hole up there while I searched the countryside for a place to practice. A manager of a nearby animal hospital that I visited begged me to work evenings. Although the pay was good, I would have accepted the job no matter what the pay. The vet I worked for was never present and I soon found out that he stayed in the basement of the hospital, most often in a drunken stupor. He would surface during the day to attend to what was left of his practice. The hospital manager handled the cash and provided for his needs. I did not know it at the time, but I was being groomed to be heir apparent.

A job at a V.A. Hospital caring for laboratory animals, rats, mice, rabbits and guinea pigs, presented itself. I knew very little about these creatures but found them to be fascinating animals—another learning experience had begun. Metabolic, surgical and cancer studies were performed on these animals. The experiments were not in anyway frivolous and every care was taken to minimize their discomfort. The end product of every experiment had mankind as its beneficiary.

Physical inactivity had become a way of life in Chicago. As a diversion, I reverted to the only sport in which I had achieved some degree of proficiency—handball. My days as a bronzed lad on the Brighton Beach handball courts were once again relived when I partnered with Miltie, my roommate, in a four-wall handball tournament. We were a successful duo, winning a handball championship and were rewarded with silver trophies.

Although Miltie had a girlfriend, he was not above going out with other girls. He persuaded me to come to a charity dance for Chicago's poor in spite of the fact that I couldn't dance.

I found an unobtrusive corner and stood watching Miltie do his thing. He was a great dancer. Nearby was a small tented area with a sign "Fortunes Told—$1.00." Having nothing better to do, I entered the tent. Seated on a chair was a radiantly beautiful blonde girl with a warm smile. Perhaps I was emotionally desperate, but an avalanche of desire swept over me—call it love at first sight. My pulse rate increased, my face flushed and I was aware of a slight tremor. I was guilty of every trite lovesick platitude imaginable. Our eyes met and she beckoned to me.

"Have your fortune told. Discover your future now. Only one dollar for a private consultation, Sir."

I clumsily extracted a dollar from my wallet and gave it to her. I was happy to see that she wore no wedding band. She proceeded to ask a few questions regarding my background, profession and social life. I answered, but in a voice that quavered.

"Don't be so nervous. I promise this won't hurt a bit," she said, smiling up at me as she took my hand in hers and proceeded to read my palm, but I hardly heard what she was saying.

"Calm down…why are you trembling so? You're quite flushed, are you sure you're not ill?"

I muttered that I was okay and saw the amusement in her blue eyes. She had me—I was hers for the taking. I had to find out who she was, where she lived and what her telephone number was. This was more stressful that the first incision I had made into an animal's abdomen.

"Can I phone you sometime?" I blurted out. "I really would like to get to know you better. I want to see you again."

I could barely look at her, but I felt her examining me in greater detail, trying to make a decision. This girl had the power to divert me from any future plans I would make. Sweat began to trickle down my brow and I heard her say, "Sure, give me a call. Here's my number. I always wanted to date a vet."

Delighted with my success, I hastened out of the tented area before I would say something foolish.

The courtship had begun. We met for breakfast every morning and dinner every night. There was no Dutch treat mode in this relationship. The next three months were among the most joyous periods in my life. Mary was truly a kindred spirit, as beautiful inside as she was outside. Her presence dissipated my taciturn nature, and I found conversation with her easy and fulfilling. To my amazement she thought that life as the wife of a country vet would be idyllic. I didn't think she understood all the ramifications, but I did nothing to discourage her.

The fact that this highly popular young woman—former Navy veteran, political activist, fund raiser for Jewish organizations and innumerable causes and events—was willing to run off with me to a rural hinterland to suffer the indignities of a vet's wife was indeed a puzzlement. The culture shock would be severe—then what? Would she forsake me and return to her previous life-style? Her sister in Chicago said she was making a terrible mistake. Would I end up like Tom Swingley with dirty dishes and filthy laundry—alone and depressed without the good fortune to be rescued by a Rose.

These thoughts did not consume me for long. I had captured my quarry... now to keep her caged.

OUR HOME ON THE PRAIRIE

My resolve to practice large animal medicine continued undiminished. I thought I had fortified myself with sufficient training to open my own practice and my entrepreneurial juices were flowing. Mary was supportive as ever, as we continued our search through the countryside looking for a suitable location. In one tiny farm community, we were greeted with great enthusiasm. I had heard that the veterinarian, who had been a virtual legend in this area, had died three years ago and a replacement had not been found.

We thought it might be a good idea to visit the veterinarian's widow. She should be able to acquaint us with the practice potential and the general community. I phoned and explained my interest in practicing in this area.

"Come on over, Doctor." Her voice suggested that she'd like to get it over with as soon as possible.

She lived in a colonial salt box type of house. Most houses in this town seem to fit within that framework. Only the little schoolhouse was made of brick.

Mrs. Hayden met us at the front door, her face grimly trying to smile a greeting. The door was stiff and creaky—hardly ever used. She struggled to open it. Most visitors use the side door, the front door being an architectural insistence that all houses have front doors, perhaps as an emergency exit. She seemed to endure our entrance with a coerced cordiality saying, "Please sit down while I go and brew some tea for us."

We found the living room to be rather austere and stark. A somber, colored braided rug covered much of the oak wood floor. The couch was barely padded, the chairs were small and straight backed. Comfort was not a consideration. She had an oval oak table with a glass top for tea service. A hutch with crown beveled glass was a startling piece of furniture that transformed the room, giving it sparkle and radiance.

"That I would like to have," I heard Mary say, pointing to the hutch just as Mrs. Hayden entered with tea and home made cookies.

"You actually want to practice in this area? The winters are bitter cold, the summers are torrid. Dr. Hayden practiced here for thirty years, and while he did not complain—he was not that type of man—he could not disguise his suffering. He lived a life of torture."

I examined this hawk-faced woman, wondering what she looked like as a girl. A picture on the mantel of Dr. and Mrs. Hayden, showed a good-looking man with a stern face, and a small, attractive woman forcing a smile—not a happy looking pair.

"If it was so difficult here, why did you stay on?" Mary asked.

Her annoyed expression suggested that she might have asked a too personal question.

"Dr. Hayden always felt his obligation to his clients was more important than his personal comfort."

"I think I understand how he felt," I replied.

"I don't see how you can," she answered, her voice becoming increasingly icy.

"Do you have any children?" Mary asked, trying to change to a more pleasant subject.

Mrs. Hayden looked startled, her privacy had been invaded.

"I'm afraid that's all I can tell you about Dr. Hayden. They don't make men like him any more. I don't think you will measure up to him. He was a saint."

That was our cue to leave. We said our goodbyes and were ushered to the side door. Here was a woman sustained by reverential memories, who wanted no other vet to diminish her fantasies.

As I listened to this embittered woman, I could not help but worry that what she said might be substantially true. It was a tough life, but this was what I wanted. I had succeeded in bewitching an innocent woman to come to this outpost to comfort and love me in the years ahead. Perhaps, alone on a cold winter night, the reality of where she was and what she had given up would descend upon her. It would stew within her... and one day she would forsake me.

Our visit to Mrs. Hayden was disquieting to say the least. We never even got to drink our tea. I later learned that she did have a child, but it died under circumstances unknown. Yet in spite of her hostile attitude I was in no way deterred. I liked this little town and the quilting of farms throughout the countryside. I hoped that Mary was not unduly disturbed by our encounter with Mrs. Hayden.

Other than Mrs. Hayden, the entire community continued to encourage us in every possible way. We met with the manager of the feed mill, Jess Waggoner, and he couldn't have been more enthusiastic.

"You'll have a great future here. There's a large livestock population and the farmers are desperate for a vet. Ask Ernie over there. He had a calving and had to wait a day to have a vet come out. Lost the calf—almost lost the cow. Right, Ernie?" Jess asked.

"You the new vet?" Ernie asked, extending his hand. "Boy, do we need you. You got my business. Those vets that come in from Rockford rip you off."

I listened to Jess and Ernie ramble on how essential I was to this farming community. Their words were music to my ears. Every place I went to the refrain was the same: "We need you. We need you."

What finally crystallized our decision was an offer by a retired farmer, Morgan Bullard, to sell us his house on Main Street. He would move to a smaller house leaving us his gracious tree-shaded home with a lovely front porch. Images of Mary and I rocking on the porch summer evenings helped clinch the deal. I had the house examined by a Veterans Administration appraiser to obtain a G.I. mortgage. It was declared to be sound and solid, well worth the asking price of $9,000. The down payment would virtually exhaust our capital. A 15-year mortgage was available, with monthly payments of $33.33, plus an annual real estate tax of $109.00. Outrageous!

"Morgan, before we officially consummate this deal there is something I feel you should know, Mary and I are both Jewish. If you or the community have any reservations, I would have to reconsider the deal. We would not want to live and raise a family in a community where Jews were not welcome." Much to my pleasure, he seemed elated by the news.

"Our pastor says that the Jews are the chosen people and the blood of Jesus is within you," Morgan said.

For a moment, I thought he said 'the blood of Jesus is on you.' Obviously the desire for acceptance had clouded my thoughts and I was not listening.

"Doc, you and Mary will be the first Jewish people to live in this town. I am sure that you will fit in. And if you're as good a vet as I think you are, you'll have a great future here. How would you two like to meet mother? She's going on eighty, built your house fifty years ago. She's stiff as a board from arthritis, but her mind is working well—still sharp as a tack. Come on over for lunch tomorrow at noon."

I looked toward Mary and she nodded in agreement.

"Okay Morgan, we'll be there tomorrow."

The next day, promptly at noon, we rang the doorbell to Hazel Bullard's home. Morgan greeted us at the door.

"Come in and meet Mother," he said cordially.

We followed him into the living room to find Hazel Bullard seated in a cushioned rocking chair. She was a thin, ascetic looking woman, face wizened, skin brown-dappled by the prairie sun. The hands were gnarled and crinkled, the finger joints swollen, and obviously painful. Morgan made the introductions. She wore gold wire-framed glasses and peered at us intently. She extended her hands. Mary and I hesitantly reached toward them, fearful that our handshakes would be painful for her.

"You two are Jewish? You don't look like Jews," were her first words.

Mildly irritated, I asked, "How should a Jew look?"

"Jews are dark-skinned and have black hair and big noses. You two are fair-skinned, have blonde hair and Mary has a nice little nose," she said smiling, her ill-fitting false teeth shifting a bit.

"Mrs. Bullard," I asked, "have you ever met a Jewish person before us?"

"Can't say that I have, but would you please call me Hazel instead of Mrs. Bullard? I like you two young people and will enjoy having you as neighbors. But come a little closer please, and bend your heads down."

Mary and I moved closer and bent our heads expecting some sort of blessing.

"But where are your horns? I heard that all Jews have horns," she exclaimed.

"Mother," I heard Morgan say, "Jews don't have horns."

"I'm older and wiser than you, Morgan," she replied, "and I'm sure they do."

Mary and I listened to this brief exchange somewhat amazed to learn that these notions still existed. I was both amused and annoyed. How could this woman's isolation be so complete?

"Mrs. Bullard (I had difficulty calling her Hazel), Mary and I had been dehorned at an early age, just like they do with calves. In addition, I had been circumcised at eight days of age."

I looked at Mrs. Bullard and Morgan to see if my remarks were offensive to them, but to my surprise, Morgan began to laugh uproariously.

"Doc, you're a card. Wait till these farmers get a load of YOU."

Mrs. Bullard seemed puzzled by Morgan's outburst and she looked at me and asked, "What's circum... now what was that word?"

"Morgan will explain it to you after lunch," I said smiling.

"Come on Mary and Doc, let's eat. You two young people must be real hungry."

As we walked into the dining room, I could not but be amazed to learn that these medieval concepts were still stubbornly preserved in the minds of many people. The figure of the horned Jew was not uncommon during the middle ages. To further identify the Jew with Satan, he was thought to have a devil's tail cunningly hidden from view.

Michelangelo's patriarchal sculpture of Moses with two horns protruding from his head gave credence to this myth. Michelangelo was guided by a middle age Bible mistranslation of the verb "set forth beams" as "horns," and thus Moses was given horns.

We were now seated at the dining room table when I asked, "Hazel, where did you hear that Jews have horns?"

"Well, that goes back a long, long time, when I was a little girl. I was given a book of Bible stories and remember that Moses had horns. They told me that all Jews have horns. That stuck with me to this day."

"If I told you, Hazel, that Jews don't have horns, nor do they all have black hair, dark skin and large noses, would you believe me?"

"Yes, but you said both you and Mary were dehorned as children."

"Hazel, that's the price I pay for one of my bad jokes."

She proceeded to take Mary's hand in hers, and with the other grabbed a napkin to wipe some tears away. A wonderful smile enlivened her face.

"You are two young, dear people. I am very lonely. I hope you will find time to visit me often now that we're neighbors. And even if you had horns, you would be just as welcome. After all, you are the people of the book."

All I could say was, "Hazel, you are a gracious lady and we're fortunate to have you as our neighbor."

I turned to Morgan and said, "Your mother is a great saleslady. We have a deal." I was committed.

Slowly, meticulously, I began to accumulate the essential ingredients for my career as a large animal practitioner. Fortunately I had my Ford—every call I made, every medication and piece of equipment I used would be transported in this car.

And now Mary and I owned a house that we would make into a home. The adventure had begun. What would it be like?

Underlying all my plans and preparations was my concern for Mary. Perhaps I had misjudged her. She said that being with me was all she wanted in life, and I wondered how someone like myself could be that important. Suppose she suddenly said, 'I really don't want to spend my life in a rural area. Why don't you practice in the city?' What would my answer have been? I would have been crestfallen, but would have replied unhesitatingly, 'If that will make you happy, we'll live in the city.' It was always my nature to create a scenario of anxiety for myself.

A week later, we made the move into our fifty-year-old house. Our furnishings were scanty, and Mary brought along her twin bed which we shared. At our age, sharing a small bed was not a hardship. Mary was the youngest of nine children and always slept with one of her sisters. I spent my years sleeping on folding cots, so sleeping in an abbreviated bed was a delight, especially with someone like Mary.

However, it was not long before I noticed that she could not conceal her uneasiness. Coming from a small Chicago apartment, the house seemed cavernous. When the prairie winds blew, you could hear the house's arthritic joints creaking. The old planked, wooden floors groaned alarmingly when walked on, and in the silence of the night, Mary could hear their sighs. I thought it would be a pleasant home, and so what if it showed its age at times. Before long, we would begin to understand its geriatric language of creeks and groans.

To compound her discomfort, we had several monstrous black walnut trees hovering over the house. They were possibly one hundred years old and certainly predated our house. While they provided considerable shade, I would not recommend building beneath them. I learned that the black walnut is a grandfather/grandson tree. That's what the Chinese call their ginkgo tree—the grandfather plants it and the grandson enjoys it. After fifty years, black walnut wood is coveted by cabinet makers. Perhaps we were surrounded by treasure. When the wind blew, our treasure bombarded our cedar-shingled roof mercilessly with black walnuts. To Mary, it was like living below the Chicago El. The walnuts were about the size of oval peaches, green in color, and fiercely stained our hands when we tried to remove their husks. They clogged all the gutters and blanketed our half acre so that I actually had to shovel a pathway to the house. Fortunately, I was rescued by an army of farmers' wives. They timidly knocked on our side door (nobody used the front) and asked if they could collect those green beauties. Of course, I magnanimously allowed them to fill their baskets many times over.

One veteran picker paused briefly to introduce herself, "Good morning, Doctor, I'm Stella Fairhead."

I extended my hand in greeting, and after a long moment of hesitation, she gave me her hand, barely touching mine. I noticed the flush on her face and wondered how long is was since she touched the hand of a man other than her husband.

"We farm about two miles west off the state road and a little bird told me that you are drowning in black walnuts and I'm coming to the rescue." She twittered a bit and her flush intensified. "I love black walnuts. You may not know this, but after they're picked, I have to dry and then husk them. Believe me, husking corn is easy compared to husking black walnuts. The tough shells must be cracked to extract the nuts. It's not that I drink much wine, but the sweet-bitter taste of those nuts lingers in the back of my mouth like a good wine. For me, it's a labor of love."

I listened to her almost poetic description of black walnuts and smiled at her. Her blush intensified and for a moment, I thought she had found our casual conversation too intimate.

"May I pick these black walnuts?" she asked abruptly.

"Sure you can, Stella, and to your heart's content."

To express their thanks, these farm women inundated us with black walnut cookies and sumptuous burnt sugar cakes smothered with caramelized icing embedded with black walnuts. Then came small jars of black walnuts for use as a topping for ice cream sundaes. The wet nuts on sundaes at the ice cream parlor are mostly black walnuts. When I returned from calls, I would see the gleaners, their fingers purple-stained, gathering the latest hail of nuts. Stooped over, the gatherers looked as if they were panning for gold. In winter, I saw some of those nuts grimly clinging to the branches, awaiting the moment to continue their life cycle.

The medicines and tools of my trade had been delivered by a Greyhound bus that made our town a daily thirty second port of call. I outfitted my car and was ready to begin my career. After buying my equipment, our resources had dwindled to three hundred dollars. I nailed a reflective sign on a black walnut tree in front of our house, placed ads in local newspapers, had some business cards printed and was ready to go to work.

One week, two weeks, three weeks—not a single call. We spent money on only the barest necessities. I spoke with Morgan who couldn't believe what I was telling him. He would pass the word, and in addition he wanted Mary and I to come for dinner. He must have thought we had that hungry look. A good farm dinner with all the trimmings was just what we needed. When Morgan said he would pass the word, I was not exactly sure what he meant. We soon found out. Welcome packages of foods, fruits and cakes descended upon us. It was obvious that we would not starve.

Although our prospects for the moment seemed uncertain, Mary was remarkably unconcerned. I wondered if she had a nest egg somewhere to justify her disposition. One morning she gave me that great smile of hers saying, "I've done some politicking in my younger days and this is what I would recommend your doing. Get in your car and go north. Stop at every farm you see. Introduce yourself, give them your card and move on. Tomorrow you go south and so on until you've met every farmer within our area.

It's better than moping around here. And besides which you'll probably make some good contacts for the practice."

In spite of my total lack of enthusiasm for this type of soliciting, I headed out. I was greeted curiously, but politely on the farms where I stopped. I continued to make my rounds. Most didn't even know I existed and were happy to receive my card. In an effort to be cordial, I drank a lot of coffee and ate all kinds of delicious cakes and cookies.

That afternoon, I drove into the barnyard of a farmer whose name on the mailbox was Avery Knutson. Three large dogs came a-running, all barking with the intensity of unmuffled cars. In my early days of practice, I usually sat in the car until somebody emerged to placate the dogs. In later years, I learned that they were just barking a greeting, and I would get out of my car to be intensively sniffed.

A young man about my age, emerged from a shed. His greasy hands and overalls suggested that he was repairing some farm equipment.

"Hi there," he said. "If you're selling something, don't waste my time. Get along."

"No, I'm the new vet and just opened my office in town. Just going around to introduce myself. Here's my card."

He looked at me closely. "You don't sound like any vet I've ever known."

"Maybe because I was raised and went to school in the Northeast." Could this young man have detected my Brooklyn accent?

"That could be it. Since you're here, would you look at a couple of calves that are breathing hard and coughing? I'll pay you for your time. I'm Tim. My dad is over in Rockford." We shook hands. "I see your hand is still soft from schoolin'," he said smiling.

Tim led me inside the barn where two calves were penned.

"They're not eatin'—haven't for two days. They're sure to croak."

Both calves had fevers. Their chests were thumping up and down and I could hear the tell-tale signs of pneumonia through my stethoscope. The poor animals were fighting for air, mouth agape, tongues partially protruding, blue-tinged.

"They're in tough shape, Tim. Hope I'm not too late. I'll give them some antibiotic shots and something to make them breathe easier. Here's some medicine I want you to give them after you finish milking. Careful with it. I don't want it to go down the wrong pipe."

"Doc, how come these two got sick while four others on the other side of the barn look okay?"

"Glad you asked before I told you. See that broken window alongside this pen?"

"Dad was planning to fix that. In fact, one of the things he went for was some glass to repair that window."

"Tim, three nights ago, we had an early frost, the cold wind blowing through that broken window chilled these calves... gave them pneumonia. Is it okay to come back tomorrow to look at them?"

Tim hesitated.

"No charge for tomorrow, Tim."

"In that case, come on out. Okay if Dad pays you then? He'll be home."

The next day, I returned to find the calves remarkably improved and the window repaired.

Avery came into the barn and greeted me with a big smile.

"Tell the truth, Doc, I writ those calves off. No way were they goin' to make it. Losin' the calves and a vet bill to boot didn't seem too smart." He turned to Tim and said "Son, you're smarter than your old Dad."

Tim beamed. We all shook hands.

"Doc, if you didn't stop by, we'd have lost those calves. And they're out of my two best cows. Come on into the house for some coffee and a check for your work," Avery said.

This was my sixth cup of the day. I was flushed with success and caffeine. If these farmers were drinking people, I would be reeling drunk.

I struck gold in a couple of places where I was asked to treat some ailing cows. Coming home to Mary with money in my pocket was reason to celebrate. To commemorate the occasion, she made her first angel food cake. I told her it was a culinary masterpiece. What a mistake that was. Thereafter nothing could dissuade her from producing a never-ending assembly line of angel food cakes. My waist line... nor Mary's... was in need of this expansion.

Night calls worried Mary the most. To her it seemed that no sooner did I leave than the house would really begin to groan. If the sounds were coupled with black walnuts rumbling on the roof, I would come home to a very fearful young woman. Alone in our upstairs bedroom, she would imagine various horrors were about to befall her. Here was a girl brought up in the warrens of Detroit and Chicago, yet she walked those streets totally unperturbed. In our town, where violent crime or even non-violent crime was virtually non-existent, Mary had grown skittish. I realized that logic, reason and even the offer of a weapon were not the answers. Mary just had an unreasonable fear. Perhaps the realization that she was pregnant increased her anxiety. She was alone, no family, few friends—just me. I was not enough to compensate for this fear, especially if I was away on a call at night, when she was most fearful.

To further disturb her life, I had to go on more and more night calls. I attributed this to the advent of home television. Farmers who ordinarily went to sleep at eight or nine o'clock were now staying up late watching T.V. on their snowy screens. After T.V. closed down for the night, it was not unusual for a farmer to look in on a cow that was due to freshen. If he thought she was having a problem calving, he was sure to call me.

On many nights, Mary chose to accompany me. I really enjoyed her company as we proceeded on our way along dark country roads. On wintry, moonlit nights, a glistening lather of snow illuminated fields bearded with corn stubble. As we would approach a farm and see the barn all lit up, afloat in darkness, I would often conjure up an image of a cruise ship at sea.

Call completed, we would drive to the Four Corners Café, which stayed open around the clock to accommodate the feed grain haulers, milk tank truckers, and drivers of livestock semi-trailers on their way to the Chicago stockyards. After hot coffee and homemade delights, such as tawny pumpkin or tart rhubarb pie splashed with whipped cream, we headed home. For years that was our night out. After Mitchell was born, the availability of Agnes, our baby-sitter, continued to make these calls an occasion for another midnight on the prairie. These were magical moments. I was happy and hoped she was happy too.

I should have thought of it myself, but the solution to her fear was thrust upon us by a phone call from a friend of mine, Dave Brenner.

"What's all the excitement?" Mary asked.

"That was Dave Brenner calling. You remember my speaking of him?"

"Yes, I even remember meeting him once in Washington. He's very good looking and unbelievably shy—shyer than you. The two of you go back a long way."

Dave Brenner was a remarkable fellow—best friend I ever had. Our love of animals was the bond between us. His appearance was striking—tall, slender with blonde hair swept over his head, immune to any current style. Green eyes set in a contemplative face regarded the world with wry amusement. He never asked a personal question, but you could easily find yourself confessing your most intimate thoughts.

He loved the heavens and he loved dogs. Astronomy enthralled him and dogs responded to this thoughts as well as his voice. His presence put reverence in their eyes. They immediately sensed that here was a kindred spirit in human form.

Dave was essentially an apolitical person, occasionally heaping scorn on the political shenanigans in Washington. After Pearl Harbor, I was amazed when he told me that he was leaving college to enlist in the air force. His ability and leadership qualities were immediately apparent, and despite his laconic nature, he rose in rank to command a B-29 in the Pacific. After twenty missions, his plane was shot down by Zeros and only he and the tail gunner survived. Severely injured, he was hospitalized for eight months. Typically, during our correspondence, he never mentioned the pain he was enduring while undergoing reconstructive surgeries. Finally, released from the Army, he returned to his upstate New York home to complete his convalescence and to prepare for his return to college.

My trip to visit him was hastened by a call from his mother. She begged me to come. Dave was so withdrawn and depressed... he would speak to no one... scarcely a word to her... maybe I could reach him. She was told that in time he would recover completely but that was not happening. Perhaps, I would bring him back to reality. I had no such illusions, but decided to spend a few days with him. I just wanted to be with him, if only in silence.

Perhaps it was an epiphanous inspiration—I decided to come bearing a dog as a gift. Knowing Dave, I was sure he would respond to a loving dog, and I knew he favored German Shepherds. A breeder I knew sold me a gawky, friendly, exuberant four-month-old male shepherd puppy named Baron. Baron was large-boned, too big for most people, but remarkably intelligent. He would know how to handle Dave.

It was a tough drive to Dave's home. Baron could not be contained in his kennel in the car. Between his frequent naps, I was subjected to considerable face licking accompanied by ear and neck kissing. I needed a wad of paper towels to clean up after each onslaught. My stern reprimands seemed to encourage him. I was in his complete control. He had sized me up correctly. I was a pushover.

When Dave first saw the dog his eyes opened wide. Baron went right for him, licking and loving him. There was no inhibitions. Words and barks flowed between them in a torrent.

His mother and I just sat and watched—each of us experiencing a special delight. Believe it or not, three months later, Dave was back at Cornell where he eventually obtained a Doctorate in Astronomy, leading to his assignment at the Naval Observatory in Washington, D.C.

During his two years in Washington, Dave's time was mostly spent at the Observatory. Baron's isolation and loneliness almost made Dave quit his job to be with him. It occurred to him that perhaps another German Shepherd would provide Baron with companionship. After a careful search, he purchased Captain Fang Von Oldehove—a distant relative of Rin Tin Tin, no less.

Two months after Dave acquired Fang, he was informed that he was being transferred out of Washington to a new job, mapping a site for a lunar landing on the moon. What type of Buck Rogers project was that, I wondered? Somebody actually thinks they can walk on the moon?

The new job would provide Dave all the time he needed to be with Baron. In fact, the dog could accompany him to work. There was no place for Fang in the scheme of things.

"Mary, Dave just called to ask if we would take Fang?" I turned to Mary with a smile on my face and said, "What do you think I told him to do?"

"I guess we've got ourselves a dog," she said, her mind busily sketching out what new responsibilities she had acquired.

Two days later, we drove to Chicago's Midway Airport to claim Captain

Fang Von Oldehove. There he was in a large airline kennel, silent, staring, searching—searching for faces he would never see again. Although he was only six months old, I knew he was strongly bonded to Dave and Baron. Gaining his trust and loyalty would be a slow process.

Mary's first attempt to embrace him was greeted with a low, warning growl. Having lived with a bachelor, he had never been exposed to such affectionate exuberance. Fortunately, he and I got along almost immediately, and for me it was love at first sight.

I marvel at the way adults can give their hearts to animals. I have seen mature, staid owners of a new puppy tearfully despair when advised to return their pet because of a serious or untreatable ailment. There's a magical hold that a puppy can have over us. After a few moments of holding one in our arms, the bonding begins. The lick of a puppy is enough to bond a child. Adults need only to feel their aura of innocence to be equally smitten. In the briefest of moments that animal is part of us, for better or worse.

So now we had a beautiful black and silver German Shepherd, with the formidable name of Fang. Although he shied away from Mary, she knew that love and food would eventually win him over. We knew he was trained to eat on command and to respond only to Dave's voice. Fortunately, I was able to communicate with him very quickly, but he totally ignored Mary's sweet talk and gourmet cooking. Unless I touched his food dish and said, "Eat," he just wouldn't eat. Undismayed, she used her wiles to try to win him over. The situation improved after I was gone two days to a veterinary meeting. When I returned, he was eating out of her hand and seemed to have made a grudging acceptance of her. Yet when I was home, he stayed at my side constantly. He accompanied me to my car when I went on calls and excitedly greeted me when I returned. I was flattered by all this attention but wished he would show Mary at least a little affection. For no apparent reason that I could determine, dogs generally prefer one member of the family. In fact, years later another shepherd identified with Mary just as Fang had with me and they became inseparable.

Fang was now a member of the family, and I heard fewer and fewer complaints about night calls. Now when I returned home, I would find Mary reading or asleep, unafraid, with Fang slumbering on the bed. When be became aware of my presence, he immediately left the bed to continue his sleep on his favorite rug in our bedroom. Without being told, he knew that I refused to share my bed with him. However, we did have a miniature poodle later on who slept between Mary and myself, aggressively defying my orders to vacate.

One night I returned from a particularly difficult case to find her distraught.

"What's the matter? What happened? You seem so upset."

"My sister, Rose, called from Canada to tell me that her home had been burglarized."

"So why are you so frightened? That's a thousand miles away. She wasn't injured, was she?"

"No, but she's my sister."

At this point, I really wasn't following her reasoning, but it was obvious that this event had greatly upset her.

"You've got nothing to worry about. You have Fang, the great protector," I reminded her.

Fang, hearing his name mentioned, rose lazily to his feet and sighfully yawned.

Though it had taken place in Toronto, it had nullified the sense of security that Fang had given her. Fang's love, gentleness and lack of aggression suggested to her that he would not rise to the occasion were she threatened.

"Now what would this loverboy do if a burglar broke into this house?" she asked, pointing at Fang as he nuzzled her hoping to get his chest scratched.

"I believe he would protect you with his life if necessary. He's got the face of a killer," I kidded.

Meanwhile, Fang stretched out on his braided rug Mary had made from old neckties gleaned from our families and secondhand stores. What would this dog do if Mary were actually threatened? He was not trained to attack. I had never seen him act aggressively at any time. I rarely heard him growl or snarl—the floorboards made more noise than he did. His size made many people wary, but, before long, they were petting and sweet-talking him. Maybe Mary was right. I had to find out for my sake as well as hers.

"Well, Fang," I said, "We're going to put you to the test." His ears popped erect, the intelligent eyes regarding me quizzically.

"Okay, here's the plan, Mary. Next night call I get, you and Fang remain upstairs in the bedroom until I return. I'll sneak into the house wearing my old raincoat and slouch hat and hide behind the big leather club chair. When I thump twice on the wall, send him down. If he tears me to pieces, that should convince you."

The stage was set. I had my props and now all that remained was the night call. Two days later, after Milton Berle completed his T.V. show, the phone rang. It was Oscar Swensen's wife. She explained that Oscar was having a lot of trouble with a heifer trying to calve. Oscar had built a tall tower on top of which he'd placed an elaborate antenna to grope for those weak television signals. Friends and family were invited to come on Tuesdays to see "Mr. Television," as Milton Berle was called. It was an ongoing happening.

I knew Oscar could deliver a calf as well as anyone. Pulling a calf should not have required my services. Something was seriously amiss.

The steering column of my Ford chattered incessantly as I sped over the corrugated gravel road. A recent thaw had caused trucks to deeply rut and hump the softened areas. As I navigated these spots in the darkness, the ruts were so deep that if I slowed, the car would hang, momentarily suspended on the humps, the wheels barely providing traction. If I went a bit faster, my momentum would scrape me through the high spots. It's hard to believe that in the Midwest, country roads were virtual gravel pits. It was not until the 1960s that most were black-topped.

I arrived at the farm to find four cars parked in the barnyard. Oscar greeted me at the milkhouse door.

"We're all set for you, Doc. Hot water, soap, towels and lots of help."

Sure enough, four of his neighbors who had come to watch television were on hand. Bloodstained sleeves and arms, soiled ropes and a block and tackle attested to their strenuous efforts to deliver the calf.

"Don't think you ever had a tough one like this, Doc, Oscar announced. The others silently nodded.

If I seemed calm to them I was far from it. I visualized myself grappling with an unborn calf, while my restless audience watched my performance.

What could a city boy do that this group of farmers could not do? Sure, I had my training, but how could that compare with generations of experience? It would be at least a year before I would be able to control the self-doubt that haunted my dreams.

The barn was warm as I stripped to the waist. I opened my obstetrical kit. Once again, the frozen OB chains glued to my hands and only released after I placed them in a warm antiseptic solution. As I washed the vulva area and the hind quarters of the exhausted heifer, she humped her back, held her breath, and strained mightily. For a moment, two little hoofs protruded from the vulva and then were immediately sucked back as she relaxed. The poor animal had been unnecessarily abused. Curiously, in the farm world in which I lived these futile efforts could not be considered abuse, but I had different standards.

"Think she's dead, Doc?" Oscar inquired.

"Could be, Oscar," I replied.

I lubricated my arm and reached through the vagina into the uterus. It always amazed me to see animals suffer this personal invasion without a strenuous protest. Sliding past the forelegs, I searched for the head. The heifer contracted against my arm, squeezing it against the pelvis with numbing pressure. Unable to advance or withdraw, I waited until she relaxed. With my arm up to the armpit inside the heifer, I turned to Oscar and said "Oscar, we have a wry neck here. The head is turned back facing in the wrong direction."

To effect delivery, the head must be brought forward so that the calf could fit through the birth canal. With the head awry, no amount of pulling on those legs will deliver the calf unless the legs are brutally ripped from the calf. I have seen that happen, much to the detriment of the cow—not to mention the calf. I've had the misfortune of arriving at a calving where the farmer was trying to deliver a calf using a chain attached to his tractor. The results were disastrous.

"By golly, no wonder we couldn't pull that calf. We might of killed it. We pulled mighty hard, even used a block and tackle. What are you going to do, Doc?"

"Well, Oscar, with your help, I'm going to try and get a chain over the lower jaw of that calf and pull the head around."

"Anything you say, Doc. Can the boys help?"

"Not right now, Oscar. Once I get the head around, we can pull the calf."

I removed a repelling rod from my kit, positioned it on the breast bone of the calf, and gave the other end to Oscar. I placed a loop of obstetrical chain in my hand and inserted my arm into the uterus of the cow.

My audience was watching my efforts without comment. There was really nothing that they could see. This was strictly an inside job. I hoped they thought I was performing magic within that uterus.

I turned to Oscar and said, "Push, but go easy. Stop when I tell you to."

My strategy was to push the calf back within the uterus to provide elbow room, so to speak, for me to locate the head.

"Push a little harder, Oscar."

"Ain't we goin' the wrong way, Doc? If I push any harder, that calf'll come out of her mouth."

Oscar's friends laughed loudly.

"Hold steady, I got the head. Now to slip the chain around the jaw. I got it. Have one of your friends pull the jaw chain gently... *gently*, I said."

I could feel the head coming around.

"Oscar, remove the rod. The head is coming around. I'll put some chains on the front legs and we're ready to deliver the merchandise. Okay you guys, grab the chains and pull slowly. I'll guide the calf out."

The heifer bore down again. Manure extruded from the compressed anus, ribboning my arm and shoulder. I have been saturated with manure and have never seemed to mind it. It is totally unlike carnivorous waste, which is often foul and repelling. I remember Masai women in East Africa using their hands as trowels, plastering their huts with it. I have seen women in India scooping the droppings of sacred cows from the streets. Shaped into patties, dried in the sun and hardened, the droppings became a good source of fuel. Villages are redolent with their pungent odor, as they heat their homes and cook their food.

"Okay gentlemen, let's pull the calf. Slowly now, don't drop the calf when she comes out."

"By golly, she's acomin'! She's a heifer, too. I think she's alive!" Oscar exclaimed.

I could not believe how relatively uncomplicated this calving had turned out to be.

Actually, there was no sign of life, but eager hands began vigorously rubbing her with burlap sacks. She was totally unresponsive. I lifted the calf by her hind legs. The aspirated fluids drained out of her mouth and nostrils. I cleared her throat of mucous and started pumping her chest to encourage breathing. I was rewarded with an amazingly loud gurgling sound. The calf began to breath spasmodically and move her legs. The forgotten mother, unsteadied by her pain and exhaustion, turned her head in the stanchion to look anxiously toward her calf. Oscar released her and she carefully approached her new offspring. After a few sniffs to assure herself that this was indeed her baby, her sandpapery tongue began a licking process that not only dried, but revitalized the calf. Oscar and his friends offered me their words of praise, but I felt more lucky than praiseworthy.

I was exhilarated that the calf was born alive and seemed to have endured the brutality she had been subjected to. Even after I had delivered a thousand calves, it was never less than a thrilling experience to deliver a live, healthy calf. I was covered with manure, blood and amniotic fluid, trying to contain my feeling of elation, especially when I heard one farmer say to another, "That young vet did a nice job. He made it look easy."

As I drove back home, I became aware that my right pants leg had become wet and bloodied. Once again, I was returning all messed up. I tried wearing the rubber obstetrical suits made for this purpose, but like most vets, found them to be clumsy and stifling. What an assault I must be to Mary's senses of sight and smell. Yet she never recoiled at the sight of me when I returned in this condition. She would gather the heap of soiled clothes outside the shower and by her special alchemy, they would reappear immaculately clean.

Suddenly I remembered that this was the night that Fang must prove his mettle. Since I was such a stinking mess, my impulse was to abort the mission. But I decided that my disguise would be more effective if I smelled like something out of a manure spreader. I drove slowly into town in order to muffle the whine of my knobby snow tires. Fang was capable of hearing the car from way out to the state road pavement. I parked about fifty yards from my house, put on my old raincoat and slouch hat and began my walk home. I entered stealthily through the side door. The radio in the bedroom was playing louder than usual and masked any noise I might make. If Fang didn't hear me, I was sure he could at least smell me. I positioned myself behind the large leather club chair in the living room. My wet pants leg had frozen stiff and I could hear the fabric crackle as I crouched.

I gave the signal—two thumps on the wall. The radio was turned off. It was then that I heard a growl that I could not believe came from Fang.

"Go get him, Fang," I heard Mary say.

He bounded down the creaky stairs, and in a moment he was in the room with me. I peered at him in the dim light. He seemed to have grown in size since I had seen him earlier in the evening. God, he was beautiful—poised, ears erect like two spinnakers in a stiff wind, deep chest heaving, eyes gleaming. Someone was in the room, but he seemed not quite sure where. As I slowly rose from behind the chair, the hair on his neck and back seemed to porcupine erect. He looked at this looming, hulking figure as if trying to assess its intent, searching for some sign of recognition. I made no movement and he remained motionless. Suddenly he emitted a sound so primordial in its nature that I was shaken with fear. I knew that once he sprang at me, he could inflict severe damage. With my newly acquired odors, he might not know me, especially in his state of fury.

What to do? I yanked the hat off my head and yelled, "Fang, it's me, it's me."

He hesitated, looked at me intently, and with a deep gasp, his body deflated like a blown out tire. He sat there a moment, baffled, then sniffed my outstretched hand. With full recognition, he began to whimper with joy, his tail wagging so furiously that his hind end shimmied. I pulled him to me and just hugged him. I heard Mary laughing from her vantage point half way up the stairs.

"Come on everybody, angel food cake and ice cream for all. And a double scoop for Fang."

There was no doubt in Mary's mind that Fang would be her protector should the occasion demand it. I noticed that their relationship had become much more intimate. She now regarded him as a member of the family... fully capable of understanding everything she said. Her conversations with him and his whimpering responses were music to my ears. One of Fang's great frustrations was that he couldn't talk, but that was no impediment to their communication. Mary developed a profound respect and love for Fang. If only man's capacity to love animals could be found in man's capacity to love man.

Mary would still accompany me on moonlit nights, motivated not by the fear of being left alone, but by the joy of experiencing the moonglow of midnight on the prairie.

OUR DOGS, GOD BLESS THEM

We were notified that the baby furniture had arrived at a warehouse in Chicago and would be delivered in a couple of weeks or whenever a truck was going our way. Although Mary was not due for at least three months, she had to have that furniture now. The nursery was painted, delightfully curtained and graced with a cushioned rocking chair, laboriously but lovingly needlepointed by Mary.

She cleared the afternoon of all calls and arranged to borrow a neighbor's pickup truck for the two-hour trip to Chicago. While I could not share her sense of urgency to get the baby furniture, neither could I deny her wish to pick it up. She even packed sandwiches to eat on the road so as not to waste time having lunch at home. Fearful that some emergency call would abort our mission, she kept prodding me to get going.

"Just as soon as I get the dog into the house and treat my lamb in the basement," I called to her.

That morning I had been called to the Wilbur Hoffman farm. Wilbur was one of the few farmers that raised sheep in this area. About a week before he had docked the tails of some new lambs. It was not a complicated procedure, and I had even heard of some farmers biting off the tails of lambs. Unfortunately, not even a minimal effort was made to disinfect the cutting instrument or the tail, and as a result, tetanus or lockjaw may ensue. Tails are docked because the wool tends to trap the droppings, and before you know it, a large wad accumulates causing all kinds of distasteful problems. I drove over to the sheep pens to find Wilbur dumping some dead lambs into his pickup truck.

Wilbur looked up and said, "I'm gonna bury them in a hole I got dug up in that field over yonder. Now why the hell is it that the lambs get lockjaw when I cut them and I never have trouble when you do it."

"Well, I'll tell you Wilbur, it's my college education. They teach you to wash your hands and your tools when you operate."

Wilbur peered at me from baggy eye slits, and I thought my flippancy had irritated him, but he gave me a tobacco-juiced smile and said, "God damn, if you ain't right. Let's dock those lambs in that other den."

After I completed docking about a dozen lambs, he turned to me and said, "From now on, you're the only guy that's gonna dock my lambs. I can't take this shit anymore. It's a hell of a way for these poor critters to die. Can you do somethin' for these others?"

I saw that he was deeply upset, and I regretted my smart-ass remark about a college education.

The tetanus or lockjaw bacillus is spore-forming and capable of living in the soil and in the intestinal tract. The spores are the most resistant known and can survive for many years. When a wound becomes exposed to the organism, a toxin is released that is a hundred times as toxic as strychnine. The bacillus remains localized in the wound area, but the liberated toxin attacks the nervous system producing severe spasms. Involvement of the jaw muscles causes difficulties in eating and chewing, hence the name "lockjaw" given to the disease.

I followed Wilbur to another pen. Here I saw lambs in different stages of the disease. Some were lying on their sides with heads and necks bent back or to one side. Any disturbance or noise put them into severe spasms. Most had high fevers of up to 110 degrees Fahrenheit. The disease is almost always fatal. It was a distressing sight, and I could see why Wilbur was so upset.

"I'll give them some intravenous antitoxin, but I doubt we will be able to save any of them. That lamb over there seems to be in the early stages. Perhaps massive doses of antitoxin and the new drug, penicillin, will be helpful. Is it okay to take him back with me to my office? I'd like to be able to give him frequent sedation to control the seizures. The chances are that he'll die no matter what."

"Sure, go ahead, Doc. I appreciate anything you can do to give the critter a chance."

As I picked up the lamb, I felt his body lock into spasms. The legs stiffened and his head whiplashed back. He was much sicker than I had first thought. I gave him a shot of a sedative, placed him on the front seat of the car alongside of me and headed back.

By the time I reached home, the lamb had relaxed. I cradled him in my arms and carried him into my house, planning to bed him down in my basement. Our dogs were all over me, sniffing the lamb with avid curiosity.

"Remember we're going to Chicago this afternoon," Mary called. "You have two more calls this morning. Mark Grenlund has a cow off feed, and Olaf Broquist has a cow to clean and then we're off."

Olaf Broquist was a Swede. His wife's contribution to the church suppers was always a mountain of Swedish meatballs whose aroma and taste should be immortalized. A call to Olaf's farm always excited my taste buds. That feeling was immediately neutralized by a two foot piece of rotting placenta dangling from the vulva of a cow that had calved four days ago.

"Believe me, Doc, I thought she cleaned out in pasture. She never showed a thing until today. You know how careful I am," he said apologetically.

This man was a paragon of cleanliness.

"These things happen, Olaf. Don't take it too hard," I said.

The odor was fierce. I slipped on a rubber sleeve to avoid the inevitable contamination. I washed the vulva area with an antiseptic, lubricated my sleeve and entered the uterus. It took about twenty minutes to unbutton the placenta from its attachments. I packed the uterus with antibiotic bolets and hoped that Olaf would not end up with a sterile cow.

"Better you wash up in the milk house. Things don't smell so good here," Olaf said.

We entered the milk house and I heard the murmur of the compressor refrigerating the milk in the milk tank. A tanker truck was making its rounds and would soon arrive to pipe the milk into the tanker. The days of lugging milk cans was all but over.

I proceeded to scrub up and as I was toweling down, I noticed two cans of Rokeach Kosher Scouring Powder on a shelf. Ordinarily this product is found in Jewish homes. Now why would Olaf want to use kosher scouring powder? It wasn't even readily available.

"Olaf, this scouring powder is used mostly by Jews. Where did you get it?" I asked.

"I like it, Doc—does a good job on my milking equipment. I buy it in a store in Rockford."

He looked at me curiously—closely.

"Say, Doc, are you a You?"

"I sure am," I responded smiling. "I thought everybody knew."

"By golly, I knew it. There's somethin' different about you. You're the best vet I ever had. You sure know your cows."

"You think it's because I'm Jewish, Olaf?"

"My father once told me about a doctor who saved his life in Sweden. That doctor was a Jew. All the other doctors said he was going to die. When I left Sweden, my father told me to only go to a Jewish doctor. I'm a lucky man. I got a Jewish veterinary. Come to the house, Doc. Alma will make some fresh coffee, and she had some wonderful Swedish coffee cake to go with it."

"Mary is waiting for me and I better get back as soon as I can. Say hello to Alma and tell her I am sorry to miss her coffee and cake."

On my way back, I thought a lot about Olaf's testimonial. Jewish doctors do have a mystique for some people, but if I have any special gift for healing, I am unaware of it. I know I have been unable to make all my clients happy and it wasn't because I was Jewish or not Jewish. In large animal medicine, success had to have an economic benefit. Saving the life of a cow was not a measure of success if you didn't preserve her value as a milker. Saving the life of a pig was no great accomplishment if that pig does not fatten for market in the prescribed time. I was no more successful than any of my colleagues who braved the trials and tribulations of farm practice as I did. Olaf's was one of my "good luck" farms. I wish I had more of them.

I arrived to find the pickup all gassed up and ready to go. The dog was in the house, and I had given the lamb antitoxin, penicillin and further sedation.

Our trip to Chicago was uneventful. As we entered the congestion of the city, I glanced at Mary and saw her looking wistfully about. I wondered how much she missed the city's cultural delights and the stimulating social life she had enjoyed. She was a gorgeous girl and could have had any number of boyfriends. I knew that one of her suitors was an enormously wealthy young doctor, and yet she chose me, an enormously poor veterinarian.

Fortunately, she acclimated to rural life quickly and actually seemed to have thrived on it, or so I hoped. I never ever heard a suggestion of complaint from her, even though she endured many difficult times as the wife of a large animal veterinarian. However, I could never accept the thought that she was completely happy. Farmers were forever coming and going, and I often found them seated in our living room being served coffee and cookies. Mary was an inveterate hostess and any caller to our home, even if he was a client, was served refreshments. At times, I often wondered if they came to get a closer look at her. She chose to allow these invasions of her privacy as part of her job. She enjoyed talking to these men and learning about their concerns. One day, as I watched her sort out my manured, blood-stained, evil-smelling clothes for laundering, she turned to me with a grimace and said, "You have the dirtiest, smelliest laundry imaginable," then added with a smile, "At least it's not greasy. Which reminds me, if you don't pick up some Clorox, you'll be out of business."

It remains a mystery how she managed all the chores she undertook with the Home Bureau, local politics and being treasurer of our local credit union. I did not for one moment believe that pregnancy or having a baby would slow her down. She was like one of those pregnant Chinese field-workers who stopped work to have her baby, only to return with the new baby strapped to her back. She was a very busy lady, but she always had time to lavish love and affection on me.

I never tired looking at her, and having her smile at me when I returned from calls was an ineffable delight. Unfortunately, my feelings were contained in a bottle that had a minimal opening. My affections were released sparingly in spite of my wish to shatter the bottle.

My parents rarely showed any overt affection, and at times, I even thought they did not like each other. Perhaps that is why I was always less than demonstrative toward Mary. To make up for what I deemed to be a serious flaw in my personality, I would deny her nothing. Even though I was very unhappy about driving to Chicago, I went without a murmur of complaint. It was my way of showing affection.

The pickup safely loaded with blanketed baby furniture, we made our way back to our new life. The furniture seemed to symbolize a further rooting of ourselves in rural America. I pulled into our driveway and began to unload. Mary's excitement was obvious. The dog greeted us as effusively as ever, and as I bent over to pat him, Fang suddenly burped. The smell of lamb hit my nostrils like a red-hot poker. I grabbed at his collar and pulled his face toward mine, and then I noticed his muzzle was stained red with blood. I ran to the basement door and found it ajar.

Obviously in my haste to leave, I had not closed the door completely and the dog had gained entrance. If I was appalled by what I was about to see, the reality was much worse. The body of the lamb was lying in the corner of the basement like a bit of crumpled sheepskin. Entrails were snaking in all directions, but there was a remarkable absence of blood. My dog had ripped into the abdomen of the lamb and had eaten its heart and liver. In all likelihood, the lamb was dead before it was attacked and that would account for the lack of blood in the basement. I bounded up the stairs in a state of fury. I just wanted to beat the hell out of that dog. I felt betrayed, violated. That my dog should do such a terrible deed and then act as if it were the most natural thing in the world was unthinkable.

"Mary, where's Fang?" I yelled, anger smoldering in my voice.

"Why, I let him out. What's wrong?" Her face was taut with concern.

"That bastard ate the lamb in the basement, and I'm going to beat him within an inch of his life."

Before she could intervene to stop me, I was out of the house. I searched the area, but he was nowhere to be found.

I returned to find her greatly disturbed. She had never seen me quite so angry before.

"I couldn't find him, lucky for him," I said.

"Lucky for you," she replied looking very grim. "You, more than most people, should realize that our dog is doing what most dogs do."

When we begin to attribute human values to our pets, we are not facing reality. In fact, I have always felt that animals have higher ethical standards than humans.

My boiling anger was reduced to a simmer... the thought of beating the hell out of Fang rapidly fading away.

Fang returned about an hour later, but keenly aware of my hostility, he had the good sense to avoid me. However, it took a couple of days before we were again on speaking terms.

A month passed and the incident with the lamb was all but forgotten. I returned from calls to be greeted by a tantalizing aroma wafting through the open kitchen windows. I could smell the simmering onions and a mushroom sauté, but they were just the cosmetics for something sumptuous.

"Hurry and wash up. I have a feast for you. Milton, the man whose dog lost a front leg in that mowing accident, was here. He says you saved his dog's life and he's very grateful. Anyway, he didn't pay his bill, but he brought us a beautiful calf's liver as a token of his appreciation, and that's what we're having for dinner."

I had a passion for calf's liver, and no master chef could prepare it better than Mary. It was with great anticipation that I sat down at the dinner table to enjoy a meal that was almost too elegant for my simple palate.

"Let the dog in before he scratches through the door. I have a treat for him as well," Mary called.

She served dinner with the practiced flair of someone who patronized fine restaurants. The liver was broiled medium rare and served smothered with mushrooms and onions with a side dish of snow peas and a dollop of smashed potatoes, cratered with brown gravy. Mary watched me go dreamy-eyed as I tasted the liver steak. My reverie into the world of gourmet food was interrupted by the gigantic head of Fang plopping down on my lap. As I looked down at Fang, I swear I could still see some of the lamb's blood encrusted on his muzzle. I jumped out of my chair almost upsetting the table. It was as if someone had poked a finger down my throat. My appetite had been converted to nausea in a split second.

"What's wrong, what's wrong? Did you burn yourself?" Mary asked looking at me intently.

"Don't you see what I am doing? I am doing exactly what this dog did a month ago. I am eating a calf's internal organ, that a surrogate killed and eviscerated and my wife prepared for me. You were so right when you said I would never forgive myself if I had punished him. He was doing what was the most natural thing in the world. I'm sorry, Mary, I just can't eat that liver now. I have to sort this out in my mind."

Mary smiled sadly while looking at her culinary efforts cooling on the table.

"You sure have a way of making things complicated. You're going to be sorting this out for the rest of your life. Does this mean that you are now a vegetarian?"

She sure had a way of getting to the heart of a problem. She left the room briefly and came back with a Bible. She thumbed through the Bible rapidly. I remembered that she had once taken a class in Bible studies.

"Here it is, Isaiah, Chapter 11. Let me read this to you. It's about a world as you would like it.

'The wolf also shall dwell with the lamb, and the leopard shall lie down with the kid; and the calf and the young lion and the fatling together; and a little child shall lead them.

And the cow and the bear shall feed; their young ones shall lie down together; and the lion shall eat straw like the ox.'"

"Now what does that say to you?" She looked at me inquiringly.

"It's a beautiful dream. I wish with all my heart it would come to pass. Nor shall man eat the liver of a calf, nor shall our dog eat of a lamb. But evolution has provided each specie a different menu. In order to survive, a carnivore's relatively short intestinal tract requires meat, which is much more readily digested than grass. Thus by necessity, he becomes a predator. A lion cannot exist on straw nor can a cow exist on meat, without extensive modifications of their digestive systems. Therefore, the creatures of the earth must eat whatever their digestive tracts are designed for. Man, the ultimate predator, can eat anything and everything. And remember God covered the nakedness of Adam with skins, thereby sanctioning the killing of animals. When God revises the evolutionary process and makes all living creatures grass eaters, perhaps then we will be ready for the vision of Isaiah."

Mary listened quietly to my ramblings and finally she said, "What about your dinner?"

I looked at her and laughed. "Give it to Fang. He knows how to enjoy a good meal."

I swear I saw a smile on the face of Fang.

VIRGIL

Mrs. Maitland had lived in this farm town in northern Illinois as long as anyone could remember. At one time, she had run a dairy farm with a hired hand, but had given that up and moved to town. She lived a reclusive life, only emerging to obtain the necessities. Occasionally, I would glimpse her walking into town and could not help but wonder about her. How did she spend days and nights alone in that large house? Did she read, listen to music or just dream the time away? There was something about this woman's demeanor that intrigued me, but she was unapproachable. Nobody knew anything about her except that she originally came from Texas a long time ago and had waited to be joined by the man who settled her here.

Hattie Johnson, who is pushing a hundred, relates that this man returned for a visit and brought her a baby parrot he had obtained in South America. She raised this bird, hand feeding and nurturing it, and inevitably, a human-animal bond developed. Her husband, if that's what he was, never returned.

It was a lovely spring day and most of my clients were in the fields sowing oats. The afternoon was quiet and restful except for a patiently dripping kitchen sink faucet that had begun to impatiently trickle.

"Will you fix that faucet or shall I call the plumber?"

Apparently the drip was getting on Mary's nerves.

"Okay, I'll go down to Cliff's and get a washer," I replied.

Going to Cliff's General Store was always a social experience. Everybody found their way there on one pretense or another. His assortment of merchandise was absolutely astounding. It was a cavernous store, shelves extending from floor to ceiling and assorted merchandise hanging from anything that could support a hook. A tall ladder, footed with wheels, accessed the inaccessible. The wonder of it was that he knew where everything was, be it a part for my oddball washing machine, which was always balking at the bloody, odoriferous clothes it was forced to wash, or a liniment for man or beast. If you were in dire need of some item he didn't have, he somehow improvised what you needed. I loved that store and spent many happy times poking at its innards and wondering what all those devices could be used for. When Cliff had a few moments, he would take me on guided tours of his personal museum.

I entered the store and noticed Cliff was attentively showing the mystery woman his collection of fry pans.

"Hi, Doc," he called as soon as he spotted me. "Come on over. Here's the lady you were asking about. I want you to meet Mrs. Maitland. He's our new vet," he said turning to her. I felt myself blushing under her blue-eyed gaze.

Here was a woman about seventy and I was twenty nine, and this was what I was concerned about—I had not shaved that morning; and I knew I had that aura of barn and cow odors from some morning calls.

My corduroy hat was streaked with cobwebs, barn dust and flecks of manure. I bought these hats by the dozen, and when one reached the state this one was in, I would stop my car beside some unplowed field and ceremoniously let it sail to be plowed under at some future date. I figured my hats had the fertilizer power to increase the yield of many a field.

I knew I would feel obliged to remove my hat in her presence, although this was not customary. Furthermore, I knew my hair was in total disarray. I had a habit of always shifting my hat like some pitcher on the mound; and with each shift, a swath of hair clumped together, producing strange geometric patterns, accentuated by the goo I used on my hair that morning.

I approached slowly, hoping to keep a little distance between us, but Cliff brought us eye to eye. My hat was off and I swear she was stifling some laughter. I saw her scan me from top to bottom. Her eyes dwelled momentarily on my manure-clad army shoes. Obviously my appearance left a lot to be desired.

"Do you have any experience treating parrots? I have one." No pleasantries, no superfluous remarks. She got right to it.

It took but ten seconds to review in my mind what I knew about parrots.

"The only birds I get to treat out here are chickens." I was serious, but Cliff thought it was as funny as could be and began to giggle.

"Well, it was nice meeting you," and off she strode from the store, leaving me and the fry pans. Apparently, there was nothing I could do for her or her bird.

Cliff winked at me, "Don't take it personal, Doc. She's really a grand old lady. She's lived with that parrot as long as I can remember. I know for a fact that they talk to each other. They're very close."

Two years passed; our meetings were mostly by chance and noteworthy for their laconic brevity. Yet, I continued to find her a compelling person. I admired that facade of determination and discipline she evoked. I asked Mary to invite her over for tea. I'm sure she drank tea and not coffee—she had that British tea look. Mrs. Maitland politely refused. Apparently, she chose the company of her parrot and no one was going to intrude on their privacy.

That winter, on a particularly cold day, driving home through the frozen darkness, I was experiencing my typical delicious fatigue that follows a hard day of satisfying work. Dinner was waiting, but no sooner had I washed up when the phone rang. Mary gave me her disappointed look and I shrugged my shoulders, as if to say "what can I do?" She answered the phone and I watched her listen intently, hoping it wasn't something that would force me out into the night.

"Virgil is sick?" she repeated into the phone.

"Virgil? He's a Roman Poet who wrote the Aeneid," I whispered, showing off my superior knowledge.

Mary handed me the phone with a look that said you had better handle this personally.

The voice on the phone was shrill, screaming, hysterical. "Virgil is dropping blood. He's going to die. He's going to die. Come at once," the voice ordered.

I knew immediately it was Mrs. Maitland in a state of hysteria. She tried to talk, but her sobbing seemed to swallow her words. Her stern facade had crumbled. She began to talk, but it was an imperial voice trying to be friendly. I could barely interject a word. On and on she went, telling me how sick her parrot was. Finally in abject surrender, she began to beg for whatever help I could provide. I was the straw she was clutching at.

"I'll be right over," I said, but she didn't hear me.

"I'll be right over," I shouted.

"Are you really coming now? He's all I have. I won't live without him." Hysteria was slowly returning to her voice.

"Mrs. Maitland, listen to me. I'm coming now," and with that I hung up the phone. She lived only a few blocks away and I dispensed with my usual uniform—a sheepskin-lined leather vest and a hooded parka. Of course, I wore my longjohns, from which I was inseparable till early spring. It was an intimacy so profound that Mary had a problem separating us. Regretting that I had not shaved that morning, I carefully brushed my hair, slipped on my plaid mackinaw and some gloves, no hat this time to dishevel my brilliantine hair. Mary took one look at me and said, "I hope you're not going out on a date."

In a few minutes, I was at her home wondering what I would do when I inevitably confronted her bird. I had a car filled with medicines and equipment to treat farm animals, but hardly anything to treat a sick parrot. I told myself the only thing to do is to treat this bird as if it were a chicken with pretty feathers. I would do what I could.

Before I could knock, she opened the door and ushered me into a large living room. The center of the room was dominated by a round pedestalled oak table with legs carved into lion paws, each clutching a ball. Enthroned on this table was a magnificent, gilded cage within which perched Virgil. His huddled form and ruffled feathers of brilliant colors indicated he was quite ill. For a fleeting moment, I could imagine Virgil sitting in the upper canopy of an Amazonian jungle as luminous rays of light glittered through the foliage.

"There, he's doing it again, Doctor."

Bloody droppings emerging from under the tail feathers splattered the floor of the cage. Both Mrs. Maitland and Virgil were breathing rapidly.

"He's going to die. He's going to die. I know it." Her voice was shrill.

That well might be, I thought. These symptoms were indeed life threatening. In an effort to bring her back to the immediate situation, I said, "Please, Mrs. Maitland, tell me about Virgil. How long has he been passing blood?"

She did not answer. I turned to her and she seemed transfixed. She was standing motionless, eyes fixed on some space in time, probably playing out some memory tape of a happier time.

I placed my hand on hers, which she quickly pulled away, but it did bring her back to reality.

"I'm going out to the car to get some medicine for Virgil," I said. "I'm coming right back. I'll do the very best I can," I said reassuringly.

Once again I told myself, "This is a chicken with colored feathers." With that in mind, I selected a preparation I had used with some success in chickens with hemorrhagic diarrhea. I decided to use the injectable and oral form of this antibiotic. I loaded the syringe with what I thought to be an appropriate dose and returned to the house ready to do battle with Virgil.

Neither Virgil nor Mrs. Maitland had moved since I left. Were it not for Virgil's shallow, rapid breathing, I would have thought I was looking at a still life. An overhead, electrified, antique lantern concentrated the light over the cage, leaving all else in shadow.

I carefully opened the cage and reached toward him with my gloved hand. He gave a half-hearted squawk and turned toward me menacingly. I knew his powerful beak could actually bite off a finger, and I also knew that handling a bird in this condition could have dire consequences. He was too weak and miserable to put up much of a protest. Fortunately, it was no trick at all to grasp him with my gloved hand and administer the medicine, both orally and by injection. I carefully released him, praying that the restraint had not put him into shock.

"Well, that wasn't too bad, Mrs. Maitland, now was it?"

I turned toward her, but she was nowhere to be seen. I scanned the room and as my eyes adjusted to the shadows, I saw her lying on the floor in a dead faint. It took me but a moment to scoop her up in my arms and place her on the divan. I thought she scarcely weighed more than the Holstein calf I delivered that morning. She felt cold and clammy and I covered her with an afghan that lay folded nearby. Slowly she began to stir and her eyes flickered open. She stared toward her parrot and then back at me.

"Is he all right? Don't leave us," she implored, "He's all I have."

"So far, so good," I responded.

Her eyes stared into the shadows. They began to mist with tears as she seemed to contemplate a life without Virgil. A haunting loneliness haloed her face. I had seen that look in nursing homes where old people are warehoused until they die.

Parrots live forty to fifty years and I could well imagine her emotional dependence on Virgil. Mrs. Maitland's life had reduced her to this single consuming relationship. It was sad in a way, but that was the lifestyle she had chosen. Perhaps she was still waiting for the lover who never returned. There are many of us who wait a lifetime for the return of love lost.

"Mrs. Maitland, I'm going out to my car for some more medicine for Virgil. I'll be back in a moment."

I doubted whether she heard me. I hurried out of the house and went next door to her neighbor, a retired farmer and his wife. I explained the situation to them.

"Oh, yes, we know about her heart problem. It happens all the time. We'll call her doctor."

They placed the call, and to my surprise, her doctor said he would be right out. And I thought only veterinarians responded that quickly, but it was the 1950s and doctors did make house calls. I returned to Mrs. Maitland with news that her doctor was on his way.

"Oh, him," she said. Apparently, she was less than happy with her doctor.

I found a lamp on a table next to the divan. A pull on a beaded chain produced an illumination of exquisite multiple colors. It had a leaded glass shade, depicting a profusion of fruit blossoms set in luminous blues. The base was a sculpted, cast bronze tree trunk. This had to be a real Tiffany lamp.

Deciding to wait for her doctor, I sat down on a chair beside her. Her breathing had eased and she seemed more alert and less anxious.

"Can you save him, Doctor? He's never been this sick before."

We both looked toward Virgil, perched in his cage. About two hours had elapsed and he was still alive. There was no further evidence of bloody droppings. Perhaps it was my imagination, but he looked better—less huddled, more alert.

"I think he looks a bit better."

Sometimes those words "a bit better," especially when you're talking about a creature this critically ill, is seized upon to mean that the animal is on its way to recovery. At times, you're so desirous to relieve the anxiety of a client that the first glimmer of improvement is mistakenly brought to the client's attention, but that can boomerang with disturbing consequences.

While I sat wondering who was more ill, Mrs. Maitland or her parrot, a car crunched onto her gravel driveway. In a moment, a florid, rotund man entered. He was neatly dressed and introduced himself as her doctor. After a cursory examination, he asked me to help get her into bed, but by now she had sufficiently revived as to need minimal assistance.

To further help relieve her anxiety, I promised to look in on Virgil first thing in the morning. Her doctor assured me that she would be okay, but seemed slightly annoyed when I suggested that somebody be with her through the night.

"She has these spells frequently and always recovers nicely." However, he will try and locate a companion for her. Failing that, he himself would spend the night with her. I thought that was more than reasonable and my disquiet about him evaporated.

After many voluble assurances that all would be well, I decided to leave. However, I could not help feeling that he was reassuring me about Mrs. Maitland's condition just as I was reassuring Mrs. Maitland about her parrot's condition.

Before I left, I grabbed hold of Virgil and gave him another swig of medicine. I was happy to hear him protest. Virgil was feeling better. I cleaned out the floor of the cage, put some fresh water and seed in his dishes and headed home for a late dinner with Mary. I knew she would not eat without me.

That night I slept fitfully. My phone rang at 5:30 a.m. It was Tom Vogel.

"Doc, this cow freshened yesterday and this morning, her bag is hard as a rock. She's off feed, too. Get to her as soon as you can."

Undoubtedly acute mastitis, I thought.

"Be there this morning, Tom."

Over morning coffee, I outlined my schedule to Mary, or better yet, she outlined it to me. My first stop would be the lady and the parrot. It would only take a few minutes, and perhaps, I could provide the old girl with some comforting words.

My car went through its usual sputtering protest before it started. A frosted morning had blanched whatever color this little town possessed. Even the red and white sign out in the middle of Main Street, showing a little girl clutching a loaf of Sunbeam bread with its grammatically incorrect admonishment *Drive Slow – School – Eat Sunbeam Bread,* was suffering from a winter pallor. And why couldn't our school board buy a proper sign as I had suggested, instead of taking the freebie from Sunbeam? There was a principle involved, but somehow it seemed too arcane for the school board.

I was mildly irritated as I drove into Mrs. Maitland's driveway. I rang the side-door bell, but no response. I knew it was early and figured she must be asleep. I was sure her doctor had somebody spend the night with her. I circled round to the front and heard chimes inside the house as I repeatedly rang the doorbell. I tried the door and it was unlocked. It was not unusual to leave doors unlocked in this small farm town. We were a community of innocents. I peeked into the living room and was overjoyed to see Virgil moving about in his cage.

"Hello, Mrs. Maitland," I called again and again. The silence worried me. I walked toward her bedroom, and after a moment's hesitation, I decided to look in. I opened the door, softly calling her name. The room was suffused with a soft, morning light that peeked through the lace curtains. It was sparsely furnished, and except for the elegant curtains and a colorful, braided rug, it had a monastic ambiance. On a small bed in the corner of the room, I saw Mrs. Maitland... apparently asleep. I felt like an intruder as I approached the bed. I feared that if she suddenly awoke and found someone in her room, it could be very frightening indeed. A loud screech blasted the silence. My guts just about flipped over. "Sue, Sue, Sue," Virgil shrieked. But Sue did not stir. I moved closer to the bed and began to look for a sign of life. Did she have a stroke or was she in a coma? Her wizened face had a wonderful serene expression. Age had not entirely diminished what once was a beautiful woman. I reached for her hand and my worst fear was realized. She was dead. Sometime, in the stillness and darkness of the night, she passed away... alone. No one should die alone. I always felt that when death took you by the hand, someone should be there to hold your other hand. Unkind thoughts about her doctor, who promised to have someone spend the night with her, consumed me. Where the hell was he? He said he would stay if he had to.

"Sue, Sue, Sue," Virgil screeched again. I left the bedroom and walked over to the cage. Virgil stirred restlessly, eyeing me with suspicion and dislike. Suddenly, he humped his back and passed some blood-tinged droppings. There was no doubt that he needed another shot. I prepared the injection and reached into the cage with my gloved hand. He squawked and screamed, bit at my fingers, and it was quite a scramble before I could corner him and administer the medication. I daresay that in his forty years of life, he had never suffered such indignity and I doubted if he would ever forget it.

I went next door and awakened the Johnsons to tell them that Mrs. Maitland was dead. And again, they seemed to know exactly what to do. It was as if they had rehearsed it all before. First they called the doctor, then they called her lawyer, and third, they placed a call to a funeral home. Everything was arranged, they advised me. No need at all for me to trouble. I found the whole situation disquieting. I thought it most curious that no family member was called; perhaps there were none, or her attorney would notify next of kin.

I decided to go back into the house and at least await the arrival of her doctor. Near the window, I found a lovely chair graced with a needlepoint chair pad. It had a leaf design that depicted elm, maple and locust leaves swirling in a sunlit background. It was so exquisitely done, I was reluctant to sit on it. Nearby, facing Virgil, was what looked like an early American rocker. Lovely decorative designs were carved into the back of the chair. The seat pad was alive with sunny yellow and whites daisies. They seemed to bring in all the outdoor freshness of a spring day. Alongside the rocker was a large quilted bag. Poking out of it was some lacy material and assorted crochet hooks. Obviously, most of what I saw was her own handiwork. As the morning light filled the room, I saw Virgil's form reflected on folds of the white window curtains. A spear of sunlight on a glass-enclosed bookcase caught my attention.

What did this woman read? There were books by Jane Austen, the Bronte Sisters, Thomas Hardy, Wordsworth, Shelly, Byron and tattered volumes of Shakespeare's plays. How appropriate I thought. I heard her neighbors say that on warm, summer days, she sat on the porch with Virgil and read aloud in some strange language they could partially understand. I presumed that she had been reading Shakespeare to Virgil. In a corner was a hand-wound phonograph standing on a cabinet filled with records. A record of Mozart's Jupiter Symphony was on the spindle. It was obvious that she enjoyed Mozart as much as Mary and I did. Once again, I regretted not being able to share a friendship during her lifetime.

Alongside the bookcase was a colonial style table that supported that magnificent Tiffany lamp with its succulent stained glass of fruits and blossoms cascading down the shade. I pulled the light switch and the vivid colors illuminated the room. The decor evoked the personality and elegance of a very special lady. Within this room was evidence of a rich, full, creative life shared with a parrot. It was not an island of despair and loneliness as I had imagined. It evoked a vibrancy and richness as vivid as the color of Virgil's feathers.

An hour had passed and finally her doctor arrived. I greeted him with my best expression of displeasure. After a brief examination, he returned to the living room to announce, "She's very dead, you know. I doubt whether anything could have saved her."

What an inappropriate and insensitive way to announce someone's death, and at the same time use the occasion to cover his negligence.

"Her lawyer will take care of all the details," he explained.

"Got to run now." With that, he abruptly left. The visit took him all of five minutes. His attitude seemed to say, "She's dead and that's all there is to it." But there's a lot more to it.

I was way behind my schedule. Fresh water and seed for Virgil and I was on my way, leaving only him to mourn his mistress. I think he sensed her death.

A feeling of despondency accompanied me on my rounds that day, but dinner with Mary brightened my spirits—nothing more invigorating than a beautiful wife. I retired to my large, leather chair to smoke a King Edward cigar. This leather chair and ottoman had been a surprise birthday gift from Mary. Although it eroded our assets, I must confess that I spent many a blissful hour cushioned in its recesses. The foul, acrid smoke that emerged from that nickel cigar was patiently endured by my wife and our dogs. Those King Edward cigars assured me a lot of privacy. Nobody wanted to get too close. The ring of our phone brought me out of my reverie. Mary came in to announce that some lawyer wanted to talk with me.

"I'm Jim Benson, Mrs. Maitland's lawyer. I understand you are the vet that treated her parrot. Please send your bill to me. There are funds available for you to be paid. Mrs. Maitland's will provides for her to be buried in Austin, Texas, in a family plot. That's where she came from, you know."

"No, I didn't know."

"I would appreciate having you come over sometime tomorrow and put her bird to sleep."

I recoiled at the thought of having to euthanize Virgil. I could just see myself reaching into the cage, struggling to grab Virgil to administer a lethal injection. I was positive that was not what she would have wanted.

"Mr. Benson, did Mrs. Maitland make any provisions in her will for her parrot?"

"Uh, as a matter of fact, she did. It was her desire that upon her death, the bird be put to sleep and buried with her in the same coffin."

"Well, why not honor her wishes?" I inquired.

"You see, Doctor, this coffin's going to be sealed here, and it's against the law to ship a human body and an animal in the same coffin. So be a good fellow and take care of this matter for me," and with that, he abruptly hung up.

In no way could I persuade myself to euthanize this bird. Benson will have to find an executioner elsewhere. Feeling very self-righteous and now having unkind thoughts about lawyers as well as doctors, I decided to ignore the whole matter.

The next day, I returned to the routine of practice, feeling strangely uneasy. Benson wanted the bird dead, and for that matter, so did Mrs. Maitland. While I was unwilling to euthanize the bird for her lawyer, I was willing to do so if the provisions of the will were carried out. How often we respect the wishes of the dead before those of the living. And how often it is that the hand that heals is the hand that kills. Animals are legally classified as personal property, and consequently, their owners have the power of life and death over them. Most domestic animals are led to slaughter and consumed by us.

This is their life cycle in our society. Pet animals have a kinder fate—living out a comparatively short life span, often euthanized when they become terminally ill. A parrot on the other hand, has a life span almost the equivalent of man and will often outlive its owner, especially if purchased in the owner's middle years. My continued misgivings merely served to confuse me further. My work-saturated brain had little room for ethical niceties.

Meanwhile, Benson repeatedly called, but I made myself unavailable, hoping he would get someone else.

One evening, I returned home to find Mary impatiently awaiting me. There was more than the usual twinkle in her eyes when she said, "There's a surprise for you in your office." Her amused demeanor worried me. I was unprepared for the sight I was about to see. There was Virgil, cage and all, ensconced on my exam table. After Mary was fully satisfied that I had recovered from my shock, she informed me that lawyer Benson had personally delivered Virgil and said, "Tell the doctor to get rid of him," and with those words, he dropped the cage and took off.

I looked at Virgil, and as if expecting another shot, he cringed to the back of the cage. With his health restored, a sheen on his feathers gave vibrancy to their colors.

"Tell me beautiful bird, do you wish to live on with us or not?"

Now it was Mary's turn to be surprised. After all, the care, feeding and reeducation of Virgil would be her responsibility.

Generally, we would discuss a matter such as this. If she had an objection, I probably could find another home for this magnificent animal or even leave him at Benson's front door... that would shake him up a little! In this case, I was positive she would not part with Virgil. The look in her eyes told the whole story. He was ours.

During the following weeks, she spent a lot of time with Virgil. Outside of a few squawks and whistles, not an intelligible sound emerged. Mary could now tickle his head and neck as he sat dreamy-eyed on his perch. My presence still agitated him. His beady eyes locked into my movements and never wavered until I left the room. I tried some sweet talk, but he cringed pathetically as I approached the cage. To make matters worse, on one occasion I had to manhandle him in order to trim a broken nail.

Meanwhile, Mary continued her one-way conversations with Virgil.

"How are you today?"

"My, you look pretty."

"Virgil want a polly seed?"

"I love you, Virgil."

On and on she would prattle. There was no end to her patience. I began to see an element of perseverance in her that I never knew she had. She was resolved to communicate with this bird. She just knew that he was a highly intelligent, affectionate animal with an extensive vocabulary.

It was a radiant, spring morning as I returned home for a late breakfast. As I pulled into the driveway, Mary came running from the house terribly excited.

"He's doneit. He's done it."

The last time she came running from the house this excited was to tell me that she had just returned from the doctor and was pregnant.

"What's he done, sweetheart?" I thought an expression of endearment might calm her.

"Virgil is talking," she beamed.

"What did he say?" I inquired.

"He said, *'I Love You, Sue.'* He may be identifying me with Mrs. Maitland. He keeps saying *'I Love You, Sue,'* over and over."

The word dam had been broken and Virgil became an increasingly articulate member of our family. His vocabulary was enormous, and at times, I could swear he was responding to questions. He even learned to tolerate me, but I had to entice him with food bribes and lots of head tickling.

Virgil lived with us for another six years before he died of kidney failure. When that happened, Mary became terribly distraught, since she assigned human characteristics to Virgil. This is a terrible mistake many of us make with our animals. Mary was no exception. Our pets are such wonderful creatures, capable of giving us moments of great pleasure and serenity. We just can't help ourselves. Virgil was ceremoniously buried, and it was our hope that he would be reunited with the Sue he loved.

Large Green Mat

Hemstitch Bed Skirt in Ivory

42101 Valance $19.95

Hemstitch Bed Skirts Are Sized To Fit

The crisp, clean good looks of our gathered cotton Hemstitch Bed Skirts have a refreshing effect on a room. Daybed Bed Skirt has a 14" drop. Split corners accommodate footboards. Coordinating **Shams** tie the look together. Choose from lengths listed below and SPECIFY IVORY or WHITE. Imported.

42279	Standard Sham	$24.95	
42278	European Sham	$29.95	
42815	Daybed Bed Skirt	$49.95	
14"L	42362	Twin	$49.95
	42363	Full	$59.95
	42364	Queen	$69.95
	42365	King	$79.95
18"L	42366	Twin	$59.95
	42367	Full	$69.95
	42368	Queen	$79.95
	42369	King	$89.95
21"L	42370	Twin	$69.95
	42371	Full	$79.95
	42372	Queen	$89.95
	42373	King	$99.95

1•800•627•1712   plowandhearth.com

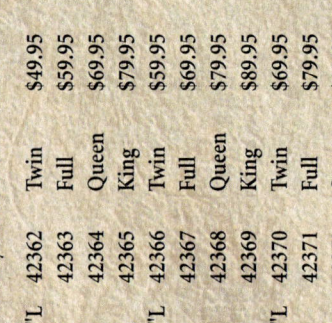

TWO DOGS AND A MONSTER

Although I shouldn't speak so irreverently about them, all of our dogs were hand-me-downs. For one reason or another their owners could not keep them. There were five dogs that spanned our lives and each had a remarkable personal impact upon us. Unfortunately, dogs have an abbreviated life span compared to humans, but we have always managed to eke out at least fifteen years of devotion and pleasure from each of them.

Our dogs were always a source of joy and occasionally, sorrow. You love them so unreservedly that it is impossible not to forgive some of their flagrant violations of etiquette. Poop on the carpet, a squirt of urine on the leg of our rock maple dining room table are forgivable, especially if I do not step into it. Fortunately accidents are uncommon, most animals being more fastidious than their masters.

Their lives are accelerated, consequently so are their problems. They endure pain stoically, and pain is often a forgotten component of treatment. They age rapidly, but gracefully. We had one old dog, a miniature poodle named Charlie, who became incontinent. The problem depressed and distressed him just as it would any human. I was able to control his incontinence for about a year with medication and diet, but finally he lost control altogether. He stayed with us for another year, finally he died while cradled in Mary's arms, enveloped by her sobs.

We had another dog named Nicky, a dog we adored. In our eyes, he was the most beautiful Beagle in the world. His appearance and coloring were crafted by a master creator. Nicky was a Chicago firehouse dog who rode to fires perched on top of a fire engine hook and ladder. Maybe he was replaced by a Dalmatian, but at any rate he was sent to Mary by a fireman she knew in Chicago. He said the dog needed more space than a firehouse, and since we now lived in farm country, he persuaded her to adopt him. The more likely story was that his howl was louder than the fire engine's siren and caused confusion when they were racing to a fire. In Chicago, traffic would never slow down for a howling dog. In our home, he was as calm and beautiful as a Persian rug. Take him outside, his energy was boundless. He had a bark, or should I say voice, that resonated from an Ezio Pinza to a Mario Lanza. He was designed to be a mighty hunter, and that he was, much to my displeasure. The tracking of wildlife was his greatest joy, as its preservation was my greatest joy. Keeping Nicky's pursuits within reason was a time-consuming job. The vast fields and pastures were his playground. He was responsive to my commands and our walks together were invigorating occasions. For every half mile I walked, Nicky would cover five. He was indefatigable. I could not begin to describe the many geometric patterns his nose led him to create. The zigs and zags, the sudden turns, all in pursuit of a tantalizing scent.

Among my vices was the cigar. Its objectionable emission permeated the entire house, even the closets and bathroom. Mary never complained. She smoked cigarettes. In those days, I thought cigar smoking to be a benign habit, and cigarette smoking something malignant. There was nothing I could do or say that would deter her. She was addicted.

I noted that Nicky avoided my office whenever he saw me smoking. Once I blew some smoke at him and he looked as if he were going to have a panic attack. He let out a yowl that would have made Bugle Ann proud and bolted out of my office. His reaction caused my devious mind to hatch a plan that might discourage Mary from smoking.

Behind our house was a large hip-roofed garage that could easily accommodate three cars. The farmer I bought my house from used it to store a tractor and assorted farm implements. Since our house was becoming rapidly engorged with the medicines and implements of my profession, I had converted half of the garage into an office and storeroom. The decor was knotty pine, and I knotty pined everything in sight—walls, cabinets, shelves and even the ceiling. It was within this environment I sequestered Nicky. Every chance I had, I would isolate myself with Nicky and light an ugly cigar stump, blow the smoke toward him, observe his panic and encourage him to yowl. It became so ear shattering an experience that I stuffed cotton in my ears to dull the sound. After three days of dog abuse, I thought Nicky might experience some serious psychological damage. Finally it occurred to me to reward him for his cooperation. When Mary was away at a Home Bureau meeting, I surreptitiously broiled some liver, well done, cubed it into chunks, and gave bits of it to Nicky when he yowled on cue. Much to my pleasure, he became a willing participant in my scheme.

He was ready. I was ready. We were sitting down to an early breakfast when Mary said, "Where's Nicky? I've hardly seen him around lately."

"Oh, he likes to spend time with me in my new office. He likes the smell of knotty pine among other things."

Mary looked at me curiously, immediately perceiving that another one of my shenanigans was in the making. Before she could say a word, I said, "Give me a minute. I'll bring him into the house."

Glory be, she was just about to light up a cigarette. I rushed to my office and returned at a gallop with Nicky. He entered the kitchen, took one look at Mary, and began to howl at a decibel that would have shattered a crystal glass, if we had one. I saw the fluster in Mary's eyes.

"What's wrong with him? I have never known him to behave this way," she shouted.

"He can't stand cigarette smoke. Put out your cigarette and I'm sure he'll stop."

She hastened to the sink and plunged the cigarette into a soaking frying pan. Meanwhile I slipped Nicky a cube of liver. His barking stopped immediately.

"Sorry, Mary, no more smoking in this house. You see what it does to Nicky."

Mary looked at us suspiciously.

"What's he chewing?" she asked.

"Oh, some breakfast food I suppose." I could not contain a guilty smile.

"Come here, Nicky. Let me see what you're chewing."

Nicky approached hoping for another treat, but instead Mary opened his mouth only to see and smell the remains of liver.

"Ah ha, so you two have devised a plot to make me stop smoking."

She picked up Nicky and gave him a kiss on his lips, liver breath and all. I didn't believe what I was seeing—she used to be so squeamish about animals. She then cornered me and gave me a kiss. I could smell the liver on her breath. Ugh.

"I love you both. I'll see what I can do about stopping smoking."

She did cut down quite a bit, especially when Nicky was in the house. It wasn't until she became pregnant with our son that I was able to convince her that smoking could be damaging to our baby. There was minimal information at that time about the evils of smoking, but whatever information I could glean from the press and scientific literature, I brought to her attention. Her addiction (I thought it to be an addiction) was compelling, but I had inculcated some guilt into her thinking. I did light up a cigar at times, but never seemed to enjoy it as much as I did before. Apparently Nicky's reaction to smoke provided a similar reaction in me. While I did not howl, I did smoke less.

During her pregnancy, I did my best to persuade her to limit her activities, but she was more active than ever. An increase in our social life became troublesome. After a grueling day of practice, I was rarely in the mood for after dinner company, but I did my best to be cordial to all who came by. It was obvious that Mary encouraged visits from her friends. Pregnancy was a period of joyous anticipation. She was never more beautiful.

It was about 10:00 p.m. when the phone rang. Mary answered, and I heard her speaking to Emma Whitehead. I was relieved to know that it was not a call for me and proceeded to get ready for bed. About ten minutes later as I lay in bed reading a book, Mary entered the room—a Mona Lisa smile on her face. It was a smile that needed interpretation.

"Here's the story," she said. "Jack Whitehead has been at the Phil Bossert farm for the last few hours trying to deliver a calf. He's exhausted and needs help. I volunteered your assistance. I was positive you wouldn't refuse."

"So why did you let me get undressed and ready for bed if you knew I had to go out?"

"Wasn't it worth reading a few more pages of that book you're so excited about? It's so easy for you to get undressed and dressed. See that—two minutes—you're dressed."

Looking at her, I really wanted to get undressed but not for reading or sleeping.

Once again I drove into the darkness. I remember how strange and desolate the prairie used to be. As the years went by, it was no longer dark and forbidding, but familiar and comfortable. On wintry nights when snow clogged my way, each farmhouse became a beacon of security and warmth. Alone in sub-zero weather, survival was a consideration, but I was young, strong and as yet unchallenged by fear.

Now why would Whitehead call for help? He was a crackerjack veterinarian. What sort of a problem could have prompted him to make this request? Obviously, he found himself in a difficult situation. If it was a problem for him, it would certainly be a problem for me.

In my first year of practice, I would tremble with anxiety when called for a calving. When I was advised that the farmer always delivered his own calves but just couldn't handle this one, my anxiety escalated. If he can't do it with all his experience, what can I do? In most cases, these calls turned out to be relatively uncomplicated. But when an experienced vet calls for help, things are going to be very complicated.

I drove up the long blacktopped road leading to the Phil Bossert farm. No dirt road here. This was the access to the most elegant farm I had ever seen. There were two wonderful barns, four silos, innumerable corn cribs and storage facilities for all kinds of farm implements. This farm was as self-contained as any I had ever seen, and Jack Whitehead was their exclusive vet. They were smart enough to know the qualities of a great veterinarian.

I drove up to the lighted barn and entered to find Jack seated on a three-legged milking stool in front of a maternity pen. He was stripped to the waist, arms smeared with blood and mucous, while obstetrical chains soaked in milk pails filled with antiseptic solutions. How well I knew the look on his face—fatigue, frustration and a tinge of embarrassment when he saw me. A magnificent but exhausted Holstein slowly moved about her maternity pen, stopping to labor in a desultory manner.

"Glad you were able to come. I'm exhausted. I can't do a thing with this calf. The legs are contorted and rigid. The spine is twisted and inflexible. I thought I would do a Cesarean, but I didn't think I could get the calf out. I think an embryotomy is in order—we have to take that calf out in pieces and I'm beat and need help."

"Here I am Jack, and I'm all yours. First let me take a poke in there and see if I can get some landmarks. Have someone put the cow in a stanchion."

"How about you?" I said, as I turned toward a middle-aged overalled man standing nearby. "Would you please place the cow in her stanchion and hold her tail?" I said dryly.

Jack came over and said, "I want you to meet Phil Bossert."

We shook hands. His grip made me wince. I guess I should have been a little more friendly, but I was beginning to anticipate the problems of the delivery and social amenities were forgotten—never a good excuse. The cow was put in her stanchion while I stripped to the waist and lubricated my arms. My right arm entered the uterus (I am left handed and always save that arm for the most difficult parts of the delivery) and confirmed what Jack had said. The legs had no flexibility, and the joints were fused making manipulation and positioning impossible. The calf was lying crosswise, with the legs tenting the uterine wall. Tugging on these legs could easily rupture the uterus. The spine was curiously angulated, reptilian, also in a locked position. The head was not palpable and I could only assume where it was.

My feeling was that we were dealing with a type of monstrosity known as a muscle contracture monster. Many of these abnormalities are caused by an incestuous sire-daughter mating. While inbreeding constitutes the shortest path to the stabilization of type, the consequences can be disastrous.

I turned to Jack. "Afraid we have one of those monsters that can turn your hair gray. We'll have to take this calf out piecemeal."

Phil Bossert winced and Jack said, "I knew that would be your decision."

I have in my obstetrical kit several feet of wire called "Gigli wire." I can attach a handle on each end, loop one over the part I want to amputate, grab both handles and begin pulling firmly back and forth. This wire will cut through tissue, bone, whatever, sparing adjacent tissue. It's remarkable. Jack and I began sawing off the limbs to avoid a uterine perforation. Our plan was to cut the animal in half, thereby making extraction easier. Getting the Gigli wire over and under the spine was a difficult matter, but we did it somehow. We had cut the calf in half and it still would not budge. Jack finally located the head and we were able to saw that off. I noticed considerable hemorrhage ensue as we sawed through the bones, suggesting that the calf had been alive when we started the procedure.

Once again we attached obstetrical chains and were able to extract a segment of the calf. It was a piece-meal process, but we delivered what might be called a calf.

The veterinary literature described this calf as a monster. The severe skeletal changes and gross abnormalities of the head certainly fit the terminology. But looking at what we had delivered, I could only feel compassion for the animal. It was regrettable that we had to kill her, but her death was inevitable. The choice was not ours to make if the cow was to survive. Rooted in my mind was the thought that this indeed had to be the result of inbreeding. I would let Jack discuss that with Phil Bossert.

We made a final examination of the cow and found her to be in pretty good shape. Jack would give her all the necessary follow-up care. Hopefully she was not sufficiently damaged to prevent her from breeding again under happier circumstances.

With our hands, arms and bodies soaked in blood, fetal fluids and sweat, Jack and I shook hands. It was a memorable case that neither he nor I might have handled alone. It linked us together in an extraordinary experience.

As we cleaned up, we smiled, we laughed, we joked with Phil Bossert—three happy men exulting in a barn. He insisted we join him for a snack. I was starving and readily accepted. It was hardly a snack, but rather a sumptuous meal that we had no difficulty devouring. Mrs. Bossert looked on with awe and delight as Phil, Jack and I consumed the feast that she had prepared. I said my goodbyes and shook hands with Phil Bossert, but this time his powerful hand was warm and gentle.

As we walked to our cars, the moon was bursting in its fullness and a soft spectral light illuminated the landscape. It was midnight on the prairie.

About two weeks had passed when Mary received a call from Emma Whitehead. She braved my cigar smoke to inform me that we had accepted an invitation to be the guests of Emma and Jack at the Wagon Wheel for dinner and dancing in celebration of their tenth wedding anniversary. The Wagon Wheel was about twenty miles north in Wisconsin and was the grandest log cabin I had ever seen. It was the most elegant restaurant in the area and easily the most extravagant. Without being forewarned, I had taken Mary, her sister and husband up there a couple of years earlier. I still had not recovered from the shock I experienced when I received the bill.

I put my cigar stub in a large test tube for suffocation and reclamation and said, "Did she say 'guest'?"

"That's what she said, 'guest.'" She said that since you refused to accept a fee for your services at Phil Bossert's, they would like to reciprocate in some way, and this is it. Jack asks but one thing from you—take it easy on the wine."

I laughed. "He's worried about the bill."

Mary gave me her mischievous smile and said, "We're going next Thursday evening so have everything cleared. And we are unavailable for emergencies that night, right?"

I winced but said, "Right."

"Morrison will cover for you," she informed me.

Well the day arrived. Mary had acquired a pretty dress, and I had exhumed a suit and tie from the attic. We were ready. Our dogs seemed to share in the excitement, probably wondering how they would fit into the scheme of things. I promised each of them a doggy bag from the Wagon Wheel—no bones.

The Whiteheads arrived a little early, and I sat on our porch chatting with them. Our dogs were in the house looking after Mary. There was always something she couldn't find—be it her butterfly pin or a bracelet or whatever. Finally the door opened and out she came with Fang and Nicky. Emma rose to greet her, and I couldn't help observing how beautiful these women were. Emma was wearing an elegant black dress with a ruffled skirt, glistening black patent leather shoes with a bow, and a lovely pearl necklace with matching earrings.

Our dogs were not remiss in their greetings. I noticed Fang sniffing Emma's shoes with unusual interest. Then in the blink of an eye, he raised his leg and urinated, I said urinated, on Emma's skirt, left stocking and shoe. Not in my wildest dreams would I have thought him capable of such gross misbehavior. I bolted out of my chair to make a kill, but he was gone with what you might call mercurial speed, with Nicky following. I suppose Nicky thought we might not consider him an innocent bystander.

Mary and I smothered Emma with apologies.

"It's nothing, it's okay, don't worry about it. I'm fine." Emma spoke calmly as if this were an everyday occurrence. For a moment I expected her to say, "Dogs do this to me all the time." She was truly the epitome of grace and good manners.

"Let's get you cleaned up, Emma. Come into the house," Mary said.

I turned to Jack. "You do small animal work. How do you explain this behavior?"

"I've never seen a dog do something like this, but I've heard of it happening. I do know that Emma went into the kennel to give some medication to a sick dog before we left. Maybe she stepped in something that reminded Fang of the call of the wild."

Meanwhile Fang was nowhere to be seen. Nicky returned looking a bit sheepish and bewildered. Some kind words and a pat on his head absolved him of any complicity. I circled the house and found Fang sulking under the rear steps. He approached me with trepidation. He had shrunk to half his size and his eyes begged for mercy. I grabbed his collar and yanked him along with me to the front of the house just as Emma and Mary were coming out the door. The damage had been repaired as much as possible.

"Oh, there you are Fang," Emma exclaimed.

She turned to me and said, "Would you mind if I had a private conversation with Fang?"

"Certainly not," I answered.

She took Fang by his collar and led him to a nearby tree. I saw her bend down, take Fang's head in her hands and begin whispering in his ear. After a few minutes, she released him and he exploded with joy. Apparently all was forgiven.

"Emma," Mary asked, "what did you whisper in his ear?"

"Oh, it's our little secret. If Fang wants to tell you, it's all right with me."

MITCHELL

Each season has its own weather pattern. But in March each day can be sufficiently varied to confuse even the *Farmer's Almanac*, the best weather prognosticator around. Weather vagaries from Arctic blizzards to the sweat-soaking heat of summer were a fact of life. The weather can be as unpredictably fierce as it can be gentle. I was concerned about having to drive the 22.6 miles to the nearest hospital with Mary in labor. It was a daunting thought—especially if I would have to do it in a snow storm.

Early March I was awakened at 6:00 a.m. by Ralph Ralston who had a cow off feed. "No great emergency, but she seems to be bloating a wee bit. Get here as soon as you can," he said. A glance out my window revealed yet another March landscape—a fine sheet of ice had veneered everything within sight. It was as if the earth, the trees and the houses had been dipped into a freezer and had emerged ice-clad. With the rising sun, the world had become a glittering, prismatic fantasy land. It was a challenge, but

I decided to get to his farm right away. The cow might be sicker than he imagined. Once out on the pavement, driving might be easier. I virtually slid to my car and barely made it out of my driveway. There was absolutely no traction. My rear tires spun wildly even when I attempted to creep along. Out on the deserted highway, the road was a sheet of glare ice, and I crawled along at fifteen m.p.h. My radio was playing a lilting Strauss waltz, and I tried to increase my speed. The car skidded to the right, but I was able to bring it back on course rather easily. I found that with a little squeeze on the accelerator and a turn of the wheel I could cause a slide to the left. It was a pleasant sensation sliding back and forth to the rhythm of the Strauss waltz. It was on that icy morning in March I discovered the joy of road dancing with my car.

In mid-March we had a monumental snow storm. It was as if a tidal wave of snow had swept across the prairie and obliterated everything in its path. Massive drifts climbed walls, winds howled, and our house trembled during the onslaught.

At the height of the storm our dog Fang decided that, no matter what, he just had to go out. I expected him to return as soon as he completed his ablutions. After waiting an hour, I went out into that raging blizzard to look for him. I yelled, whistled, banged on an oil drum, but was only able to rouse my neighbor, Morgan Bullard.

"He's safer out here than he is in your house," he shouted.

"Hey Morgan, you sold me this house. Don't tell me it's about to collapse."

"C'mon Doc, you got the deal of a lifetime when you bought that house. Now get yourself inside and go to sleep. I'll plow you out in the morning."

Now that was an attractive offer not easily forgotten. Although Morgan was a retired farmer, his security blanket was a tractor and plow in a shed back of his house. He was a gracious man and a wonderful neighbor. When I purchased my house from him, I asked if he knew a lawyer to represent me. In all innocence, he recommended his lawyer and in all innocence, I accepted. While it might not have been ethical for the attorney to accept the buyer and the seller of the house as clients, it does guarantee a harmonious closing of the deal, but not necessarily to my advantage.

The storm continued unabated. During the night I must have gone out a dozen times. I could not think of anything surviving this Arctic blast. Fang, our beloved dog, was lost in the storm. At about 5:00 a.m., the storm's howl became a whimper, and the rising sun began to smudge the clouds. The whole town was inundated by this avalanche of snow. Red-eyed and exhausted, I once again forced open my snow bound door and began to slog through the area, the deep snow creeping into my boots. My plaintiff whistle sounded like a dirge. I expected it would be days before I found his body. I plodded along whistling, calling, not caring whom I woke this morning. Tears flowed, congealing and freezing on my cheeks. My nose was dripping and icicles hung from my nostrils. A northwest wind began to nibble at my ear tips. Feeling terribly cold, I turned toward home to warm up a bit and then continue my search. I knew wildlife could survive such punishing weather. Some were holed up underground; some were hibernating. Beef cattle were out in frozen pastures, huddling in windbreaks or copses awaiting hay and feed from ranchers. But Fang was none of these. He was an exaggerated lap dog, acclimated to human comforts. True he had a magnificent hair coat and a body temperature of 101.5 degrees Fahrenheit, which should stand him in good stead, but he was no match for a storm of this ferocity.

As I trudged back toward home, I could not help but admire the wind's handiwork. It coiffured the trees and bushes, and on its windward side, snow drifted in elegant, graceful sweeps on anything it encountered. An eight-foot wave of snow leaned broadside on Morgan's shed. The wind began to blow strongly and snow powder dusted the air making it difficult to see. Was it my imagination or did I actually see the base of the drift give a sudden heave? A black nose emerged, sniffed the air, and with a final heave, a white body disentangled itself from the drift. Could this be Fang or was it some other creature holed up to survive the storm? As the snow dust settled, I noted that this animal had no ears or visible eyes.

"Fang?" I tentatively called.

The creature became rigid, and in a surge of excitement, rushed toward my voice. His eyelids were frosted closed with ice and snow, his ears were battened back over his head. Snow had plastered his coat, caking it white. I reached toward him with my gloved hands, and then I heard his exultant bark. The next thing I knew I was rolling in the snow; he was all over me, kissing my face and giving forth yips of joy. I clutched him in my arms and pressed him to me. I brushed the ice from his eyes, and he began to shake vigorously, flaking off the snow from his coat. I removed my gloves and began to stroke him with my hands. He was as warm as toast and seemed not to suffer from his exposure. We headed home for a joyous reunion.

There was no way I could make calls that day. The whole area was quilted with snow. Snow plows were clearing the main roads, and farmers were attempting to plow the roadways leading to their farms so that at least the milk trucks could get through. The business of farming had to go on. Animals had to be fed and milked, and the milk had to be picked up and taken to the dairy for processing.

Veterinarians had to function as best they could. Sometimes, after a heavy snow storm, I found I could wrench my way to an emergency call using tire chains and a hundred pound sack of limestone in my car's trunk for traction. Once, a snow plow escorted me to a farm during a blustery snow storm. I was marooned on that farm for two days and used that time to examine every cow for pregnancy, Brucella test the entire herd and tell stories to three rapt kids. No matter how severe the storms, we rarely lost electrical or phone service. I never, ever thought of power or phone failure and took them for granted. The providers of these services were cooperatives and were not as appreciated as they might have been.

One vivid adventure occurred when, after a particularly bad storm, I heard a voice yelling at my door, "God damn it, Doc, get out of bed and come on out here." I rushed to open the door which was unlocked in any event. Apparently the caller was not too indelicate to just burst in if I did not respond promptly. I opened the door to be enthusiastically greeted by Ken Peterson, a farmer who lived three miles west.

"Hi, Doc. Saddle up. I got a cow down with milk fever. I got Bob and Bing chilling out, so let's get going."

Ken had a team of magnificent Percherons, and he often used them to pull a wagon or a sled to town. Essentially they were pets, for the days of work horses were rapidly giving way to mechanization. Yet the mightiest of farm tractors would not venture where a team of horses could go.

I grabbed my kit, first making sure I had a few bottles of calcium gluconate, and accompanied Ken to his sled. The road was duned with snow, and the plows had not made it out this far. I sat beside Ken on the open sled as Bob and Bing chugged along like twin locomotives expelling mighty gusts of steam into the air. I felt their prodigious power as they romped through drifts, pulling the sled as if it were a mere toy. They seemed to revel in their unchallenged strength, and for a fleeting moment, I thought how fragile they really were. They had fifteen or more years of productive life... yet could easily succumb to a host of disabling and fatal illnesses.

Ken, as if sensing my thoughts, said, "You sure pulled Bing through his colic last year. I don't think he enjoyed you putting your arm up his hind end or pumping that stuff through his nose with that hose. He gets spooked when he sees you, but he's doing great."

We arrived at Ken's farm and sure enough a bottle of intravenous calcium gluconate did its magic. A hot cup of coffee from Ken's wife, Doris, and we were on our way back.

I barely returned home when another milk fever call came in. It was always strange how these cases came in groups. This call came from Tom Bolton, who farmed ten miles south over rough terrain that was unpleasant even in good weather. There was no way get to his farm under present conditions. It might be twenty four hours before I could break through, and by that time, the cow would probably be dead. I called Tom to discover that the cow was comatose and lying on her side. She could easily regurgitate food and develop inhalation pneumonia. Under these circumstances, she might only last a few hours. I knew that while a cow's blood calcium was low during milk fever, the calcium level in her udder was very high. I had heard from the old vet I worked for of an old treatment to inject air into the udder, thereby forcing the reabsorption of calcium back into the blood stream. It was worth a try.

"Tom, do you have any teat tubes?"

"Sure do, Doc, all sterilized and ready to go. They're soaking in a jar of alcohol."

Teat tubes are inserted into injured teats either to inject medicine or to drain milk from teats too painful to be milked.

"Tom, I would like you to place a teat tube in each of her four quarters and pump up each of the quarters with air until they feel firm. Tie each teat gently with gauze to prevent the escape of air. Are you still with me, Tom?"

"Sure am, Doc."

"After four hours, remove the gauze and partially milk her out. If she is not better in six to eight hours, you can repeat the procedure. Be sure you prop her up with some bales of hay. Good luck, Tom. I'll come out as soon as the roads are plowed."

"Thanks, Doc, I'll call you later."

It was a pleasant day at home. Everyone was occupied digging out and the phone did not ring for me once. There was no way I could make a call and everybody knew it. I was dead tired and the prospect of a nap seemed pretty good. Maybe I'd be able to burst from this cocoon of snow tomorrow. As I languished about the house, I managed to create my own scenario of anxiety. Suppose Mary had gone into labor during this storm, what would be my options? Call Ken Peterson and take her the 22.6 miles by sled? Out of the question. Locate a midwife? Who in this little town would qualify for that job? The nurse who had lived here had moved to be near the hospital. Deliver the baby myself? It was an option but not a viable one. My God, what am I thinking? Now wait a minute, there are a lot of very aged people in this town, and I bet some were even born on a wagon train. Now Agnes Johnson is one hundred years old. I wonder how and where she was born. First minute I have to spare, I'm going to speak to these old folk. There's over two billion people in the world and everyone was born one way or the other—can't be too difficult.

"Hey, Mary, how are you feeling?" I called.

"Oh, I'm just fine. I hope you enjoyed your nap."

After a week passed, the weather turned mild. The storm was an unpleasant memory. My greetings of Mary were becoming increasingly clinical. She usually put my mind to rest with "Sorry, nothing doing." She appeared calm. I could detect no apprehension, just excited anticipation. She continued to answer the phone and do some household chores. I had never known her to look more radiant. She insisted on painting the nursery and was always having me rearrange the baby furniture. We were love birds fussing with a nest. I continued my work but was having trouble concentrating. The *Farmer's Almanac* promised an early spring and the weather seemed to confirm it.

It was a clear, crystalline sunset. The sun had spent the day mellowing the countryside, but the brittleness of winter was returning with evening shadows. The snow melt puddled the scrub board roads, but by late evening, they would be slithered with ice. I had completed my calls and was driving home once again, filled with that delicious fatigue that occasionally overcomes me after a day's work. It is not a fatigue that requires sleep, but rather a state of utter relaxation, a limpness of mind and body. For a brief time, I was able to unload my duffel bag of stress and tension and enjoy true tranquillity.

I walked into my house still suffused with this tranquillity. I called to Mary, "I'm home. How are you doing?" Her response was hesitant. "Oh, I'm okay, but I'm having twinges."

The duffel bag was reslung over my shoulders and I bent under its weight.

"Did you call the Doctor?" I inquired, endeavoring to be calm.

"No, not yet," she replied. "I'll wait until they are more frequent."

We sat at the dinner table picking at our food. Conversation was desultory, and I noticed that she periodically glanced at the wall clock. Fang had eaten dinner earlier and just couldn't find a suitable place for his after dinner nap. He tried a variety of throw rugs and even the hardwood floor, but he sensed the tension we felt. Nicky was asleep, hind legs spasmodically twitching, probably dreaming of exotic scents yet to be explored. It was 8:00 p.m., and I noticed that her peaches-and-cream complexion was becoming strawberry. Her flushed face began to grimace periodically.

"It's about time to call the doctor," she quietly informed me. "Contractions are coming ten minutes apart."

I placed the call and was relieved to learn that her doctor, as he put it, "had nothing to do that evening and would be honored to officiate at the delivery of our first born." In a more serious tone, he said, "Head for the hospital when labor pains are coming at about five-minute intervals."

Okay, we were all set. Doctor alerted, weather good, car gassed and ready, and her bag in the car. I figured I would notify those invisible ladies who manned the telephone co-op switchboard. This was the era of the crank phone and the party line. Mine was five short rings. If I was urgently needed, they would firmly, but politely, clear all parties off the lines so that I could receive the call. They would hold calls, and in an emergency, ring farm after farm in an effort to find me. The central switchboard was in another town, and had never met them personally. I only knew them as Mabel, Frances, Agnes and Loretta. There was always one of them on duty. Their voices all had a sort of nasal twang and I wondered if that was supposed to be some sort of a telephone voice they affected. I enjoyed their folksy inquiries about Mary and even a cow I was treating. When finally the system was automated, they disappeared from my life. I deeply regretted always being too busy to personally meet and thank them for services above and beyond the call of duty. The flowers, candy and even the heater for their office had been little tokens of my appreciation. I still have that large oakwood phone with its double bell eyes, long mouthpiece, earpiece on the left and crank on the right. In the years that I practiced under the umbrella of the Telephone Co-op, I had never known it to fail me.

Somehow two hours elapsed and Mary was becoming increasingly uncomfortable. Finally, after some hesitation, she said, "Let's take off for the hospital. I am anxious to see our baby."

As I helped her on with her coat, I remembered that I must call one of my telephone ladies and advise her of my unavailability. I approached the phone and it suddenly rang. Ring, ring, ring, ring, ring—louder than I had ever heard it. Oh no, not a call at this time. Mary said, "Pick it up, sweetheart." As I hesitated, she said emphatically, "Pick it up."

After a moment's hesitation, I picked up the receiver and managed an almost subvocal "Hello."

"Is that you, Doc? Can't hear you too well. This is Joe Campbell. I got a cow calving. Seems the calf is coming tail first. I'm gonna need you. Come on out and bring the wife."

I recalled that I had been there with Mary on a night call, but that had been when she was afraid to stay in the house alone. Joe and his wife asked us in for coffee after I treated a colicky horse. It had been a Saturday night and I remember telling Mary that this was our Saturday night out. I shall never forget the coffee Mrs. Campbell served. She had put some freshly ground coffee in a pot of boiling water, added a couple of cracked broken eggs, shells and all, a pinch of salt and had stirred vigorously. After having allowed the mixture to steep a few minutes, she had served a mug of coffee that was pure ambrosia.

I guess Joe was planning to make another social evening out of this calving. Ordinarily I would have enjoyed an evening with them, but now... Damn! Damn! Damn! "What's his problem?" Mary inquired.

"Oh, he wants us to stop by for coffee after I deliver a calf. It's out of the question. He'll have to get someone else."

"I think he'll have a difficult time getting a vet at this hour. His farm is right off the pavement on the way to the hospital. Suppose we stop, you deliver the calf, and then we'll go on to the hospital. We'll make the supreme sacrifice and skip the coffee. At any rate, my contractions are not as frequent as they were."

I looked at her suspiciously. She forced a smile, but I noticed the tension in her face. "We'll make the call. How long could it take? I insist on it." she said.

"Oh, you do now, do you? We have a baby to think of. Sure the calving might be easy, then it might not."

"Look, my contractions have subsided and you're wasting time. Let's go—I know I'll be fine."

She well knew my obsession with coverage of the practice. The thought of being unavailable for a call would gnaw at me until I checked in with one of my telephone ladies interrupted many a social affair to call in my whereabouts. It was as if I wanted to be omnipresent. I have been known to charge into raging storms to reach a beleaguered animal. Sometimes I would end up in a ditch and would have to hike to the nearest farm and roust some poor farmer out of his hibernation. We would either use his tractor or a team of horses to pull my car out of the ditch. Riding an open tractor in a blinding snow storm and then trying to attach large frozen chains to the undercarriage of my snow-impacted car is a miserable frost-biting experience. There were times that I could go no further and had to take shelter on any nearby farm.

"Come on. Make the call. What are you waiting for?"

Her voice became impatient, insistent. Despite feeling that I was betraying some basic instinct, I agreed. We hurried to the car and within ten minutes we were at the farm. The farm was right off the state road, so Mary was not subjected to the standard veerings and jostlings of country roads. I drove in close to the barn door and quickly reached for my OB kit. I winced as I removed Mary's overnight bag in order to reach it. I hurried into the barn and found Joe there with two buckets of hot water and a towel. The cow was in active labor. As she bore down, the mucous-pomaded tip of the calf's tail protruded. It was obviously a breech presentation with the hind legs retained. I prayed for an easy calving. The big Holstein should provide plenty of room to manipulate the calf into a normal position. I planned to deliver the calf rear legs first and be on our way. My efforts to reach into the uterus and straighten out the rear legs were met with labor so intense that I could make no headway. She would hump her back like some dromedary camel and pushed with a force I had rarely encountered. I was in trouble. How could I have performed this triage and selected this cow before my wife? As the cow took a deep breath before another Herculean contraction, I quickly entered the uterus and attempted some manipulation. I was up to my armpit inside this animal when I turned my head toward Joe. Out of the corner of my eye I saw Mary seated, not in the car, but on a bale of hay a few yards away. Here I was with my arm inside a laboring cow, while I'm looking at my laboring wife. Something had to be wrong with my value system. Our eyes met and she gave me a reassuring smile.

Meanwhile my unsuccessful struggle continued. By now I knew that the cow's name was Faye. Periodically, Faye would turn and look at me as if to say, "Don't worry I've had six calves without a problem and I'll manage this one." With that, she turned to nibble some alfalfa hay Joe had pitchforked to her. Little did Faye know that if I didn't get that calf out of her one way or another, she was going to be meat loaf.

My heart sunk as I heard a commotion behind me. Mrs. Campbell had come into the barn and was noisily insisting that Mary move from where she was sitting.

Don't tell me the baby is coming right here and now. The thought trembled in my mind.

"Now let me get you out of this barn. You are not to watch this. It can mark the baby," Mrs. Campbell said.

"Please Mrs. Campbell, I want to be with my husband."

"At least turn around and look the other way. Let me fix you a nice cup of coffee while you're waiting."

Mrs. Campbell was the yeoman type of woman that could bale hay, cook, plow a field, milk cows, make babies and, I prayed, deliver a baby if the occasion demanded.

I used my right arm, my left arm, and would have crawled into Faye's uterus if that were possible to effect a delivery. In fifteen minutes, I was utterly exhausted and had accomplished zero. I sat down on a milk stool to think about a new strategy and get some strength back in my arms. For the briefest moment, I forgot that Mary was here in the barn with Mrs. Campbell waiting for me, and then my mind walloped back to reality.

"How're you doing, Mary," I yelled out.

"Nothing doing with me," she called back.

I didn't believe her, but now I was going to do what I should have done in the first place. Faye turned in her stanchion, looked at me indifferently, and swish, the end of her urine soaked tail slapped me resoundingly in the face. It was a whiplike, stinging, soaking slap, like a reflexive flick at a fly on her rump. A fury I could scarcely remember surged through me. I heard Joe say softly, "Easy Doc, easy. Sorry, I should have been holding her tail." I could barely contain my anger. I wanted to lash out at Faye in the worst way.

Just last week a farmer was kicked by a cow I was treating. In his anger he punched the cow right in the head and, as a result, broke his right hand. As for the cow, she didn't miss a chew on her cud. In this business you're going to get bitten, kicked, stomped on, butted—and sometimes just being squeezed by a thousand-pound-plus animal feels very life threatening. And be doubly careful if they have not been dehorned.

What a predicament I had placed myself in. Perhaps I was endangering the life of my wife and baby. What was I doing in this business anyway? Some other vet would have delivered this calf long ago. My mother always said I should have been a teacher. They get such wonderful paid vacations. They sure do, and their wives are not subjected to such indignities while they're in labor. This was my frequent refrain when I had problems. I'm not a farm boy. I'm a product of a ghetto to which I'm still attached by an umbilical cord.

Okay, before I go home to mother and become a school teacher, I'll try a new tack. I washed up, walked over to Faye and said, "The game is up. No more labor for you, and if anyone labors in this barn, it's going to be Mary. Joe, raise her tail." I prepared a syringe with procaine and quickly injected it into the epidural space of the spinal canal. It took but a few minutes for the anesthetic to work and Faye's labor to cease. I easily positioned the calf and effected delivery of an eighty-pound bull calf. I cussed at myself for trying to take a short cut and persisting even when I saw I would not prevail. My poor judgment under pressure was inexcusable.

I quickly cleaned up and rushed out to find Mary and Mrs. Campbell seated in the Campbell kitchen sipping coffee and exchanging recipes. My thumbs-up look brought smiles to their faces. We loaded up and were on our way to the hospital.

As I drove, the enormity of what I had done overwhelmed me. I had my wife sit in a barn while she was in labor, about to bear our first child, while I delivered a calf. Sure, she sanctioned what I had done, but that was because she loved me. I would remember that night as long as I lived. I know I'll never forgive myself for what happened. Looking at Mary, I wondered if she would ever forgive me. The expression on her face seemed to say this was standard operating procedure for a vet's wife. Her husband had a job to do, and she would happily endure so that he could get it done.

Five days later, I brought her and our son Mitchell home from the hospital. The birth of our son was a glorious occasion, but I was still drenched with guilt and misgivings. Mary seemed totally unperturbed by the whole episode. She did her best to lessen my feeling of disquiet.

One night after I insisted on talking about it again, she turned to me and said, "There's one thing I never told you."

Now, I thought, her real feelings would emerge.

"What's that?" I asked.

"You remember that night when I sat drinking coffee in Mrs. Campbell's kitchen? Well, it was the greatest cup of coffee I ever had. I shall always remember it. Now stop beating up on yourself. You did what you were supposed to do. The world didn't have to stop turning because my labor had begun."

SWEET CLOVER, THE BLANKET AND PERRY

It was another long day, a hasty lunch, a gobbled dinner and I was on my way to a final night call. Ted Atkins had called to explain that he had dehorned some heifers, a job I detested, and that one heifer continued to bleed despite all his efforts to staunch the flow. I arrived at the farm to find the heifer in a stanchion engulfed in blood. Head shaking had splattered blood everywhere, and of course Ted was a bloody mess. He had packed the dehorned area with cobwebs, wads of cotton and milk strainer pads. Farmers generally believed that cobwebs are good clotting agents, and barns are the mother lodes of cobwebs. While I cannot dispute the clotting capacity of cobwebs scientifically—I thought them to be more of a contaminant than anything else—I have learned not to scoff at home remedies a farmer, and possibly his father, have used. Who was I to suggest that a remedy going back to biblical times might be of no value?

The blood continued to seep from the dehorned areas, creating little rivulets that ran down the heifer's face, finally dripping into the concrete feed trough. Once again she vigorously shook her head, and this time I was targeted with a fusillade of blood hitting me square in the face. The poor animal had to be enduring a furious headache.

"How long has she been bleeding, Ted?"

"Well, I clipped her horns about three hours ago. I'm fearful she could bleed out. Couldn't let her go the night."

"Let's take a look, Ted. Use my nose lead to control her head."

Nose leads were cast iron clamps that hooked into a cow's nostrils. A piece of rope attached to the nose lead permitted you to snub her head to any nearby post. When bull calves were young, I was often asked to ring the bull with a permanent brass ring placed through the nasal septum. Leading a bull by a nose ring usually afforded some control over the animal, but I have seen agitated animals tear their nasal septum's apart escaping the restraint. No determined animal weighing one thousand pounds or more is going to be restrained by a nose lead or a nose ring. Fortunately most of their aggression has been genetically discouraged through the ages, and a nose lead provides a very effective and humane device for the restraint of cow or a bull.

Nose lead in place, Ted pulled the heifer's head to one side, securing the rope to an adjacent stanchion. With my forceps at the ready, Ted abruptly yanked off the padding he had applied. Four streams of blood shot up into my face temporarily blinding me. This was not my day. Ted pushed an empty feed bag into my hands, and I proceeded to wipe the blood from my eyes, effectively smearing it all over my face. I did my best to contain some four letter words that imploded within me. I should have known better than to be caught in this way, and Ted should not have ripped off the padding. I applied a large gauze packing to control the bleeding and slowly lifted part of it to expose each individual bleeder. I pried into the bone, locating and clamping each blood vessel. Since it was impossible to tie off a bleeder within the recesses of the bone, I yanked the blood vessel out with my forceps. Fortunately, this always seemed to stop the hemorrhage. I smothered the open sinus with antibiotic powder and firmly applied a gauze packing. I had Ted turn the heifer's head to the other side and repeated the procedure.

Having controlled the bleeding, I turned my attention to the heifer. She was bright and alert, and her mucous membranes were a healthy pink. I didn't anticipate any further problem, but why would a heifer bleed so profusely?

"Hey Ted, did you get more bleeding than you expected when you dehorned the other heifers?"

"Come to think of it, it was more of a bloody mess than I ever could remember."

"Do you think you might have fed these heifers some sweet clover hay or silage that was a little moldy or spoiled?"

"I've been dumping some old sweet clover hay into these animals. There might have been some mold. What's mold got to do with it?"

"I'm not sure Ted, but an anti-clotting substance might be a cause of the bleeding. If your heifer continues to bleed, I might have to give her a blood transfusion to help her clot."

"Where do we get this blood from, Doc?"

"I think you should be good for a pint or so."

"I hope you're kidding, Doc, because I'm not gonna do it."

"Just joking, Ted. I'd probably take it from one of your cows."

Ted began to laugh halfheartedly. Once again one of my jokes had gone awry. Standing there with blood-soaked face and clothes was no time to tease a farmer.

"C'mon to the milk house. I've plenty of hot water and I'll clean you up before you return home. You might put Mary into shock when she sees you."

"Thanks Ted, but I'll clean up at home. I really need a shower. Mary has seen me in worse shape. At least I don't smell too bad this time."

Once again I returned home bloody, but unwounded. It was 11:00 p.m. and I knew by Mitchell's howling that something was wrong. I galloped up to his bedroom to find Mary trying to placate him to no avail. One look at me brought Mitchell's crying to an abrupt stop. I stood before them streaked with blood from head to toe, an apparition from some horror movie. Most any family would gasp in terror at the sight of me, but not my family. This was just another variation of one of the costumes I occasionally returned home with. It was just not sufficiently unusual to cause more than a momentary distraction.

Mary gave me one of her amused smiles, and Mitchell resumed his crying. I suppose she was wondering how she would get all the blood out of my clothes or was she thinking, 'Are all vets this messy?' Mitchell resumed his howling.

"What happened? Is he sick? Did he get hurt?"

"None of those. Would you like to make some further guesses?" she asked, forcing a smile.

"I give up. What happened?"

"You wouldn't believe this but I decided to wash his filthy, tattered security blanket. I made the colossal mistake of putting it into our washing machine. That did it—it's now spaghetti, and you hear the result. He's been howling like this since you left."

Mitchell, pausing either to listen to our conversation or catch his breath, began to cry with increased intensity.

"Mary, did you check Spock?"

"I'm afraid there's no chapter on security blankets."

"Well, let him cry. How long can he last?"

"I think he can outlast either of us. He's in good voice tonight," Mary said.

"I'm headed for the shower. I'm a mess."

"You sure are. Be sure to soak your clothes in cold water to loosen up that blood."

She knew her business well. Amid Mitchell's crying, I headed for the shower. It was a long and laborious shower the dried blood was terribly tenacious, clinging to my face and arms with great determination. Finally satisfied that I had scrubbed myself clean, beet-red clean, I toweled off, got into my pajamas and was ready for bed. I opened the bathroom door only to be greeted by Mitchell's crying. I tried playing with him, got into a wrestling match with Fang, to which he always responded with uproarious laughter, all to no avail. He was inconsolable.

"We have to get him another satin blanket," Mary said. "I can't take this anymore."

"It's midnight. Where am I going to get a satin blanket? We don't have a store in town. Rockford is shut tight. We'll have to wait till morning."

"How about calling Sam Shep?" Mary asked. "I bet he has a satin blanket in his store. Maybe he'd open for us—I know he's asleep, but this is an emergency. I'll call him."

Sam Shep ran a mini-department store and was a very good friend. He was in his early forties, and we often got together to discuss world politics. His ultra-conservative views often clashed with mine, but it never diminished the profound respect we had for each other.

Sam lived in Harvard, Illinois, fifteen miles east. Its residents called it, "The milk center of the world." Once a year, they whitewashed their Main Street, held a parade with all the trimmings—floats, fire engines and marching bands. Large crowds came from as far as Chicago to enjoy the festivities. How well I remember my favorite cow, Sarah, leading the parade, led by her beaming owner. How proudly she walked, flaunting her magnificent udder, tail switching happily, turning her head side to side, like a queen, bestowing her cow-smile on the admiring crowds. This was a lady in her glory moment. She was yet to know the demons that awaited her three months hence.

"I have him on the phone," I heard Mary shout. "He says to come on down. He has just what we want. Will meet you at the store in half an hour. Get dressed and go."

I dressed hastily and sped to Harvard. Sure enough Sam was at the store. I explained the problem and selected a satin blanket. Sam absolutely refused to accept payment saying it was his good deed.

"Okay Sam, I owe you one—a big one."

I hurried to my car and raced back home.

Entering the house, tightly clutching the blanket as if it would escape my grasp, I could hear Mitchell whimpering. I leapfrogged up the stairs and entered his room. With great fanfare I presented him his new blanket. He seemed spellbound, overwhelmed by his good fortune. He clutched the blanket like a drowning man the proverbial straw, pulled it to his face, avidly sniffing it like our dogs at my boots after a messy farm call. Suddenly he took the blanket, like it was some odious, evil shroud and flung it as far away from him, with as much force as his little hands could muster. From deep within him emerged a scream so primordial in its nature that Mary and I were aghast.

Needless to say this was going to be a rough night. I went downstairs to fortify myself with a glass of milk. Pacing the kitchen, I noticed the washing machine lurking in a corner. I lifted the top and noted that within its bowels were some shredded remnants of Mitchell's blanket. I scooped out what I could, wrung them out and tied the pieces into a clump. The material was quite damp, but I brought it up for his inspection. Red eyed, exhausted, he eyed the clump with interest—even reaching out for it. I placed it into his hands and he immediately began to sniff it avidly. For a moment I wondered what kind of animal we were raising.

Apparently satisfied with its odor, he pressed the damp remnants to his chest and in an instant he was asleep.

For me sleep was not so readily forthcoming, but I managed a few hours before my trip on the South Road to see some coughing Angus feeder steers that Perry Simons had just purchased. This road south of town was the most irritating road in a county where all roads, except state roads, left a lot to be desired. It was built as a narrow strip of pavement barely wide enough for one car. Shoulders were virtually nonexistent, and when you were confronted by oncoming traffic, somebody had to get off or at least half your car did. The absence of a shoulder made that drop a challenging maneuver. Trying to get back on required some acrobatic driving. During a night-time snowstorm, the road would white out, and in that pitch black whiteness, I would do battle with all those precipitous drops and careenings, encouraging my car to make all kinds of unimaginable gyrations. Once after a most difficult trip I walked to the front of my car and patted her hood saying, "You performed beyond the call of duty. Many thanks."

I drove thirty thousand to forty thousand miles a year and was obliged to trade what was left of my car every ten to twelve months. My car at that time was a two-toned Oldsmobile, blue with a white top. After a couple of weeks of springtime farm calls, her colors would defy identification. It looked like she had been troweled with a coating of mud. Nature had camouflaged her to be indistinguishable from the prairie.

Washing a car was a chore no vet engaged in unless the occasion was a wedding or a funeral. There was an occasional eccentric who routinely washed his car, but that was quickly negated by the next few farm calls he would make. I confess to having washed my car's windows but only when visibility decreased to less than fifty percent. A car's appearance was a badge each country vet wore with unmentioned pride.

When a car performs well under all kinds of absurd conditions a kinship develops. As she ages and begins to protest, when her joints become arthritic, and her front end trembles, it is difficult to endure her pain. The time has come to depersonalize her—ship her to market like an ailing cow.

A car was an integral part of my work and trading it in was like losing a good friend. I was always concerned about what poor soul would be persuaded to buy this vehicle. A week after I traded her in, I happened to drive past my dealer's used car lot. There she was, exhumed from the prairie mud, scrubbed clean and simonized, glistening in the mid-day sun. My, she was a good looking corpse.

I arrived at Perry Simons' farm to be greeted like a visiting celebrity. He was a super-friendly man and every sentence was punctuated with laughter. But today laughter was hard to come by. Perry had the worst possible cold. Flushed face, blood shot eyes, and a nose that dripped like a leaky faucet. He blotted his nose with a soggy handkerchief and used it to throttle his frequent sneezes. He was a sick man.

"Sorry Doc, I got one hell of a cold. Caught it from those Goddamn feeder steers. Ha, ha, ha." His laughter was forced and gargly. "Those steers are coughing—eatin' good though. Probably need a vaccine shot and some sulfa medicine. Come back tomorrow and bring what you need. I'm no good today, but I'll be okay tomorrow. Ha, ha, ha."

"Perry, there's no way you'll be able to function tomorrow. If you get some help, I'll be back."

"Doc, I guarantee I'll be okay, so don't worry."

"Whatever you say, Perry." This guy was sick and would be so for days.

"While I'm here, let me take a quick look at your steers."

"They're behind that fence I just put up. It ain't too strong, needs some posts. It's okay for now. I have a squeeze chute in case we have to handle them singly. Now that's a job. Ha, ha, ha."

I walked over to the five-foot-high board fence Perry had put up. I leaned over it to see thirty young Angus steers eyeing us nervously. The fence did need further support as Perry had said. It bent under my weight. I heard the typical, moist bronchial cough and saw the occasional snotty nose. I continued watching the steers, trying to determine if any were in critical condition requiring immediate care. All in all, they seemed to be in reasonable shape and postponement of treatment for a day might not be too detrimental. Suddenly one of the larger steers froze in his tracks and emitted a cough of monumental proportions. It sounded like a blast from a ram's horn followed by an inspiratory hollow echo. This must be the sound that made the walls of Jericho tumble down. For a moment I thought it had arisen from within the earth where the steer was standing. Startled, as much as I was, the steer bolted away from the herd.

These animals had been raised in some western state and shipped by rail or truck to the corn belt to be fattened for market. They were often crowded into cattle cars and subjected to fatigue and stress, lowering their resistance to ever-present disease organisms. The whole syndrome was aptly called "shipping fever," a disease that could produce pneumonia, unthriftiness and even death.

There was a vaccine called a "bacteria," a combination of killed bacteria often present in shipping fever. It was an aid in the prevention and treatment of this disease. I used it in conjunction with sulfonamide to treat shipping fever.

As Perry and I leaned over the fence, Perry's sixteen-year-old son, driving a tractor pulling a manure spreader flanked by two barking dogs, came chugging into the adjacent barnyard.

"Goddamn it, Kevin is gonna spook those steers something awful." "Kevin," he croaked, "get the hell out of here. You're scaring the steers."

There was no way Kevin could hear him. The steers' eyes blazing with fright began to mill about excitedly. One steer could stand it no longer, bolted from the group and headed our way. The others, believing an escape route had been found, rushed to follow. They stampeded toward us and with one surge toppled the fence on Perry and myself. It was like something out of a western movie. I said a quick goodbye to Mary, Mitch, Fang and Nicky, burying my head in the ground as the herd trampled over us.

It was over in seconds. The clumping of hooves on boards throbbed in my ears, but miraculously I didn't think I had sustained any injuries. I turned to where Perry lay and said, "Perry, you okay?"

"I'm fine, Doc. Awful sorry this happened. Let's get these boards off of us, then I'll beat the hell out of Kevin."

"I think you'd best round up those steers first."

"You're right, Doc."

We extricated ourselves from the fence boards and saw that the steers had bunched together in a nearby field, not too frightened to nibble on some grass. It was surprisingly easy to herd them into the barnyard once we silenced the dogs.

"Come back tomorrow. Everything will be all set for you, and I'll be as good as new."

He looked terrible and I thought it would be unlikely he'd be good as new. I had wasted an hour and a half on this call and wondered whether I should charge Perry for my time. I'll let Mary make that decision. Now what did Lincoln say about time? Oh yes, 'Time is your stock and trade.' Probably talking about lawyers, not vets.

I returned the next day to find Perry to be clear eyed and dry nostriled. It was remarkable. I had to know his secret.

"So you want to know how I licked my cold? Very simple, I went to my chiropractor. It works every time. Ha, ha, ha."

"What did he do to you?" I asked.

"He stretched me out on that special table he has, punched and twisted my back, spun my head around so you can hear the bones snap and crack, and here I am—good as new. Ha, ha, ha."

I had never been too enthusiastic about chiropractic medicine. However, the fact that the medical profession frowned on it did suggest it might have some value. Perry's miraculous cure was a bit mind boggling, and I thought they only treated bad backs.

Perry had quickly done a lot of work since the incident of the collapsed fence. He and a couple of his hired hands had properly rebuilt the fence and positioned the chute for the treatment of the steers. With some gentle coaxing, the steers were able to enter the chute enabling me to efficiently administer the shipping fever medication. I checked with Perry a few days later and found the steers to be doing well. How was he getting along?

"I couldn't be better. Ha, ha, ha."

The question that burned within me was what could Perry's chiropractor do for my hayfever? I would wait till fall and give it a try.

When fall arrived and ragweed exulted within my mucous membranes, I did journey to see Perry's chiropractor, but his magic was to no avail. He did say that one treatment might not relieve my symptoms and that a few more sessions would be in order. But I figured that in two to three weeks the hay fever season would be over anyway, so why bother. Perry had no reservations that the chiropractor could relieve his symptoms, but for myself, no amount of chiropractic manipulation could penetrate my skepticism. The moral: you've just got to be a believer.

SARAH

I returned home more depressed than ever. Nothing was going right. Periodically you hit a week where unanticipated deaths occur in spite of your most heroic efforts. Yesterday, I lost what I thought was a routine milk fever case. The cow had become a downer, refusing to get on her feet. I decided she was a lost cause. The day before that I lost a beautiful mare as a result of a fatal gut torsion. She suffered unbearable pain, and I had no choice but to euthanize her. Today I felt I was losing Sarah, a truly remarkable cow.

Most people think of cows as mobile embellishments on a landscape that periodically return to the barn to fill bottles with milk. To dairymen like Frank Barnes and veterinarians like myself, cows are individuals possessing special traits. Frank milked over thirty cows, and while they are out milling about in the barnyard, he could name and identify every one of them, detail their milk production, tell you which were with calf and just about anything else you might want to know.

I know cows are not particularly intelligent, but Sarah was not only intelligent, she had charisma. She was gentle, friendly, responsive and seemed to understand just about everything said to her. Her eyes regarded you in a sweet, motherly way. I never made a visit to Frank's farm without a chat with Sarah. She never shied away from a pat on the head or even a hug. I was always pleased when she responded with a slurpy lick of my hand.

Frank had called me the previous night to tell me that Sarah had freshened. He complained that her udder was rock hard and she was going off feed. No emergency, but could I see her first thing in the morning? Did he think I should see her tonight? He assured me that the morning would be fine.

The day started with a tough one-hour calving, followed by a milk fever and the suturing of a lacerated teat. All this continued to delay me till noon. When I arrived at the farm, the disturbed expression on Frank's face indicated that all was not well with Sarah.

"I should've had you come last night, Doc. She's one big sick cow."

When I first saw Sarah, I was aghast. A purplish hue to her udder had a terrible foreboding. She stood rigidly in her pen and any movement brought on excruciating pain. With an effort, she turned her head toward me and I saw the distress in her eyes.

"Okay Sarah, stand steady and let me look you over. Is that your calf over there? She's a beauty." This was a cow you conversed with.

Sarah's temperature was 105.5 degrees and her bag was indeed rock hard. I could hear no digestive rumblings within her paunch. She was completely off feed. I tried to strip some milk from her udder, but all that oozed out was some blood-tinged fluid.

"She's pretty bad, isn't she, Doc?"

I turned toward Frank and nodded my head. Was it my imagination? The udder seemed to have increased its purple tinge. It was as if some gigantic tourniquet had been placed around the udder and was squeezing tighter and tighter. The udder was being strangulated before my eyes. My mind was racing ahead of my eyes to a terrible denouement.

"Frank, I'm going to load her up with I.V. antibiotics. You'll have to strip her out as often as you can—every couple of hours. Try some cold packs. I don't like the blue color on some parts of her bag. Keep stripping. The more milk you get out of her, the better."

"How can something like this happen, Doc? This is her third calf. She's always been fine."

"Remember, Frank, that episode she had with mastitis that seemed to clear up so nicely? Maybe she's been harboring an infection. These infections are often dormant or inactive until a cow calves, and then they explode."

I saturated Sarah with just about every antibiotic I had. It would have been nice to know what organism was brewing in that udder, but there was no way I could discover that in time to do something more meaningful. I don't know what else I could have done. I had shot off all my treatment cannons. If she had one of those gas forming bugs in her udder, she was probably a goner. The blue purplish tinge haunted me through the night. I never did like the color purple. It presaged disaster.

Frank was slumped over the gate to Sarah's pen, looking like a mother staring helplessly at her sick child. When a sentimental farmer and a sentimental veterinarian team up to treat a sick animal, economics and realty are quickly forgotten.

"See you first thing in the morning, Frank."

I wish I was able to say "she'll be okay," but in our inner hearts, we both knew the truth.

"See you tomorrow, Doc. And thanks."

The way he said thanks showed a profound appreciation of what I was trying to do. In a way, we were kindred spirits.

Death is an inevitable fact of life... so goes the platitude. I accept my losses, but not as stoically as I should. Occasionally, I question my competence and often decide I could have done a better job. When I identify with an animal, become personally involved, its death becomes especially disturbing. One hundred people die in a plane crash. If you know one of those people, the crash becomes a personal rather than an abstract sorrow.

Every couple of weeks, I played poker with several physicians in the area. I made contact with them after having driven a nurse-anesthetist to a local hospital during a snow storm. The nurse, who lived in my town at that time, could not get through to assist at an emergency appendectomy and asked for my help.

Upon delivering her to the hospital, and as an expression of the doctors' gratitude, I was invited to play poker with them. They thought I would be a soft touch, and they were exactly right. These poker evenings gave me an insight into their thinking, their compassion, their ethics. They talked about life-and-death situations, loudly declaiming their successes, and in lower voices confessing failures and bunglings. Nowhere could I discern any profound regret for the loss of a patient. If there was any sorrow or torment, it was kneaded into a nothingness and discarded. This is a learned, necessary attribute of the medical profession. How else can one live with the agony, pain and death of a patient? It would have certainly destroyed me, and even with animal patients, I have difficulty coping. I suppose physicians need this protection to help them perform unencumbered by compassion and sorrow.

I know that cows are not considered particularly intelligent. For good milk production, docility is the most desirable trait. Nervous cows are not generally good milkers. Beef cattle are less placid, and the coal black Aberdeen Angus can be a formidable patient to treat. A squeeze chute is often a necessary restraint before providing treatment.

Sarah embodied all the qualities of the ideal Holstein cow. She was a prodigious producer of milk, unusually gentle and had another exceptional quality—intelligence. Frank said he had trained her to respond to voice commands and hand signals. She certainly responded whenever she saw me, nodding her head and making strange basso sounds, which I interpreted as a greeting. I often kidded Frank by telling him if he could housebreak or barnbreak Sarah, he might revolutionize dairy cattle husbandry. Imagine training cows to go out of the barn to do their elimination. We both had a good laugh at the thought of it.

When I arrived home, I found Mary in a somewhat grumpy frame of mind.

"What's the problem?" I inquired.

"You're the problem," she answered. "Or rather you and your son."

"Where is Mitch, anyway? And what did we do?"

I smiled, and that seemed to irritate her even further.

"He's outside taking care of his ant farm."

"Ant farm, you say?"

"Yes, ant farm, I say. Do you know what he did? He brought a whole ant colony into the kitchen to eat a chocolate chip cookie he crumbled on the floor while I was upstairs straightening up. When I went to get the bug sprayer, he raised such a fuss I could hardly believe my ears. He began to scoop up the ants on a sheet of paper and take them outside. He said you told him all about ants, how they lived in underground cities with their queen, and that in most cases, they were hard-working, friendly creatures. But you didn't tell him they don't belong in a kitchen."

I had been reading a book about ants to Mitchell and apparently it had made quite an impression. Because of Mary's aversion and fear of some insects, I occasionally pointed out different insects to Mitchell. I wanted him to be comfortable with everything within his environment. It was often disconcerting to come home and have Mary point nervously to a spider who had spun its web in a ceiling corner. Why did it upset her so?

"Get it out of here. Kill it," she ordered.

Mitchell was puzzled by such incidents, especially when I suggested they were benign and that they might capture and dispose of other bugs she deplored, like mosquitoes. This evening she had discovered a large orb-spinning spider on the kitchen ceiling.

"Now, don't play games. Get it out of here. Don't give me any balance of nature stories. This situation doesn't warrant it."

I rolled some newspaper, grabbed a mason jar and lifted Mitchell onto my shoulders. I gave him the jar and the newspaper.

"See if you can push her into the jar. She can't hurt you, so don't hurt her."

After a moment's hesitation, he began poking at the spider. In an effort to escape Mitchell, the spider became frantic—scurrying back and forth with amazing speed. Finally, in desperation, she began a rapid descent to the floor by releasing a silken lifeline.

"She's getting away," I heard Mary say.

I hope so, I thought.

I lowered Mitchell to the floor and said, "Go get her."

Mitchell had warmed to the chase, finally cornering the spider and forcing her into the mason jar.

I turned to see Mary smiling.

"You sure know how to turn getting rid of a spider into a dramatic occasion. In the old days, one whack with that newspaper would have done it. Now look at Mitch. He looks like the great white hunter who just captured a tiger. Now, I want the two of you to get her outside and release her far away from here. I don't want her to return to this happy household."

The phone rang. Mary dutifully picked up the phone.

"Four legs coming out at the same time? You think it might be twins? Okay, Doc will be right over."

She turned toward me. "That's Howard Walton. I suppose you got the message. He's got twins coming."

"Bet you a dollar they're not twins," I replied.

"You're on. Now on your way. Every dollar counts."

Late in Mary's pregnancy, her doctor told us he heard two sets of heart beats. Mary bubbled with excitement, and I must admit I had shared her pleasure. Two for the price of one, I had naively thought. On her next visit, her doctor retracted his twin diagnosis and, on the side, suggested to me that perhaps one had died. Now even to this day, the thought of birthing twins still enchants her. But it was not to be.

"Wait a minute," I heard Mary call. "You forgot your spider. Release her somewhere on your way. Mitch, give Daddy the mason jar with the spider in it."

I took the jar, placed it on the seat beside me and drove off into the darkness. It was a long drive to Howard Walton's farm, and I thought how far I had come from the little seven year old that tore off the wings of flies and exploded tiny firecrackers in ant hills. I had been unsparing in the cruelty I inflicted on insects in my not too scientific search for cause and effect.

An image of Sarah bolted into my mind, and I chose to take the road that went past Frank Barnes' farm. The barn lights were on, and I figured Frank was in the barn stripping out Sarah. I suspected that Sarah was still in considerable pain and hoped my medication had given her some relief. My impulse was to drive in and check her condition, but a calving was waiting. A couple of miles down the road, yard and barn lights guided me to Howard Walton's farm. Howard greeted me with the usual regrets.

"Sorry to get you out so late at night. I just couldn't wait till morning. She's a first calf heifer and I think she's having twins."

Howard led me into the barn to a heifer that was straining mightily. Sure enough, with each contraction, four legs protruded from the vulva and then sucked back as the heifer relaxed. It was immediately obvious that one pair were front legs and that the other pair were hind legs. All four legs were positioned in the same direction and that would be unlikely with twins. We were dealing with a calf presenting in a folded position with the head extended to the side. I tied obstetrical chains to the forelegs and had Howard gently pull them out while I pushed the rear legs back into the uterus. This unfolded the calf and put her into a normal presentation for an uneventful delivery. The calf and her mother were none the worse, and I wondered about the perverseness of nature in the creation of these awkward obstetrical problems. But all's well that ends well.

"How about a good cup of hot coffee, Doc?"

It was 11:00 p.m., and I would have loved a cup, but the thought of waking Howard's wife to brew some coffee was unthinkable.

"Thanks a lot, Howard, but I'd better rush home. There's one thing you can do for me, call Mary and tell her I'm on my way and that she lost the bet. She bet me a dollar your cow was having twins. Bye, Howard."

I was passing Frank Barnes' farm, and the lights were still on in the barn. How could I not look in on Sarah? Perhaps with some luck, she was doing better, but I had no great expectations. The barking of Frank's two dogs rattled the night's silence as I drove up to the barn door. Frank came out of the barn to see what the commotion was all about, but one look at his haggard face told the story.

"What are you doing out here at this hour, Doc?"

"Well Frank, you must know we vets prowl the nights."

He did his best to force a faint smile.

"I was over at Howard Walton's delivering a calf. Saw your barn lights were on and decided to stop by to see Sarah."

"She's not good. I've been trying to strip her out, but I don't get much. Hot packs, cold packs, it don't make a difference. She's lying down now. I don't think she can get up. She's a goner, Doc."

I followed him to where Sarah was penned. She was lying down, and Frank had provided her with a liberal bedding of oat straw. She had a hollow, vacant look, and her body seemed to quiver spasmodically.

"Sarah," I called to her, but she made no effort to acknowledge my presence. I entered the pen and gently stroked her neck and back. She was icy, clammy, shrunken. The sight of her udder startled me—the invisible tourniquet had tightened. It had become splotchy blue-purple. I felt the crepitus or bubbling of gas and what I had feared most had happened—she had developed a gas gangrene of the udder. Somehow a gas forming bacteria had gained entrance and a violent destructive process had begun. If I were able to amputate that udder as I had amputated gangrenous limbs, I would have done so. But it was not an option I could entertain. It would have been a massive surgical procedure that I was ill equipped for. The operation might have been a success, but my patient would have died. In my younger and more innocent days, I amputated half an udder that had become septic, and why that cow survived my barnyard surgery is still a mystery to me.

What always continued to amaze me was that farmers would ask for procedures and life-saving measures that were totally impractical. They knew better than I the economic value of their livestock. When an animal became a liability, what other reason was there to keep it on? Why would they house, feed and maintain an animal that could provide no economic return? This was not good economic sense. In some cases, farmers would resort to extravagant efforts to keep an animal alive. It is difficult to live with animals and not love them. Behind those weather-beaten, taciturn faces, there lurked a tenderness and love of animals. Sure, I had met the brutes, those cruel and savage farmers whose mere presence made animals tremble, but fortunately they were in the minority.

I looked down at Sarah and said to myself, "Kill her. Put her out of her misery." I turned toward Frank and saw the pained expression on his face.

"Do what you have to do, Doc." His meaning was clear.

"Frank, would you mind if I did one more thing? I know she'll probably die, and if by some miracle she survives, you'll never get an ounce of milk out of her."

"Do anything you want, Doc. I'd keep her if she lives. I'd never send her to market."

"Okay Frank, she has no feeling and scarcely any circulation in her bag. Her teats are cold and lifeless. I'm going to amputate her teats in an effort to establish as much drainage as possible from her udder. If we can drain that poison out of her, maybe it will help."

I went back to my car and returned with my large autopsy scissors. This was not to be a delicate procedure—more like cutting off a piece of soft rubber hose. I grasped the cold lifeless teat—a dead appendage of a living body—pulled it down and cut it off at its base. There was no bleeding, no pain—just the release of gaseous, putrid fluids. Similarly, I removed the remaining three teats. Sarah barely stirred. I spoke to her, stroked her neck and head, but her response was the hollow, vacant stare of the moribund. Once again, I administered large quantities of antibiotics and loaded her with all the I.V. glucose and saline I had in my car. I instructed Frank to apply hot compresses to encourage drainage.

Holy smoke! It was three o'clock in the morning and Mary had no idea where I was. I had told Howard Walton to call and tell her I was on my way home hours ago. My unaccountability was inexcusable. I could imagine what she was thinking. I hustled to get my gear together to make a hurried exit.

"Frank, call Mary and tell her I'm on my way home. Maybe it will soften the blow if you tell her where I've been these last few hours."

Frank gave me one of his tired smiles and said, "Trust me, Doc, I'll give you a good alibi."

It was almost 4:00 a.m. when I arrived home. I found Mary in one of her controlled but agitated frames of mind. She had to be approached cautiously because this was when she was most dangerous.

She began by saying, "We're not communicating anymore. Here I thought you were gallivanting about with some farmer's daughter, and now I find you're in love with a sick cow called Sarah. Wasn't one of your old girl friend's named Sarah?"

I did not answer—just sat quietly, patiently, penitent.

"You smell vile. What kind of a cow have you been consorting with? Get your clothes off, take a shower, and we'll have breakfast. Just a reminder—you promised Lovell you'd be at his farm before six. You'll hardly have time for a nap."

I had expected some angry words, but she was sweetness and light. I was sure that this episode would not be forgotten. After a delicious breakfast of blueberry pancakes, three cups of freshly ground coffee that smelled and tasted better than a great Cuban cigar I was recently gifted, followed by a half-hour nap, I was on my way. Hopefully, I could get some rest in the afternoon.

At 5:45 a.m., I arrived at Harold Lovell's to open a plugged teat. Somehow this cow managed to step on her teat as she was rising. Her udder was pendulous and her narrow stall made this type of trauma possible. An adjacent cow could also have been the culprit by stepping on her teat. Ouch! Fortunately, after a few attempted kicks at my hind end—one succeeding—I was able to enter the teat with a sterile milk tube and inject medication. Many cows develop mastitis after such an injury, and if scar tissue ensues, these animals become difficult milkers. I instructed Harold to use a sterile teat dilator between milkings and to sterilize the teat before inserting the dilator.

While working on one cow, I was thinking of Sarah. I had to see her as soon as possible. I sped to Frank's farm and entered the barn. Frank and his wife were doing the milking. Dark shadows rimmed his eyes, and it was obvious he had not slept.

"She's still with us, Doc. Seems a bit stronger. Took a lick of grain, too. You can't imagine what's coming out of her bag."

I approached her pen and she turned toward me. She recognized me at once and made an effort to rise, but couldn't quite make it.

"Don't worry, Sarah, we'll get you up tomorrow."

Was it premature to think she would survive? I was genuinely elated by her progress. I felt a hand on my shoulder.

"She's gonna make it, Doc."

Sarah did make it. Her udder shriveled to a dysfunctional clump of fibrous tissue. She became sleek and fat and one year later gave birth to a calf.

Oh yes, Mary paid me the dollar she lost on the bet, and said she would never bet with me again, apparently deciding I had taken unfair advantage of her.

The spider did not survive. After all the excitement of that long day, I had completely forgotten about the spider. We found the jar under the passenger seat, weeks later.

THE FRACTURE

The most remarkable man I had the good fortune of knowing in this tiny farm town was Cliff, the proprietor of our General Store. His formal education was negligible, but I am certain he could have graduated from any university.

I was sure he had a photographic mind, remembering precisely everything I ever discussed with him. He was endowed with the expertise to repair, reconstruct or improvise on just about every implement on the farm or in the home. Imagine a guy like him with an engineering degree from MIT.... it would definitely be a better world.

While his skills were mostly used for routine purposes, he was anything but a repairman. His mechanical insights and innovations never ceased to amaze me. I often wondered how a man with his innate skills would perform when freed from the inhibitions of his environment. He never looked beyond his horizon to the technological advances that were being made. Personally I was thankful Cliff made this town his world. Without him, the quality of my life would have been seriously diminished. He resuscitated our moribund washing machine on more than one occasion, repaired our ailing oil furnace— and now he was being called on to devise a steel splint for a cow with a broken leg.

I was called to Harold Lambert's farm to look at a large Holstein that had hobbled back from pasture, severely lame on her right front leg. There was no history of injury, but if there were cars out in that pasture, I would suspect that one had hit her. Midway between her ankle and elbow was an area of considerable swelling. My examination intensified the cow's distress and the grating and crepitus indicated a fracture. There was minimal displacement of bone, but the prognosis for a fractured limb in a cow was invariably bad.

"Well, Doc, what do you think?" asked Harold.

"She has a broken bone, sure enough. There's not much I can do for her.

I'd ship her out before she becomes skin and bones."

"But Doc, she's five months with calf, and I want her calf. She's got great blood lines, and I ain't going to ship that bloodline to no market. I don't care if she dries up, as long as she gives me a calf. You gotta save her. I don't care what it takes or what it costs."

This was an impassioned statement coming from the most penny-pinching farmer I knew.

"Harold, you have to understand that it is customary to market animals with this type of injury. It's almost impossible to immobilize this fracture for two or three months in a cow weighing over a thousand pounds."

"Could you try, Doc? I won't fault you none if it comes to naught."

"Maybe I can get the University to handle the case. They have slings to keep her off her feet as well as padded pens, not to mention some very good vets."

"I can't see carting Queenie two hundred miles to the University—she's sure to lose her calf. Her best chance is to stay put and have me and my boys take care of her."

It soon became obvious that he could not be dissuaded. I began to review in my mind the available options. I could sling her in the barn. My last two experiences slinging cows were disastrous. I hated the contraptions. The most logical approach was a splint, but I didn't think I could get the required immobilization. Perhaps a plaster of Paris cast like the one I used on the O'Malley dog. Much to my dismay, he was out herding cattle the next day—but he healed fine. Okay, I'll apply a heavy plaster cast—at least I'll be doing something. Who knows what will happen? Hell, I know what will happen—it will break apart. This was one of those cases in which I was about to do something that went against my better judgment. With a guy like Harold it could only have a bitter ending. At this stage, he was sweet and ingratiating, but I had heard of his wrath from farmers and a veterinarian he had thrown off the farm—literally. Didn't he say he wouldn't hold me responsible if it "came to naught?" I'd better look up that word in the dictionary. Harold seemed to be listening to my thoughts.

"Try something, Doc. Anything."

"Okay, I'm going home to get some casting material, and I'll be back within the hour. We'll cast the fracture and see what happens."

He seemed real pleased. However, I had all the misgivings of involving myself in a doomed project.

I returned bringing my entire supply of plaster of Paris bandages. I asked Mary to place an urgent order for more bandage, lots of it. With Harold and his two sons as helpers, I applied some cotton padding and casted the leg, using my entire supply. It felt quite firm after twenty minutes and the cow seemed more comfortable. For a brief moment, I deluded myself into thinking that perhaps this would do it. Reality caught up to me when I dropped in to see Queenie two days later. The cast had slid down and was frayed and cracked. It was a complete failure. My new casting had arrived, and I proceeded to recast, virtually doubling the size. I noted with satisfaction that some of the swelling had subsided, but the pain persisted. Although it was only two days, I was sure the cow had lost weight. It was always shocking to see how cows with foot problems lose enormous amounts of weight. I expected Harold's cow to wither away.

Three days later, I made a further visit and found the second cast cracking and providing inadequate immobilization. In spite of my obvious failure, Harold kept telling me what a great job I was doing.

"Look how well she looks, and she's not hurting as much. I'm giving her an extra scoop of grain and she's eatin' well. She dried up a bit, but remember she's with calf. I was going to stop milking her soon anyway—gotta build her up before she freshens."

She did look more comfortable and was eating her extra ration with relish. I loved watching cows eat their grain. As they dipped their faces into the feed, their moist muzzles would stipple with particles of grain, their tongues lavishly slurping feed into their mouths. For a cow, this was pure bliss. Now that I come to think of it, that was the expression on my sister-in-law's face, a hardened chocoholic, when she ate chocolate.

It was obvious these casts were not doing their job. I knew this case would haunt me and now the haunting had begun. Larger casts would not do the trick, but a cast reinforced with steel rods or even caged in steel was something worth exploring. I had to talk to Cliff at the General Store, but first a stop at Spencer Murray's farm to look at a dead cow. I prayed that a postmortem would not be necessary.

I drove out to Spencer's farm and was enthusiastically greeted by a slew of barking dogs and three children, whose vivid barn-red hair seemed to have been painted with the same brush used on the red barn. How could I have blundered onto Roscoe O'Malley's farm? *He* had the three red-headed kids.

A chorus of "Hi, Doc" greeted me as I got out of the car to return their greetings.

"Hi, kids. I am sorry to say I'm at the wrong farm, although I didn't think so at first."

Four dogs avidly sniffed my army shoes. I must have stepped into something. When I returned home, my own dogs would be equally inquisitive. Perhaps I was a carrier of secret messages known only to dogs.

"You're at the right farm, Doc," the children chorused. "We just have a new daddy. He even let us bring our dogs, Moe and Paula, along."

The oldest, Sean, pulled me aside. "Doc, could you look at Moe's ear? It's become big and fat."

"Sure thing. Bring him over."

While Sean went to fetch Moe, Spencer came out of the house with a lovely red-headed woman that I had always known as Kate O'Malley. Where was Spencer's wife, Helen? Had these farmers switched wives? I knew Roscoe had been called away last winter by the death of his mother, and Spencer had come over to do the daily chores. Maybe that was when the romance began.

Sean tugged over his heavily-matted, bedraggled Springer Spaniel. The dog kept flopping his head from side to side. His right ear was indeed blown up like a balloon, with stringy, matted clumps of hair dangling from it. A smelly ear infection had undoubtedly provoked the dog to shake his head vigorously, slapping the ear like a whip. The rupture of blood vessels within the ear flap caused it to swell with trapped blood.

"What's wrong with Moe's ear?" I heard Kate ask.

I turned to face the questioning green eyes and explained the problem.

"He'll need surgery, but I'm afraid I won't be able to do it on the farm. Bring him over to the office, and I'll take care of it. Do it soon, the ear tends to shrivel if you wait too long."

"Tell me when and we'll be there," she replied.

"Okay, I'll have Mary call you and make an appointment. Might be at night if that's agreeable."

"Sure, that will be fine," she said.

"Where's the dead cow, Spencer?"

"She's out in that pasture near that wooded area. You can see her from here. You can't drive out there, so jump on the John Deere and I'll take you out."

I grabbed my autopsy kit, hopped on the tow bar of the tractor and in a moment we were jolting our way over a bumpy pasture. At times it took a bit of gymnastics to hang on, but a large animal vet is toughened by his trade.

Over the noise of the tractor, I heard Spencer shout, "There she is."

Near the wooded area, a Holstein cow lay flat out on her left side. The grass around her was undisturbed—no evidence of any struggle or flailing of legs. She'd dropped where she stood. Her collapse was sudden and fatal. I examined her carefully, failing to find any clue to her death. No injury or blood were apparent. My only alternative was an autopsy, but this was not the appropriate place. If she died of an infectious disease, an autopsy would contaminate a large area. Wildlife would further spread disease. We'd have to fashion a sled of some sort and drag her back to an area that could be isolated and decontaminated.

As Spencer and I deliberated on how to move her, a shot rang out from the nearby wooded area. We both ducked—completely startled. I heard a soft growl emerge from Spencer that escalated into a roar.

"Those bastards, they killed my cow."

Off he ran, full speed, amazingly vaulting a barbed wire fence and disappearing into the woods.

There was a good likelihood that this cow was inadvertently shot by a stray bullet, but where was the wound? With some difficulty, I flipped her over to her right side—something I should have done before. A small penetrating wound was immediately apparent over her rib cage near her heart. A bullet had probably penetrated her heart, and she dropped where she stood. I had to find the bullet—no worry about infectious disease here.

I incised the area over the wound, and using my autopsy saw, I removed enough of the rib cage to expose the heart. With careful dissection, I removed the heart which was obviously damaged. Upon opening the heart, I was lucky to discover the bullet sandwiched in the heart wall. Loud voices were coming from the woods, and I saw Spencer escorting two red-jacketed hunters carrying rifles coming toward me.

"These are the guys that killed my cow, Doc. I caught them red handed." He was wild-eyed, flushed.

"There are a lot of hunters out here. It could have been any of them," one of the men said.

"You're the shooters, I know it. There's no one else around," Spencer shouted, becoming angrier by the minute.

I was not happy with this confrontation, especially with two unknown men carrying rifles and Spencer losing control.

"Do you men have hunting licenses? Can I see some I.D.?" I asked, trying to diffuse the heated exchange.

They were momentarily taken aback, but one man said, "They're in our pickup on the other side of the road."

"Now, Gentlemen, if you look at the cow, you will notice that I have recovered the bullet that killed the cow. It should be no chore at all to match it with one of your rifles. I suggest you settle this matter here and now."

The two hunters walked away and were discussing what to do.

"Tell you what we decided. First, we in no way admit to shooting this cow, but to avoid any further problems, we'll pay for the cow. What's a cow like this worth?"

I watched Spencer contain a smile of satisfaction. "She's a fine cow and worth at least six hundred dollars, cash on the barrel."

"Hell, no cow is worth that much. We'll give you three hundred dollars, take it or leave it."

Spencer was about to explode, so I decided to cut in and call their bluff. "Show us your hunting licenses and we'll settle. Otherwise pay the six hundred dollars before we call the State Troopers."

Much to my amazement they reached into their wallets and each came up with three hundred dollars.

"You guys meant to give Spencer three hundred dollars each, didn't you?" I teased.

On the way back, Spencer asked, "You really didn't have the bullet, did you Doc?"

"Of course I did. We city boys always get the evidence to back us up."

"That cow was only worth three hundred dollars."

"But Spencer, you lost out on her milk production plus a vet bill. Well, maybe you'll come out a little ahead."

"Say, how'd you like my new family? Roscoe and I decided to switch wives. That Kate is some woman—too much for Roscoe, I guess. The kids don't seen to mind one bit."

"What about the women? Are they happy with the arrangement?" I asked.

"Well I haven't heard any complaints. If it don't work out, we can always switch back."

He said this matter of factly. This was more bizarre than any soap opera.

I knew that farm women lived lonely, isolated lives. The long, frigid winters contributed to their isolation. Yet I rarely found them to be depressed. In my occasional contacts, I found them to be opinionated, sprightly and physically tough. Most were able to do a man's work, care for children and do some innovative cooking. A few lived in quiet desperation and craved companionship, but so it is with all people everywhere. I learned one thing about farmers' wives... don't be too friendly, even if they're old enough to be your mother... *especially* if they're old enough to be your mother.

Before checking in with Mary, I headed for the General Store. I found Cliff at his work bench repairing a bent bicycle frame. I explained the situation and could immediately see his mind focusing on the problem.

"A complete break, Doc? What bone is broke and make me a sketch of the bones in a cow's front leg. Put in all the bumps and such and tell me what this bone does and what's around it. How much weight does this here cow put on this leg?"

He wanted to know about ligaments, tendons and blood vessels and was able to repeat exactly everything I told him. His remarkable memory never failed to impress me. Furthermore, he was interested in knowing how the bones might shift and in what direction. I was flabbergasted by his questions.

I felt I was being quizzed by a professor of biomechanics. In fact, I didn't know the answers to many of his questions, but I was glad to have his help.

"Come in tomorrow and I'll have some sort of splint put together, but I got something you can help me with. Wait a minute and I'll get them."

He disappeared for a moment and returned with some small ribbons of paper.

"You heard about that Chinese restaurant that opened in Rockford? My missus and me go there every Sunday night. You been there?"

"First I heard of it and I love Chinese food," I replied.

"Well at the end of the meal, they give you these Chinese fortune cookies for free. Trouble is, I don't always know what they mean. Here's one: 'That fleeting thought is worth pursuing.' What are they talking about, Doc?"

"Well Cliff, sometimes you have an idea or a thought that just doesn't stay with you too long. Just don't forget about it. It might turn out to be pretty important. That's the way I see it."

"O. K. I'll think that over. How about this one? 'Look afar and see the end from the beginning.' What do you make of that?"

"Now let's see. I think it means that you have to see the whole picture. Don't just look at what's happening now. Yesterday and tomorrow have to be considered."

Cliff looked at me and smiled. "You sure you don't make up those Chinese fortune cookie sayings. Here's a few I just like." He reached into his breast pocket and pulled out a handful of fortune cookie inserts.

"I see you're a good customer. I hope you like Chinese food as much as those fortune cookies," I said.

He gave me one of his ever-ready smiles and proceeded to read.

"A smile is the key to understanding."

"Good character guards against temptation."

"Enjoy each moment. Happiness is now."

"Confucius says, Be watchful and attentive to your own interests."

"Now, Doc, who is Confucius? You must have some idea."

"All I know about him I can tell you in one sentence. He's a Chinese philosopher, lived about 500 B.C. and is the source of their doctrines of ethics, morals, and politics."

Cliff looked at me, very impressed by my superficial knowledge, scarcely comprehending what I was saying. Yet I detected his yearning to understand ideas and events beyond this small farm community. In my pedantic way, I'd aroused his curiosity.

As I started to leave, I said, "Are you sure you'll have enough time to make that splint by tomorrow, Cliff?"

"I have it worked out in my mind. That's the biggest part of the job. The rest is easy. See you tomorrow afternoon. Say, Doc, would you and Mary join us for a Chinese dinner Sunday night?"

"Mary will love it. You'll have to drive. My back seat is loaded with my stuff."

Cliff retrieved one more fortune cookie insert to read "'What's vice today may be virtue tomorrow.' Let's talk about that at dinner."

"Glad to. See you tomorrow."

The next day, calls consumed the entire morning. I returned home to find Mary waiting with a long list of calls—mastitis, clean a cow, itchy pigs, calf scours, obstructed teat and so on. But first I had to pick up the splint that Cliff had devised for Harold's cow. Cliff had framed a steel splint that could be applied to the cow's leg. It was carefully contoured to avoid pressure points. He had fashioned a steel hoof for the cow to walk on and all I need do was to apply cotton padding, fit the splint in place and snugly cover with plaster of Paris bandage.

I knew he must have spent a long time putting this appliance together, but he denied it was a problem. A couple of stops on the way over to Harold's farm took care of only two calls. This was one of those days when I would be late for dinner.

Harold and his two sons were waiting as I drove in.

I must admit that their enthusiasm was contagious. After applying Cliff's splint, I began to feel that maybe this would do it. If this support didn't endure for six to eight weeks, Queenie was in big trouble.

It had been a busy day, and as I drove back in a silvery moonlit darkness, I felt comforted by the events of the day. Despite my weariness, I was looking forward to dinner with Mary, followed by a cigar and some music. My brother had sent me a collection of records containing the nine Beethoven symphonies conducted by Arturo Toscanini... but my plans for the evening were disrupted by the presence of a car in front of my house. Seated in our living room, I found Kate O'Malley, or should it be Kate Murray, sipping a cup of coffee.

"Mary called and told me to come over tonight. I have Moe waiting in the car."

I vaguely remembered telling Mary to call Kate and make an evening appointment for surgery on Moe's ear—the sooner the better. Apparently tonight was the night. I saw my dinner going on the back burner, my cigar smoke withdrawing back into the cigar and Beethoven back into the record.

"Oh, I wouldn't want to interrupt your dinner. I can wait, no problem."

"I operate best on an empty stomach. Kate, you wait here while Mary and I do the surgery. It's not serious, but it is a bit messy."

"If you don't mind, I'd like to watch—help if I can. I did some nursing in my early days, so I don't imagine this will trouble me."

With Moe in tow, we went into my office where a little-used small animal operating table resided. Some Nembutal I.V. and Moe was fast asleep. After cleaning up the ear, I made an inch-and-a-half incision on the inside flap of the ear. Clotted blood and debris poured out, adroitly collected by Kate holding a dish pan.

"Sorry, I think I hear Mitch calling, so I'll have to leave you for a bit. I see Kate's is a wonderful assistant, you'll manage," Mary said.

It was soon obvious that Kate did have nursing experience. She gauze-sponged the persistent ooze from the incision area, threaded suture needles and checked Moe's anesthetic level. My close contact with her made me aware of two things—she was a remarkably good looking woman (a Greer Garson type) and she wore a disconcertingly sensuous perfume. I was glad to have finished placing enough mattress sutures in the ear, sufficient to flatten the ear and close the collapsed space left by the hematoma. Finally I applied an ear bandage to secure the ear for a few days. And now to escape the bewitching excitement of Kate... I could easily see how her mere presence had seduced Spencer.

"I like the way you operate, Doc. You're a promising surgeon."

"Just promising? You're suggesting that I haven't arrived?" I quipped.

"No, not at all. You know what I mean."

The Greer Garson smile unnerved me, but I maintained my professional demeanor. I was about to ask her to return in ten days but thought better of it.

"Kate, remove the bandage in two days, and I'll stop at the farm to remove the stitches in about ten days. Call me if you think you have a problem."

I thought it a good idea to return Moe to the farm while he recovered from anesthesia.

"Make him comfortable in the barn."

I carried Moe out to her car and we said good night. I was starving and hoped Mary had some hot food around.

"I'm back. Got anything to eat?"

"I'm all set. Mitch is asleep. He couldn't wait for you to tell him a story so I did. I was a little worried leaving you alone with that woman. She's gorgeous."

"No need to worry about me. I didn't give it a thought. Say, Mary, would you ever consider switching husbands?"

I ducked as a pot holder came flying my way.

In the following weeks, I frequently stopped at Harold Lambert's farm to see his cow. The cast was virtually unrecognizable—cloaked with manure, urine and farm debris. However, despite some frayed areas, which I reinforced with plaster, it held firm. I could detect no pressure sores or their unmistakable foul odor. The cow seemed to have accommodated to her disability and was hobbling about fairly well.

Next week would make it two months, and I had scheduled the cast removal for that time. Whether healing had occurred was anybody's guess. It would have been nice to have taken an X-ray to determine the degree of healing, but that was not available to me.

A week passed and the moment of revelation had arrived. An audience consisting of Harold and his family, Cliff, Mary and Mitch watched me struggle to remove the cast. Even with Cliff's help, it took about a half hour to remove it. The leg looked remarkably clean, whitened by the plaster dust. To the cow, the limb must have felt weightless. She held it up, hesitant to place it to the ground. I gently palpated the fracture site. It felt real good, no swelling or pain. Little by little, she would try to use it. I suspected that it would take a week or two to learn that the leg would indeed support her.

Although I thought a celebration was premature, Harold had everyone come into the house for some homemade wine and assorted sandwiches. Cake and coffee followed, with chocolate milk for Mitch. It was a festive occasion and Harold took every opportunity to sing my praises. Never having the capacity to enjoy anything fully without reservation, there lurked in my mind the probability this cow might never be able to walk—then what?

A week had gone by and I had no word from Harold regarding his cow. It was with some trepidation that I decided a visit to the farm would be appropriate. I met Harold in the barn and immediately noted the absence of his smile and the stiffness of his gait.

"Hi, Doc. Come to see Queenie?" Still no smile.

"Yes I did. How's she doing?"

"Come see for yourself."

He struggled to walk. His face reflected pain with every motion. What's wrong with this guy? Finally I said, "Harold, are you hurt?"

"Yeah, slipped on some manure. I'm all banged up. Can hardly move. Come this way, Doc. I moved her to another pen."

"How'd she get there?" I asked.

"Why she walked, of course."

"You mean she can walk?"

"She sure can." Harold forced a smile from his pain-wracked body.

Queenie was munching on some alfalfa hay. Upon seeing me, she began to move restlessly around her pen. She was decidedly lame, but she had a functional limb. It would take time, but her outlook was encouraging. I could barely contain my elation.

"Makes me feel pretty good, and I know you feel the same. Queenie will drop her calf next month and that should be no problem. I hope you will be around in case I need you."

Harold tried to sit down on a bale of hay, but couldn't make it.

"Have you seen a doctor?" I asked.

"Whose got time for that?"

"C'mon, get in my car and I'll take you to Doc Schreiber. He's in his office, and I know he has X-ray equipment. You can't do any chores in your condition. Your boys will be home from school and your missus will tell them what to do."

With further urging and coaxing from his wife, he got into my car and we drove to the doctor who practiced part-time in a nearby town. I left him in the doctor's office and told him I'd be back after I made some calls.

It was almost two hours before I returned to pick up Harold.

"So what did the doctor say?"

"He took some X-rays and says that I have two cracked ribs. He taped up my chest and I can hardly breathe. How the hell am I going to pull that tape off with all the hair on my chest?"

"Don't worry, you'll get it off. The main thing is that you'll be okay."

"The Doc says I should take it easy for a week or two. Is he kidding or something? Oh, it's beginning to itch," he moaned.

I saw Harold about a month later. He looked good and Queenie was doing well, but he had an angry expression on his face.

"What's wrong, Harold?"

"That's one hell of a bill you sent me. You cost more than Dr. Schreiber. Queenie ain't even worth that much."

"There was a lot of work and material that went into treating Queenie, not to mention the number of calls I made."

"I don't see why I should pay for the calls you made when I didn't even ask you to come out for most of them."

"You're right, Harold. I took that into consideration because I did stop by on my own. Don't forget, some of that bill goes to Cliff who made the splint."

"Why didn't you tell me you wanted a splint like Cliff made? I could've made one just like it."

This conversation was getting out of control, and I was beginning to feel the anger rising within me. Count to ten, I told myself.

"Harold, you said save her. You didn't care what it cost."

"That I did, but I didn't expect to be robbed."

That did it. Rather than explode, I walked to my car and drove off.

Mary, my chief bookkeeper, took over the matter and after considerable haggling, settled the account, giving Harold a ten percent discount on his bill. Harold did call me to treat a cow that was off feed one snowbound day, but Mary discreetly explained that it was impossible for me to get through. He never called me to his farm again.

KETONES AND CHOLERA

Jane Nelson was an amply-packaged, capaciously bosomed woman. Her body bulged her overalls and her hatless, short curly hair was usually flecked with barn dust. Rain or shine, she always wore unbuckled galoshes that clattered noisily as she walked. Her hands were tough and callused; her handshake was formidable. She must have been about forty, her brown eyes leveling with mine, and I'm six feet tall. She was brought up in a small Midwestern town, married a farmer and soon discovered she had more passion for farming than her husband. She neglected him as well as her three teenagers in her determined efforts to provide the ultimate care for her dairy cattle and hogs. I could not help noticing the cluttered appearance of the barnyard—scarcely anything seemed to be in place. Farm implements lay scattered, slowly decomposing as layers of rust flaked off. The dairy barn was the most viable building, the others being in variable states of disrepair.

Jane escorted me into the dairy barn and the transformation was dramatic. The barn sparkled like a blue-white diamond in the morning sun. I marveled at the immaculate condition of the cows, and it became very apparent where Jane spent her time. My army shoes crunched the freshly limed floor, and cows turned in their stanchions to see who the intruder might be. Others reclined on thick beds of oat straw chewing their cud. These were happy, contented cows.

Jane had called me this morning to look at a cow that was off feed. "And wouldn't you know it, my best milker." It's an expression that I invariably heard. Cows that are efficient producers of milk require special care, special nutrition and an adequate dry period to prepare for the birth of a new calf. When you can consider that milk contains about thirty five percent protein, three to four percent butterfat, five percent lactose, calcium, phosphorus, plus other minerals and vitamins, it is easy to see why cows need a carefully balanced ration to sustain production. Failing that, they become unproductive, often ending up being shipped to market. Large producers are often found to be somewhat lean, barely able to sustain their heavy milk yield, giving of their own bodies to supply the protein found in milk.

Just ahead I saw an especially large-framed cow lying down. Her unthrifty appearance starkly contrasted with all those sleek cows around her.

"That's Annie," Jane said. "I can't believe how gaunt she's become. Look how rough her coat is and look at her bag, it's all shrunken. It hardly pays to milk her."

Apparently my presence alarmed her and she hastened to get to her feet—a major effort for this sick cow. Her eyes twitched occasionally, and I thought I detected some muscle spasms. She humped her back and began to pass ribbons of scanty mucous-covered manure. In another moment, she was urinating. I quickly pulled a tube I carried in my breast pocket for this occasion and collected a sample. Collecting urine this way made it unnecessary to catheterize the cow, but it did subject me to getting my hands and clothes splattered with urine.

"Believe it or not, she's my pride and joy. I think she has hardware. She's jumpy as all get out. Must be a piece of wire poking her stomach."

Baling machines tied bales of hay with wire. Pieces of that wire can find their way into hay and are easily swallowed during feeding. The wire will often lodge in one of the forestomachs of the cow, occasionally penetrating the stomach wall.

"When did she calve, Jane?"

"She had her third calf three or four weeks ago and has been giving a can of milk each day. Best milker I have. She's going off feed and drying up. Look at her, she's becoming a skeleton."

I began my examination of Annie, always listening to what Jane was saying. She had suggested a diagnosis and hoped I would not confirm it. Dairy farmers like Jane, milking forty cows, knew each one intimately. Any departure from normal feeding patterns or behavior is immediately noted. No veterinarian will ignore what a farmer is telling them about an animal. Their words in many cases contain the diagnosis. How often can you be really sure what you're dealing with? Most of the time you have a treatment before a diagnosis. The wisdom of doctors is not in their diagnosis, but in their selection of treatment. A fairly large percentage of the time, they don't have the foggiest notion of what they're dealing with, in spite of the assurance and wisdom they exude. Of course, future technology will hopefully define what is obscure, but in the '40s and '50s, the door to wisdom was barely ajar.

My impression was that Annie suffered from a carbohydrate metabolism dysfunction called acetonemia. Her history and examination neatly fitted this diagnosis. The urine sample I had collected was strongly positive for ketones. However, any abnormality which causes a cow to go off feed may result in a positive urine test. Where fats must be metabolized in excess by the cow in order to supply energy requirements, an accumulation of ketone bodies is likely to occur.

There were many theories as to the cause of acetonemia. When nobody knows the cause, there are always many theories. I did know that these cows had high blood ketones and very low blood sugars. The customary treatment was a liter or two of a concentrated dextrose solution given intravenously. After several daily doses, these cows usually made a complete recovery.

I had made my diagnosis, but felt obliged to check for "hardware." A World War II spin off was the metal detector. It was mostly used to detect land mines. A veterinary company modified the unit for use on cows, and I was one of their first customers. The probe of the detector was held over the area where hardware usually lodged and a hand on a dial responded when metal was detected. While it was not everything I expected, it did help me make a decision in some cases. Annie's response to my metal detector was negative.

I had completed my call, having given Annie two liters of dextrose intravenously. I intended to repeat the treatment the next day.

"Doc, come into the house and let me pay my bill. I know I haven't paid you for months, and you're going to stop coming when I call next."

She led me to the kitchen where most farm business is done. A large kitchen table served as a desk, with record books strewn all over. She insisted that I be seated at the table and hastened to pour me some tarry coffee in a cracked cup of questionable cleanliness. The rubble of many a meal and numerous unwashed dishes were scattered about.

"Try the coffee, Doc. It's a Colombian bean and I get it special."

Reluctantly, I took a sip of the coffee; it tasted as bad as it looked.

"Good, isn't it, Doc?"

"Unusual," I conceded, wondering where I could wash the grit out of my mouth.

Jane sat down beside me and began sorting out a stack of bills. She came up with four that Mary had sent her. Never once did Mary advise any of my clients they were delinquent. That was just not done.

"All I can find are these four, so I'll make a check for them. If you got anymore, let me know."

Seated next to her, I became aware that although she was a bit weather-beaten, she was indeed an attractive woman. Except for her awful galoshes, her dress code was entirely acceptable under the circumstances.

"Doc, I got a hundred feeder pigs coming in and I want to get them vaccinated against hog cholera. Get your stuff together, and we'll vaccinate them next week. Aren't you gonna drink your coffee? It's real good. It'll put some color in that pale face of yours."

Trying to immobilize my sense of taste and smell, I took another sip.

"Thanks a lot. Got to get going."

"Wait a minute, Doc. Here's your check."

I returned to my car and remembered I had an after dinner mint in the glove compartment. Perhaps that would neutralize the taste of that awful coffee. Mary's greeting kiss was followed by, "What have you been eating, and what are you covering up?"

"Just that after dinner mint I found in my car," I replied. "What do you think I had?"

"Tastes like some coffee that has been disinterred with a mummy."

"At least it's not perfume. Jane Nelson paid her bill, and I was forced to drink her coffee in order to get her check. She's getting a hundred feeder pigs, so remind me to order some hog cholera vaccine tomorrow."

I've heard it said that a dog will look up to a human, a cat will look down, but a pig will look you straight in the eye. However, close human contact with a pig from an early age will give them a dog-like quality. There is a widespread belief that the pig is a glutton. The fact is that pigs don't eat like pigs at all. A pig never eats more than he needs and always knows when to stop. Pigs are not scavengers, preferring ground corn, oats and mowed clover. They enjoy fruits like apples and pears. Man has corrupted the pig by feeding slop and garbage, thereby creating some of their gluttonous behavior.

For centuries, farmers thought that pigs had to have muddy sties, and a mud hole was an easy thing to provide. Pigs roll in mud to keep cool, not because they like dirt. If they are raised on properly planned runways of concrete with plenty of clean running water, they are the cleanest of all domestic animals. They will make a noticeable effort to keep their quarters clean by segregating their excrement to a secluded part of an enclosure.

I enjoy watching pigs—their joyful abandon as they eat, their total ability to relax, the base fiddle grunts of nursing sows, their wallowings in mud (sometimes on a hot summer day I think I would love to join them), the ecstatic expression on their faces as they rub against a post and, of course, their intelligence (highest I.Q. among the farm animals). What I didn't like was their high-pitched, eardrum-withering screams and squeals when held for examination or vaccinations. Somebody ought to do a study to see if pig farmers become prematurely deaf. And try to corner or catch one in a field—forget it—my dog will attest to that. A running back on a football team should be that nimble.

Hog cholera vaccination consisted of giving each pig two injections—one being the live virulent virus and the other its anti-serum. Not only was this an effective way of vaccinating pigs, but it was an extremely effective way of perpetuating the disease. In effect, I was seeding the area with live virus. The pigs themselves would shed the virus for weeks and anything or anybody coming and going from this farm could be a vector in the spread of the disease. I was always very careful to decontaminate myself before going to other farms.

All was going well on that bright sunny day when I arrived to vaccinate for hog cholera. The pigs were crowded into pens, and Jane and her husband Lou were grabbing the scrambling, screaming pigs, lifting and holding them against their knees for the two injections. One of their sons, who was kept home from school, had a red marker, which he used liberally on the back of each pig vaccinated. It didn't take him long to realize that he would rather be in school than endure this dusty, sweaty, ear-piercing chore.

After it was all over, Jane invited me in for coffee, an invitation I politely declined. My ears were ringing, and as a result of the dust stirred up by the frightened scrambling of the pigs, I continued to blow my nose and clear gunk from my mouth all the way home.

About a week later, I returned from morning calls to learn that Jane Nelson had telephoned. Apparently some of the pigs were somewhat sluggish and a few had diarrhea. A post-vaccination reaction was not unusual in three or four days, but overt symptoms in my experience were uncommon. A feeling of dread consumed me, and my heartburn ignited in a flash fire. A gulp of milk on the flames and I was on my way.

I knew that a week ago these were healthy pigs, free of disease and parasites. I even knew where they came from and exposure to hog cholera was most unlikely. Jane had told me that they had an outbreak on the farm over five years ago, but I did not believe that was a concern.

I drove slowly, never wanting to reach my destination. Jane greeted me pleasantly enough, but it was a veneer to cover how she truly felt.

"I thought something was wrong yesterday afternoon. Some seemed a little sluggish, didn't want to move about; others were scouring," she said quietly.

We walked to the pigpens. A deadly silence cast a pall over everything. My worst fears were realized. I had seen this disease many times before, but never had I felt that I was its viral messenger. The scene was devastating. Pigs were depressed, disinclined to move, feverish (105 to 108 degrees Fahrenheit). Most refused to eat and were hiding in their litter undergoing gut-wrenching pain. Splashes of bloody diarrhea were everywhere. I euthanized a pig that was obviously moribund. An autopsy should provide convincing evidence that I was dealing with hog cholera. Purplish patches streaked the abdomen where I made my incision. The lungs, abdominal organs and lymph glands were unsparingly attacked. There was no escape from this killer. Searing gastrointestinal inflammation and hemorrhage engulfed the entire gut. The characteristic "turkey egg" kidneys were in evidence—small hemorrhages dotted the capsule of the kidneys, giving them the appearance of turkey eggs.

I looked for some escape from my culpability. Was my vaccination at fault—insufficient or inactive anti-serum? Had they been exposed in transit on a contaminated truck? Were they fed uncooked garbage? Unlikely. The overwhelming massive involvement of almost all the pigs continued to suggest that I had administered the disease. The immediate question was what could be salvaged? Large doses of anti-serum might help those who were not in an advanced stage of the disease. Grimly I gave anti-serum to any pig I thought had a ghost of a chance. After hours of exhaustive work and further autopsies, I started toward my car.

"Doc," I heard Jane calling, "I want a word with you before you leave."

Well, here it comes. I didn't think I could feel any worse than I did, so she might as well have a go at me. There were tears in her eyes as she approached. I was totally unprepared for what followed. In one rapid motion, she took me in her arms and I found my head pressed against her bosom.

"It's not the end of the world. I'm sure it's not your fault. It'll all work out."

I felt tears fall on my face as she continued to hold me tightly. Suddenly she bent over and kissed my cheek several times. Finally, she released me and headed rapidly toward her house, the buckles of her galoshes chattering excitedly.

"I'll be back tomorrow," I yelled at her departing figure.

When I arrived home, Mary was waiting for a complete report. I went into the details, but decided to delete the goodbye kisses. You never know how that might be interpreted.

"Why not call the drug company that sold you the virus and serum. Perhaps they have some thoughts on what happened," she suggested.

"Good idea. I'll call them right now."

I placed the call and after being catapulted from one person to another, I finally was able to present my situation to a bored voice somewhere in Iowa.

"Of course, you know we are not having any such problem anywhere. Undoubtedly, your pigs were exposed to cholera before vaccination. Happens all the time. I say, did you refrigerate your virus and serum?"

"No, I leave it in a hot sun a few hours before vaccination."

"Oh, that's not the thing to do," he replied quite seriously.

What kind of a nincompoop does he take me for anyway? Everybody knows that stuff must be refrigerated. In fact, I keep it on ice all the way to the farm. If a shipment arrives that's not completely cold, I send it back to the lab. You can't be too careful."

"Could you send out one of your field vets? After all, there might be a problem with the vaccine."

"Most unlikely, but I'll try and send somebody out as soon as I can free one up. Well it was nice talking to you. Call me if you have any further questions."

"Hey wait a minute. I have more questions right now. I am sending back the remaining serum and virus, and I want you to field test it. Maybe you have a serious problem."

Mary brought over a couple of antacids for me to chew on.

"We'll need more evidence before I can authorize a field study. However, I'll credit your account for any unused serum and virus you choose to return. Good day, Doctor," and with that he hung up.

"Call the University. Perhaps they might be willing to help," Mary said.

"Fat chance," I replied. "With all the money they get from this company for different projects, they'll be reluctant to do anything that would jeopardize their relationship."

As I sat beside the phone feeling dejected and inadequate, Mary came over, took me in her arms and tenderly kissed me. I shall always remember this day because this was a day that two women tried to comfort me with their kisses. I must have been truly pathetic.

"Now it seems to me," Mary reasoned, "if something is wrong with that vaccine, there should be breaks all over the place. There's a regional vet meeting in a couple of weeks, so go up there and see if your colleagues have had similar disasters."

There I sat paralyzed by guilt and self-pity, while my wife used the logic and reason I should have been using.

The next morning, I drove out to the Nelson farm. The disease had continued to gallop through the herd. Death was everywhere. The remaining pigs continued to have severe bloody diarrhea and staggered drunkenly if they tried to rise. The scene was a battlefield—the dead and wounded had not been removed. It was obvious that any survivors would be severely stunted and of little economic value. This was a virulent, triumphant virus, pillaging every living cell.

"Well, Doc, I guess it's just about a total loss."

"I believe you're right, Jane," I responded gloomily.

To emphasize the situation, a pig struggled to his feet, staggered about and fell, apparently dead.

"I've been thinking about this disaster, and I want to reimburse you for your losses."

"Look Doc, we've had crop failures, all kinds of animal losses, even been hit by a tornado, and we manage one way or another. If I thought for one minute you were responsible for what happened, I would accept your offer gladly. So forget it."

I knew I would feel better if she accepted payment. When I returned home, I wrote a check for what I thought to be the market price of the pigs and mailed it to her. She continued to use my services, but never cashed the check.

Meanwhile, I pursued the matter with the manufacturer of the vaccine and two universities, but received polite rebuffs from all of them. However, I continued to be haunted by the specter of dead and dying pigs. I have vaccinated thousands of pigs since then, but the disquiet I feel never leaves me.

With the advent of attenuated and killed vaccines, hog cholera vaccination has become a safer procedure. Banning the use of a live virus has been a most positive development.

In 1950, the U.S. Bureau of Animal Industry reported that a new form or variant type of hog cholera virus "never before recognized" may have been responsible for recent middlewest losses in swine immunized with serum and virus.

Bureau tests of immunizing products used on swine herds showed that regular serum alone provided adequate protection against the regular hog cholera virus, but failed to protect against this variant. I can't say that the companies that produced this variant virus were at fault. I am sure that they had no idea that their virus was a variant. When they did find out that they had disseminated a deadly virus, they were remarkably uncommunicative. The brunt of this disaster was felt by the farmer and the veterinarian who administered the vaccinations.

It took a government agency to discover the variant virus and the American Veterinary Medical Association to report it in their journal. Of course, the drug companies abdicated any responsibility. The corporate character in its anonymity has no conscience.

I have no idea when and how the vaccine producers became aware of the problem. It was of minimal interest to them that thousands of pigs died as a result of vaccinations containing the variant virus as long as there were no ripples in their financial statements. Once again, the fatalism and stoicism of farmers' psyche muted their response.

ODORS

Veterinary medicine is one odoriferous profession. Hardly a day went by that I was not confronted with a repulsive odor. Debriding the cloying, rotted tissue between the hooves of cattle, removing a decomposed after-birth from a cow, cleaning up suppurating wounds, dealing with diarrhea or impactions, sniffing the acetonemic breath of an animal, or inhaling some of that tongue-biting medication I occasionally dispensed, all were part and parcel of my trade.

Every month or so, Mary and I escaped to a movie. One evening, after our sitter, Agnes, was instructed as to our whereabouts in the event of an emergency call, we headed fifteen miles north to a movie house in Rockton, Wisconsin. The movie was *Casablanca*, with Ingrid Bergman, Humphrey Bogart, Paul Henreid, Claude Rains and Peter Lorre, very special actors in my time… or any time.

Although it was still hayfever season, we drove with the windows down, enjoying the cool rush of field-scented air with only an occasional sneeze to mar the serenity of the early evening. It was pure enchantment sitting next to Mary, my right hand entwined in hers, just feeling good all over. Sneeze, sneeze, sneeze. Mary had given up the "God bless you."

We arrived at the movie house and were ushered to our seats, but not before I identified myself to the usher, instructing her to notify me in the event I was called on the phone. No sooner had the movie begun when I felt a tap on my shoulder.

"Doctor, you're wanted on the telephone. Some sort of emergency," the usher explained.

I turned to Mary. "Will probably have to go out on this one. Stay put, enjoy the movie; will be back as quickly as possible."

In the darkness, I could sense her disappointment. She had endured this situation before and would undoubtedly again. Once in an exasperated moment she said to me, "Why can't you once say you're unavailable. You can't always be the answer to everybody's urgent requests. What did they do before you came?"

I listened to her, but could not do otherwise. It became a compelling response on my part. I had come to the conclusion that most of my clients were wholly dependent on my services. I was clearly convinced that I was indispensable and my continuous availability was a critical factor in their lives. Consequently, we never took a vacation, much less a day off. On rare occasions, I attended a nearby veterinary meeting but first canvassed the area to see what vets might be available in an emergency. During the meeting, I frequently called Mary to see if everything was under control. As a secondary thought, I inquired about Mitchell. In retrospect, I don't recall asking Mary how she was coping. She always ended our phone conversations with "Love you, Irv," while I invariably said, "Got to get back to the meeting." Even a telephone was too public a device to mention love. She never really complained and was always delighted to see me on my return. She endured me, she sustained me, she loved me.

This was my mission in life. This was my parish, and I made my rounds doing my best to bring aid and comfort to those who needed me.

I left Mary at the theater, hastened to my car, and began the ten-mile drive to the Herbert Lomas farm. I had been to Herb's farm several weeks ago to blood test his cows for Brucellosis. The test results indicated that he had a high rate of infection in his herd, certainly suggesting why a cow was trying to abort a fetus almost two months before her term. Darkness had enveloped the prairie when I reached his farm. Hot water, soap and towels awaited me in the barn.

"She's been straining for hours," Herb explained. "She's a stinking mess."

An absolutely repulsive odor emanated from the cow accompanied by a thick, yellowish discharge from her vulva. My stuffed nose did not sufficiently insulate me from that awful smell.

Undoubtedly, I was dealing with a contagious abortion. I stripped to the waist and slipped on a pair of rubber sleeves that stretched over my shoulders to protect myself from the inevitable exposure to infection and odor. I inserted my gloved hand into the uterus and was greeted with a jumble of legs plus a great straining effort from the cow. The yellow fluid sprayed all over me and the smell virtually nauseated Herb, who was holding the tail. Obviously this calf had been dead for some time and was in a state of decomposition. It took only a couple of minutes to straighten the small calf and effect delivery. I should have been wearing my protective rubber suit, which I almost never wore. I used it on one lengthy occasion and sweated so profusely that I suffered a mild case of heat exhaustion. In this case, I fervently wished I had worn it, no matter what the price.

Herb fire-brigaded me with buckets of water as I scrubbed with an antiseptic soap, finally drying myself with towels. This had to be an overwhelming exposure to Brucellosis. However, I felt that I had been repeatedly exposed on previous occasions and must have acquired some immunity. I gave it no further thought.

I discarded my soiled hat, removed my rubber boots, washed and soaked them thoroughly in antiseptic solutions, dressed, discussed a disease control program with Herb and was on my way back to join Mary at the movie.

An hour and a half had elapsed before I rejoined Mary at the theater. I found my seat beside her just in time to hear Claude Rains say to Peter Lorre, "Round up the usual suspects." In the semi-darkness, I noted that people alongside, in front and in back of us were vacating their seats. When the film concluded, a considerable area around us had been vacated. Some patrons were staring at me with considerable displeasure and muttering words I was fortunate not to hear.

"Mary, why do all these people seem so upset with us?"

"It's not us, it's you. I guess they all forgot to bring their gas masks."

"You mean I stink so badly?"

"My God, what have you been rolling in? I don't think I have experienced quite that bad an odor from you before. It's going to be a problem sleeping with you tonight. I think we had best skip our coffee nightcap on the way home."

The night air was chilly, but we proceeded homeward with all the car windows wide open. We arrived home and the baby sitter, Agnes, reported that all was well. There were a few calls, but nothing urgent. On her way out the door, she turned to Mary and said, "What's that awful smell?"

"Oh, that's Doc. He forgot to use his deodorant."

I heard her giggling all the way out to her car. Although Agnes was ordinarily a discreet person, I was sure the whole town would avoid me for the next few days. It took two days and innumerable baths for Mary to announce that I had attained complete purification.

Five days previously I had made an appointment to castrate some pigs for Karl Meier. Karl was a barrel of a man, about sixty, lived with a sister, who had recently died. Karl raised hogs—only hogs, and he was good at it. On recent visits to his farm, I found him no longer to be the jolly, friendly man that I knew. Totally withdrawn, his ever-ready laughter stifled, his face reflected intense sadness and loneliness. He performed his chores, not in that happy energetic manner I had known, but in a plodding, indifferent fashion. The pleasures of living, working, taking care of his hogs and above all the companionship of his sister were irretrievably gone. I had hoped that after a few months, life would begin to have some meaning for him, but there was no indication that this was happening. I brought Mary along on one call, but the despair in his voice and the tears in his eyes suggested that I probably made things worse.

Karl's pig farm was made up of a group of low-slung buildings in which he penned his pigs. His sows were kept in pens where they farrowed and nursed their piglets until weaning. Most were sold locally to various farms for fattening until they were ready for market.

I drove to a small corral he used to gather pigs for castration or vaccination. Usually he had one or two hired hands about to help, and the pigs he had selected for the procedure would be restlessly milling about sufficiently aware that something undesirable was about to happen. Karl was a precise, punctual man, and I could only think I came on the wrong day. Nevertheless I honked my horn, but nobody responded. I noticed an open door at one of the pig houses and figured that Karl might be inside watering or feeding his hogs. I entered, calling Karl by name, but only the squeals of baby pigs and the grunts of sows answered. A feed cart was parked in the aisle between the pens, and I walked toward it. A minor commotion occurred as my presence undoubtedly disturbed the pigs. The mash in feed pails had a disturbing sour odor, but there was another overriding odor—that putrescent sickening odor of death. I looked about. A combination of apprehension and nausea began to churn within me, but everything looked normal as I walked the corridor separating the pens.

I actually walked past it, but I was suddenly transfixed. A body was lying up against the wall of a pen. I entered the pen and a closer look assured me that it was Karl, obviously dead and probably for a few days. To my horror, I noted that he had been savagely attacked. A grunt behind me was the confession of the perpetrator. I wheeled about to be faced by a monstrous sow rapidly waddling toward me. It took but a moment to vault the pen's partition and put me out of harm's way.

Behind her, in a corner of the pen, lay her piglets, fast asleep, unperturbed by the drama that was taking place. The sow turned, took a few sniffs at Karl's body and looked up to stare at me. Our eyes met. We stared at each other for at least a minute. Within fatty-lidded recesses, her eyes glowed with anger, arrogance and challenge. She charged the partition behind which I stood; it shuddered, but withstood her weight. As I stepped back, our eyes met again. Her expression was fierce—hypnotic. Her message was loud and clear, "You eat me—I eat you."

I called the authorities. Obviously a complete investigation was in order. After an autopsy was performed, I learned that Karl died of a massive heart attack. I was comforted to know that the sow's attack had taken place after Karl's death.

Perhaps there were mitigating circumstances that could explain the sow's behavior. The coroner said that Karl was dead for at least three days, certainly enough time to make her one hungry sow. Her attack and ferocity could be explained by her hunger and her need to nurse a demanding litter of baby pigs. There are innumerable reports of starving men eating dead men, so why not a starving pig eating a dead man?

On this occasion, I carried the odor of death only in my mind, not on myself. I returned home anxious to tell Mary what had transpired, but we had a visitor, Becky.

Becky was a teenager who lived on a farm just outside of town. She was interested in exotic animals, be they birds, snakes, turtles, ferrets, fish—just about any living thing excited her interest. It was not unusual to see her bike parked in front of my house when I returned from calls. I knew immediately that I was about to face some challenging questions about subjects I knew little about. She was always probing into my ignorance.

Becky had a rare, inquiring mind. Her curiosity was boundless. I daresay she knew more about her pets than I did. Her questions often sent me to reference books to find answers. At a recent veterinary meeting, I had even purchased several books dealing with exotics so I could better deal with her questions. Needless to say she taught me a lot.

Mary greeted me with, "Becky's here. She brought you a litter of baby skunks. I had her leave them outside. I'd rather you didn't bring them into the house."

Becky gave me a cheery, "Hello," and said, "Let's go and look at my skunks. Their mother was run over by a car, and I found these in the woods nearby. My daddy says I can't bring them into the house until they are descented."

Tired as I was, I obediently followed her outside, where she uncovered a basket containing three baby skunks. Their tails immediately raised, ready to express their displeasure. Becky's voice, which they immediately recognized, seemed to calm them. Without hesitation she reached into the box and lifted one out.

"This is Oreo," she said, nuzzling the little creature with her nose. "Isn't he the cutest thing you ever saw?"

The animal was totally relaxed in her hands.

"Here, hold Oreo while I bring out Shadow and Striper."

She pushed Oreo into my hands while she reached in for the other two. Oreo sniffed me curiously and fortunately decided I was no threat. As we handled the three skunks, I detected the faint but infamous aroma of skunk. I made no mention of this lest my comments offend Oreo.

"Daddy says I can keep them if they are descented. That's why they are here, Doc."

"Becky, I have never descented skunks. Call Dr. Whitehead. He does small animal work and has more experience than I."

Becky blushed a bit and said, "To tell the truth I did, and he said absolutely 'No, no, no,' three times in fact."

She turned to me and said, "If you won't do it, Doc, I'll have to turn them loose, and then they will surely die."

As she continued to chatter on, I began to visualize the procedure. I had seen it done some years ago and decided at that time it was no big deal. Now that I was being asked to perform the surgery it was a big deal, a very big deal.

"Of course you'll do it Doc," Becky implored. "Please."

"I'm not really the man for this job," I responded.

Much to my surprise Mary chimed in, "Do it, Doc. It would greatly please me as well."

It was two against one, and I succumbed.

"Okay Becky, I'll do it. You have to understand that it is very new to me and things might go wrong, but I'll give it my best shot. Surgery will start tomorrow at 4:00 p.m.—in the back yard, just in case we have problems. Be sure you feed them only breakfast tomorrow. I want them here on an empty stomach. Becky, you'll be my surgical assistant."

She beamed with excitement, "I knew you would. I knew you would," she repeated. "Wait till Daddy hears about this."

She gathered up her babies and bicycled off.

Frankly, I was disturbed by the whole situation. Once again I was involved in something I should have avoided. Whitehead said "No," and that was it. I should have said the same thing. Okay, I was committed, but I had terrible misgivings.

Anesthetic would be administered by placing each skunk in a jar with ether-soaked cotton and covering the top. When an anesthetic level was reached, I would remove the animal, and with Becky positioning the tail, the operation would proceed. But first I would have to improvise a tiny ether cone in the event the skunk started to come out of anesthesia before surgery was completed. Maybe I could persuade Mary to participate, but she was already making squeamish remarks. However, I knew my powers of persuasion would induce her to assist. She almost always responded to financial inducements. She agreed to split the fee.

The next day during morning calls, I must confess that I was distracted by my afternoon skunk surgery. Perhaps it was a foreboding, but I was uncomfortable with myself. The animals I treated sensed my vulnerability and seemed more restless and difficult than usual. On one farm, the dogs were unusually aggressive, and instead of standing my ground, I made a dash for the milk house. The farmer said the dogs were just being playful. I returned home about 3:30 p.m., scrubbed the day's dirt from my body, brought an old table out to my backyard, prepared my ether jar and instruments, and awaited Becky. In spite of my wishes otherwise, she appeared with her babies right on time.

I had Mary, Becky and myself glove up because you never know where that skunk juice might go. Becky placed the first skunk into the jar and in a few minutes it was asleep. She removed the animal, placed it on the table, and proceeded to elevate the tail as I had instructed. The small openings containing the skunk sacs were soon evident. Using a tiny forceps I spread the opening, enabling me to grasp the sac with another forceps. I tugged lightly, but it was not forthcoming. I widened the opening, dissected away some connective tissue that seemed to be holding it, and slowly it began to emerge. It was a yellow sac, tiny grape sized—much larger than I would have imagined. Mary and Becky were so focused on what I was doing that the patient was completely forgotten. The skunk began to stir. "More ether, Mary," I pleaded.

She placed the ether cone over the animal's face and in a few minutes she said, "Proceed with the surgery, Doctor."

I operated on the second skunk and finally got to the third. Everything went well. I had only one more sac to remove. Somehow this sac was more tightly attached than the others. I bent closer to discover the problem, tugging more firmly and impatiently at the sac. Suddenly a silent, violent explosion. The sac ruptured! Skunk fluid spritzed my face, my hair, my left eye. The effect was instantaneously catastrophic. My whole respiratory apparatus shut down. I couldn't speak or breathe. I clutched at my throat gasping for air. My eye felt as if it were on fire, the cornea crinkling in flames like tissue paper. My blindness was certain—no eye could withstand such a flagrant insult. For one fragmented moment! I tried to think what the chemical components of skunk material might be, but in my agony I found no reprise.

Curiously, I don't recall any odor. Perhaps its intensity had dulled all my senses as a protective mechanism. With great effort, I sucked in some air and after, a few moments wheezed it out. In a minute or two, I whispered to Mary, "Bring the garden hose—quickly."

I flushed myself with the hose, lavaging my eye, soaking my hair. This was the pain of torture but a confession would in no way mitigate it. I doubled over doing my best to contain the moans that were bursting out. The pain in my eye had subsided somewhat. It was an angry red, but I had vision... I had vision!

Mary and Becky were standing nearby looking at me with expressions of horror.

"Damn it, I'm going to finish this operation. Becky, hold the tail up."

The odor was forbidding, but they approached to resume their assignments after having placed clothespins over their noses.

I grasped the ruptured sac with my forceps and had no problem removing it. Operation completed, I placed the last skunk in the basket and Becky sped off, undoubtedly to escape the skunk odor and to relate to her family the details of my surgical disaster. Mary confiscated my clothes so they could be destroyed—burned, buried or whatever. I showered for over an hour, shampooed my hair, saturated my head with quarts of tomato juice that I heard would neutralize skunk odor—no help! My reflection in the bathroom mirror was ghastly. Mary suggested a hair cut and shampoo. I drove downtown, but not before I heard my neighbors complaining of a terrible skunk odor in the neighborhood.

I walked into the barber shop reeking.

"A short, short haircut, Al, and a strong, strong shampoo. I got to get rid of this smell."

Al looked at me and said, "Okay Doc, but I don't smell anything."

A patron entered the barber shop, gave a gasp, and quickly left. Al gave me the shortest haircut since my army days. "Looks pretty good," Mary said. After this incident, Al and I became good friends. Any man who says he don't smell a thing when a guy reeking of skunk comes in for a haircut and shampoo is truly a gentleman.

The skunk odor clung to me with unbelievable tenacity. When I entered a barn, the farmer would invariably say to me, "Do you smell a skunk?" At this point, I didn't smell a thing, and I would answer, "Afraid I don't."

Undeterred, I had occasion to de-scent skunks again, but never repeated my previous disaster. In fact, I became the best skunk de-scenter in the area. I got at least one request a year, even a referral from Dr. Whitehead, and my fee had risen to ten dollars each—it had been five.

I gown up for this surgery. My head is hooded and I wear protective goggles. In addition, Mary pins a white sheet over my body. The first time she surveyed her handiwork, she broke out into laughter.

"You look like you're ready for a Ku Klux Klan meeting—and don't forget we still split the fee."

LEONA AND LEO

An incident occurred that caused me no small amount of grief. A small town, eight miles east, had a mini-drug store (no pharmacist) with an ice cream parlor. Toothpaste, aspirin, cosmetics and other sundries necessary to our western civilization were available.

An elegant soda fountain, surfaced with rose marble and rimmed with mahogany, greeted your entry. Padded stools with cast iron floor rests made it a comfortable place to plop down on a hot afternoon between calls and order a black and white soda—hold the cherry. All that was needed were some brass spittoons to complete the prohibition era ambiance.

Leo had found the counter in the Chicago warehouse of a secondhand restaurant supply store under decades of dust: He had it shipped to his store by cattle truck, cleaned it up, and converted it into a show piece soda fountain. I had to admire Leo for his daring and imagination in transforming it from beer and booze to soda and ice cream.

"Doc, I wonder if we can work out a deal. Lots of farmers are coming in looking for mastitis medicine for their cows. I heard you have some of the best stuff around. Can I buy some from you?"

I knew lots of farmers were coming to the house and Mary was dispensing the medication. She was constantly interrupted by their comings and goings. Perhaps a deal with Leo would lessen her burden. I knew other vets were doing this, but I wondered about the ethical implication since this medication was designed for veterinary distribution only. However, many mail-order catalogues were featuring this very product for sale to any farmer who would place an order.

"Here's your black and white—no cherry, Doc" Leona said, giving me a big smile.

"Leona, that scoop of vanilla can barely fit into the glass. I think she likes me, Leo," I said jokingly.

Leo gave her a disapproving look and walked away.

"Leo thinks I gave you too big a scoop. He's a real penny-pincher." She laughed loudly as she edged toward me, flirtatiously. I turned to see Leo glowering from the rear of the store. This was not someone to go into business with.

I went back to Leo and said, "There are mail-order companies selling mastitis medicine plus other veterinary supplies. It would be a good idea to get it directly from them. Certainly would be more profitable for you."

"Tell you what I'm going to do, Leo. I have some vet supply catalogues that I'll drop off. They'll show you what's available, even send down a salesman to sell you the merchandise."

"That's great, Doc."

"Tell Leona how pretty I thought she was."

Leo's face tensed and I knew I had committed a cardinal sin in our relationship. I should have known better.

I returned a few days later to be effusively greeted by Leona. My black and white was enormous and I could not avoid her constant chatter. Leo was slinging arrows at us. I could not finish my soda and decided to leave the catalogues with Leo and be on my way.

Leo was at the back of the store pretending to sort out some supplies he had received. I approached him with the catalogues and he turned toward me. His usual ruddy complexion was ashen. "Get the hell out of this store. I never ever want to see you in here again," he hissed.

There was nothing I could do or say to diffuse his anger. This was a fiercely jealous man. What ugly impulse had prompted me to provoke him in this way? How often I had told myself to be extremely discreet in my communications with the women in these tiny farm communities. I was keenly distressed, and promptly left the store, never to return. I would miss my black and white respites on hot summer afternoons and so would Mitch whom I had occasionally brought with me.

A year later, I heard that Leona had left Leo, taking off with a traveling salesman. It was rumored that he sold veterinary supplies.

THE STINE BROTHERS

"You won't believe it, Doc, but she's making manure from her pisser," Ollie said.

"Her pisser, what's that?" I inquired teasingly.

"Aw, you know, Doc. That's the hole below her ass where the piss comes through."

Ollie was doing the talking while his younger brother Alvin nodded his head in agreement. The Stine brothers stood outside my new office, their faces in an unbroken grin. They had remarkably large front teeth and sometimes I wondered if it were anatomically possible to bring their upper and lower lips together.

Alvin and Ollie were born on a farm about ten miles north of town. As soon as they could toddle, they were given farm chores. Their father, describing his sons as "morons," made them learn every aspect of farming. They were frequently beaten, especially when their chores were not done in a manner to his liking. His bitterness toward them intensified after the loss of his wife. She had been a timid soul who nevertheless had a mitigating influence over her husband's violence.

In a way, it was his tyranny as a teacher that gave them the expertise to continue farming after his death. They had barely survived a grade-school education, but could read and write sufficiently to handle the business of farming. They may have been crude and simple, but they had a degree of shrewdness and suspicion that made it unlikely for someone to cheat them more than once.

On the farm or in town, they were unkempt and often dirty. They tromped about in manure-encrusted boots and wore soiled locomotive engineer caps. I had recently converted my garage into an office, and to have these two fellows come in was instant gross contamination.

"Hi Ollie. Hi Alvin," I heard Mary greeting them in her cheery, friendly way. They turned toward her, and I could swear their lips curled into leers.

"Harry Ray has a milk fever and wants you out pronto," she said.

I watched with disquiet as Alvin's and Ollie's eyes followed her back into the house. I had always felt that these two fellows were a little weird, but who can blame them for staring at Mary? Yet, I could not contain my disquiet when they were on my home ground, and they seemed to be there more frequently than ever. They had no phone, so they came knocking on my door when they needed my services. Ollie once told me, "Heck, I cain't think of nobody that would ever call us, so what do I need a phone for?" The presence in town of their mudcaked red pickup was their calling card, and I kept noticing it more and more.

"I'll be out your way as soon as I treat Harry Ray's milk fever... and be sure she's in the barn." The Stines never had the cows they wanted me to look at in the barn. Sometimes I was sure they left the cows to be treated outside just to tease me. Once as I was giving vent to my exasperation after waiting twenty minutes for them to bring in a sick cow, I had caught them smiling at each other. This had been their joke at my expense. When I told them that I would charge them five dollars for every fifteen minutes I had to wait for them to bring in a cow, their demeanor became serious.

"You cain't do that," Alvin said. "It ain't right."

"You had your warning. Next time you keep me waiting, I'm going to charge you waiting time." I felt myself really getting angry. "And if you don't like it, call another vet." I wasn't going to let these yokels play games with me.

"Gee, Doc, we wouldn't call anyone but you. You been good to us. And don't we pay our bill on time?" Ollie said.

They sure did, and this bit of flattery calmed me down.

I hustled out to Harry Ray to treat the milk fever. The cow had calved a day ago and now she was down. She showed the classic symptoms of milk fever: she was down, her head and neck were drawn acutely to one side, eyes dull and staring, pupils dilated, and she was in a state of semi-consciousness.

A pint of calcium gluconate intravenously and in ten to fifteen minutes the cow would be up enjoying a scoop of grain. However, nothing is without its problems. After I waited about fifteen minutes, she refused to get up. She seemed bright enough, but in spite of our urgings, she just could not get to her feet.

"Give her another bottle, Doc," Harry said.

"I'd rather play it safe and wait," I replied.

There was hardly a vet I knew that hadn't killed a cow with that extra bottle of calcium gluconate.

"Harry, I'm going out to the Stine farm to look at a cow. I'll stop on the way back."

"Do me a favor, Doc. When you come back, would you please clean up thoroughly before you enter the barn. That whole farm of theirs is one big pig sty, even if they don't raise hogs. I would really prefer you to change clothes." Now that was going too far, I thought.

Harry was obsessively clean, a meticulous farmer who took pride in his animals. The farm was a showplace, and it was a pleasure to enter his barn and see the immaculate condition of his cows. Obviously the prospect of me going to the Stine farm and returning to his farm was disturbing. He was a man who saw his farm as a disease-free island in a world of filth and infection. His Holsteins were among the finest in the state, and he never purchased livestock for fear of introducing diseases. All replacements to the herd were home grown.

He was a small man, but his small size could never diminish that sense of authority you felt in his presence. Cropped hair, a just-shaved look, well-fitted, white coveralls (which I suspected were custom made by his wife) gave him a fresh milk look. His voice had a Jew's-harp twang that resonated in your ears. Blue eyes hidden behind a prominent nose gave him a caricatured appearance, but that dissipated as soon as he spoke.

"Harry, when I come back to this farm, you will find me clean enough to shake my hand." I knew Harry disliked shaking hands, and I once saw him use a handkerchief on a door knob to enter a room. I often wondered how he came to be so fastidious and a farmer to boot. Although Harry shied away from personal contact with people, he held no such restraints toward animals. He once said to me that the purity and honesty of animals was rare to find in humans. He would not hunt or fish and refused to allow his farm to be used for such purposes during hunting season. He treasured every wild creature, even those that raised havoc with his crops. "They gotta eat too," he said. "Hell, there's enough for everybody."

Harry looked at me intently. "I see you got my message loud and clear. Just get my cow up when you return."

"You bet I will, Harry." As I said those words, I wished I had swallowed them. Milk fever cows that don't get up promptly can be a problem. I've seen some that never get up, in spite of major efforts on my part. I treated a down milk-fever cow for weeks without success. She continued to eat and drink, but ended up an emaciated hulk that had to be euthanized.

Now, burdened with the thought that this cow might never get up, I turned to Harry and mumbled, "See you soon."

I hurried over to the Stine farm to find the cow that was supposed to be in the barn out in a muddy barnyard. I managed to control my displeasure as they hustled her into a stanchion. Sure enough, manure began to seep out of the cow's vulva.

"How long has she been doing this?" I asked.

"Oh about a week," replied Ollie.

"More like two weeks," Alvin chimed in.

"Now you shut your big mouth, Alvin. When I say it's a week, it's a week. Now, you don't even know what day it is. Now, what day is it? Come on now what day is it?"

Alvin hesitated a moment, "You see, Doc, he doesn't even know what day it is."

"I just know it's longer than a week," Alvin replied, his face wreathing into a sheepish smile.

"When did she calf?" I looked towards Ollie. "About four months ago," he replied.

"More like five months," I heard Alvin say quietly.

Before they could start another argument, I said, "Look, it doesn't matter."

"Alvin, fetch the cows. It's time for milking. I'll stay here with Doc," Ollie said.

I had expected another argument on who should bring in the cows, but to my surprise Alvin promptly left. I proceeded to examine the cow. In spite of manure caking her flanks and clumping the hair on her abdomen, she seemed to be in good condition. If she had calved recently, there was a possibility that the calf's hoof had poked a hole in the roof of the vagina and penetrated the rectum during delivery. There was no telling what Ollie and Alvin might perpetrate to deliver a calf. Since the cow had calved months ago, I had to consider other causes. Ollie brought me a pail of hot water, a chip of dirt-impregnated soap, and a filthy towel. I held up the dirty towel in front of Ollie's face and shook my head.

"We just didn't have no time ai'tol to do the laundry this week," Ollie said.

I would've bet these guys hadn't done laundry in a year.

"Hey Doc, what about a nice clean feed bag we just emptied?"

"Never mind Ollie, I have a towel in my car."

I made eight to ten calls a day, and it was customary for the farmer to provide hot water, soap and a towel. If I had to provide a towel on each call, Mary would be inundated with laundry. Having a husband as a large animal vet is worse than having a bunch of kids playing in a mud puddle each day.

I went back to my car to get antiseptic soap and a clean towel that I kept for these special occasions. When I returned, the cows were filing into the barn and were being directed to their stanchions by Alvin.

"God damn you, Anna. You know that ain't where you go. Now Rose, git the hell out of there. C'mon Elsie, move it along."

A resounding slap on Elsie's hide didn't bother her a bit, but I was sure that Alvin's hand must be smarting. Finally, twenty eight milking cows entered their stanchions and began to slobber-lick the grain that had been placed in the trough in front of them.

"Ollie, you didn't breed this cow with a bull recently?" I asked.

"Naw, we got rid of our bull a couple of years ago. We use a artificial co-op. Ida was bred two months ago and should be with calf."

I stripped to the waist, soaped my right hand and arm and entered the rectum of the cow. The rectum contained voluminous quantities of manure, and I began to scoop out as much as possible, flopping each handful into the gutter.

I have never found the manure of cows to be particularly objectionable. It has a soft, granular consistency and an odor that is certainly not unpleasant. On one occasion, during the delivery of a calf, a dollop of manure plopped into my open mouth. While I did hasten to wash my mouth, I must confess that it had somewhat of a bran cereal taste. However, I would not recommend it as a breakfast food.

Since it is possible to palpate the uterus through the rectal wall, I was able to determine that the cow was indeed two months pregnant. Further examination revealed a one-inch tear in the floor of the rectum. As I probed with my finger, I soon discovered the tear penetrated the roof of the vagina through which the manure was entering. I could find no evidence of a disease process and had to assume that this was the result of some sort of trauma. I turned to Ollie and said, "Any idea how something like this could happen?"

An expression of innocence masked his face. His lips clamped over his teeth.

"No idee at all. That's why we called you out. Kin you fix her, Doc?"

"I don't know Ollie, but I'll try."

"Gee, Doc, I don't wanna lose this cow. She's a good un."

My mind, for the moment, was not on the cause but rather on how I could repair the damage. There was a chance that I could close the rectal tear using a spinal anesthetic. There was a lesser chance that I could repair the vaginal laceration, but without manure passing through, that might heal itself.

"I'll get a few instruments together and be back tomorrow," I said.

As I walked down the barn, I saw Alvin removing a milking machine from a cow.

"See you tomorrow, Alvin. Keep Ida in the barn for me."

"Sure thing, Doc."

As I walked by the cow Alvin had just milked, I was assailed by a putrid odor.

"What's that awful odor, Alvin? It smells like rotting flesh."

"This here cow smells a bit from her hind end, but she's eatin' and feels good."

A closer look at the cow revealed a putrefactive discharge emerging from the vulva and creeping down her manure clumped legs.

"Ollie," I yelled, "Come on over here. Do you know about this cow discharging and smelling this way?"

"I sure do, Doc. And if you want to examine her, you gotta understand that I didn't call you for her, and I ain't gonna pay you if you do."

"Okay, it's a deal, Ollie. No charge. Just bring me some hot water. I have my own soap and towel, remember."

I slipped on the rubber glove and sleeve that I used for stinky jobs such as retained afterbirths, soaped up the hand portion and tried to enter the vagina. It was obviously painful to the cow, but I managed to make the examination. Multiple infected lacerations greeted my fingers. Fortunately, the vaginal wall was not perforated. I irrigated the vagina with an antiseptic solution and packed it with an antibiotic powder. Ollie was watching me treat the cow. He seemed very uncomfortable and kept staring over at Alvin who was busily engaged in milking. Alvin finally looked up.

"C'mon Ollie, get on with the milking. I cain't do it all myself," he whined.

"Oh, shut your mouth, Alvin. It's all your fault anyway," he whispered in a voice that I could just make out.

On my way out of the barn, I noticed the last cow nearest the barn door reeking with that same putrefactive stench and copiously discharging pus from her vulva.

"Ollie," I called. "I'm going to check this cow as well. No charge."

This was the third cow with a lacerated vagina. All kinds of possibilities were running through my mind. It was not too difficult to observe Ollie's and Alvin's discomfort and their nervous whisperings. But how could they have perpetrated these injuries? Was this the result of some strange sexual perversion?

This cow had a similar problem, a lacerated vagina. However, I was not to escape gross contamination of my clothes. As I approached the cow, her pus soaked tail began to switch nervously back and forth. In an effort to grasp her tail, I was thrown off balance, slipping on some manure on the barn floor. In the blink of an eye, I fell forward and was draped over the hind end of the cow grasping at her prominent hip bones to keep myself from falling. Meanwhile, the startled cow began to shift and stomp her legs in an effort to shake me off. It required some real gymnastics to regain my equilibrium. Ollie and Alvin began to laugh in a wild hysterical way, jumping up and down, slapping their thighs and saying to each other, "Did ya see that? Did ya see that?"

I was a total mess. I would have to go home, shower and change. Nevertheless, I proceeded to examine this cow and treated her as I did the last cow.

Ollie and Alvin came over to gape at me.

"It sure was funny watching you try to hold on to Angel. You must have scared her half to death," Alvin said. "She don't get riled like that too often. Nothing more we can do for you, so we're goin' back to our milking. See you tomorrow, Doc."

I was streaked with pus and splattered with manure and was in no condition to set foot on Harry Ray's farm. I would just have to make the drive to my home, clean up, and drive back to Harry Ray—twenty five miles in all. Then it occurred to me, just suppose I strip down to my longjohns and take off my boots. I'll leave all my dirty clothes and boots here in the barn to be picked up tomorrow. I think Harry Ray will greatly appreciate the lengths I am willing to go to avoid transmitting infection from one farm to another. The more I thought about it, the better I liked it. I would make the call in my longjohns. Maybe Harry won't even see me.

Ollie and Alvin were busily milking at the other end of the barn and took no notice of me. Nevertheless, I walked around Angel to the corner of the barn out of their view and proceeded to undress. I rolled my clothes into a bundle and was about to place it in the corner when I noticed a broomstick standing there. As I picked up the broomstick to place my clothes in the corner, I saw that the top of the broomstick was covered with dried blood. The suspicions I was suppressing became a reality.

"Ollie... Alvin," I boomed. "Come on over here right now."

I heard a clatter of pails and clunk of milking machines being removed from cows. They came running, alarmed by the sound of my voice. I confronted them clad in my longjohns and wool socks holding the bloodied broomstick aloft in my hands. They must have thought I was about to swat them with the stick because they began to back away.

"Have you guys been poking this stick into these cows?"

They did not respond. There was fear in their faces, and their lips were actually clenched over their teeth.

"I told you not to push so hard, Alvin."

"Ollie, you pushed harder than me."

"Now if you didn't leave that broomstick around, Doc might never have known and all would be okay. Ain't that right, Doc?" Ollie said turning to me.

As I listened to their little exchange, my anger began to abate. I had to remind myself that although they looked like grown men, they were actually children mentally, living a simple, lonely life. Yet they were able to function. They could plant corn and oats and supply the basic needs of their animals. But they had disgustingly abused these cows. It was a titillating experience for them, but abhorrent, nevertheless.

Ollie and Alvin were looking at me strangely.

"Where's all your clothes?" Alvin asked.

"I left my clothes in the corner where I found the broomstick," I replied. "I'll pick them up tomorrow."

"Now listen to this you guys. If you don't promise to stop broomsticking your cows, all kinds of bad things can happen."

"I tell you, Doc, Alvin started the whole thing." And then seeming to hear me for the first time, he asked, "Wadduyeh mean bad things, Doc?"

"Well, your neighbors won't be too friendly if they knew."

"Well, they ain't friendly nohow, never were."

"Your pastor would be unhappy if he knew."

"Hell, he don't like us nohow. Never did. Come here once or twice. Never even asked us to come to church, and we got church clothes too."

It was now obvious that I was not communicating. I had to tell these fellows something that would threaten them if they didn't stop broomsticking their cows, but I just could not get to their level of understanding.

"It's against the law to hurt your animals. There are people that will take you to court for just what you are doing now."

"How they gonna find out? It's only you, Alvin and me that knows."

"Ollie, if you and Alvin don't promise to stop broomsticking your cows here and now, I'm going to report you to the American Society for the Prevention of Cruelty to Animals." Then it occurred to me that they probably never heard of an ASPCA.

Feeling totally inadequate and not knowing what else to say, I blurted out, "I will never, ever come to your farm again. You will have to get another vet." I was shooting in the dark.

Ollie looked at me closely. Tears formed in his eyes and he began to sob.

"Does that mean that Alvin and me cain't come to your house and have Mary serve us coffee and cookies and talk with us?"

I had no idea that these fellows came to my house and were served coffee and cookies, but I responded, "That's right, Ollie."

"But Doc, you and Mary are the only friends we got and we don't wanna lose you. Your wife is always nice to us. She treats us like other people. We ain't ever gonna hurt our cows again. Ain't that right, Alvin?"

"I heard what you been saying and I agrees with Ollie." Anxious to conclude this awkward situation, I said, "That's great. I'll be back tomorrow to sew up that cow." Ollie extended his hand. I felt his callused palm and some grit within his fissured fingers. He held my hand tightly, almost refusing to release me.

Feeling quite relieved, I walked to my car. I was not surprised to learn that Mary had shown some special kindness to them. I knew she was raised with a retarded brother and that undoubtedly gave her an insight into their life. She understood their limitations and their loneliness. She knew their behavior was partly in response to how they were treated by the community.

In a way, they were institutionalized on a farm, cut off from all relationships. For myself, I knew they were backward, slow, simple minded or whatever their designation. Given a little more understanding, their lives might have been substantially enriched.

Mary and I would just continue to treat Ollie and Alvin with judicious compassion and allow them to think of us as people they could trust. They seemed to worship Mary. Maybe my threats and promises would be enough to encourage them to take better care of their animals and themselves.

In the meantime, a bright sun in a cloudless sky had warmed the afternoon by the time I arrived to treat Harry Ray's cow. I had hoped to sneak into the barn, give the cow another dose of calcium gluconate, get her up, and be gone before Harry discovered his longjohned vet. When I returned home, a phone call to him confirming what I had done would complete the matter.

Usually when I arrived at a farm, I'd beep my horn once or twice to announce my arrival, or better yet, a couple of howling dogs would come charging at me out of nowhere. In spite of all their frenetic activity, I have never been bitten by a farm dog. I probably smell like a cow to most of them. I knew Harry's collie dog Ginger pretty well, having once spayed her and later on having sutured a large laceration on her back. She and I were the best of friends. It was no problem at all to sneak into the barn without the usual commotion.

I entered the barn and headed for the maternity pen where Harry had kept the down cow, but to my surprise the pen was empty. Don't tell me he got tired of waiting for my return and called another vet? He was a great client and I'd hate to lose him. At any rate, I would get in the car and beep for him. As I opened the barn door, I was confronted by Harry and his wife, Helen. They looked at me startled, and then began to roar with laughter. Now that was the second time today I was the object of laughter.

"But where are your clothes?" Helen said.

She had a son as old as I was, so there was no embarrassment in her face as she examined my longjohns.

"You see, Helen, Doc was out to the Stine farm, and I made him promise not to return here wearing the clothes he wore there. He's true to his word. I'm just glad he's at least wearing his longjohns."

Harry's laugh sailed into the rafters of the empty barn and echoed back. My face flushed crimson.

"Where's the down cow, Harry?" I asked with some trepidation.

"Oh she got up about ten minutes after you left and she's out in the barnyard. I had no way of calling you at Stines, but I did call Mary. I'm taking Helen to a Home Bureau meeting and we're late. I'll be seeing you, Doc."

I slid into my car and drove home, eager to take a bath and recover my equanimity. I had hoped to avoid my wife's critique of my uniform of the day. Her laughter proclaimed that I had been caught a third time.

As I went up the stairs to our bathroom, I heard her call, "Say, Doc, do you know there's a button missing from the rear of your longjohns?"

ETHEL AND RAGS

There are some farms where you have a magic touch. The animals always recover, sometimes miraculously. And then there are other farms where it's gloom and doom. In fact, you wonder why you are called back. There are many farmers whose strong sense of fatalism insulates them from their problems. If a cow dies, well, that was preordained. If a hail storm ruins a crop, well, that is an act of God and there's no sense dwelling on it. Now that's good, healthy thinking. How I wish I could subscribe to it.

The attitude of equal acceptance of both the good and the bad is a trait I often see in farmers. Perhaps it helps them deal with the unpredictability of farming. As for me, I'm a worrier. I cannot accept the loss of an animal without some degree of guilt. I get up in the middle of the night wondering what I should have done, and knowing that I did everything possible does not assuage the sense of loss I feel.

When Ethel Mulvey stops by in her pickup truck with her gold and white Springer Spaniel Rags, it is a happy sight. Her words are an antacid to my heartburn, balm to my soul. Ethel, like some farmers in this area, did not have a phone and would drive to town to contact me.

"Doctor, you have a healing touch," she said to me on more than one occasion. "Do you remember when you placed hands on Rags when he was out of sorts and how sprightly he became. He has not been that way since he was a puppy. And let me tell you one more thing, when you come into our barn, our cows give more milk. A sick cow feels better when you just touch her."

I smiled at her. She was a small woman and I rather foolishly patted her head. She blushed with pleasure. This was a big heap of admiration and trust Ethel unloaded on me. I knew that the glow in her face could turn to a glower as soon as my healing powers waned. However, my infallibility as a vet continued unabated on the Mulvey Farm.

I usually went out on calls between 6:00 a.m. and 7:00 a.m. and returned to breakfast with Mary about 9:00 a.m. It was not unusual to find

Ethel and Rags parked in her pickup awaiting my arrival. A bushel of sweet corn, apples, asparagus, peas, strawberries, tomatoes, string beans or whatever else was seasonal leaned against my front door. There was nothing I could do to dissuade her from this generosity. All she wanted was for me to pat Rags. I explained that I was fond of Rags and would do so in any event.

"Rags is getting old and your touch makes him feel so much better."

On a torrid August afternoon that only the corn that smothered the earth for miles around could love, Ethel knocked on my screen door.

"Thank goodness you're home. Mabel just had her calf, but then she done cast her withers, Doctor. I'd be beholden to you for coming as soon as possible."

She was remarkably calm, considering the dramatic nature of the case. It certainly roused me from my summer torpor. Apparently her cow, Mabel, having given birth to a sixty- to seventy-pound calf, had turned her uterus inside out. Imagine having a deep pocket with a glove in it, and upon pulling out the glove, the pocket came out as well. That is a prolapse of the uterus, or in the local vernacular, the cow "cast her withers."

I arrived at the farm to find Elmer Mulvey trying to prod some oat straw bedding beneath the down cow. Her uterus lay behind her, emerging from the vulva as a monstrously engorged organ, perhaps two-and-a-half feet long and watermelon round. It lay in the gutter smothered with manure and urine. Although the cow had delivered her calf, she continued to labor forcefully. Each time she strained, manure would creep from her anus contributing to the contamination.

"Mabel is a great cow. She's a real charmer. I would be most obliged if you could save her, Doc," Elmer said as he patted the cow on her haunches.

"Don't worry, Mabel, the doctor will make you well," I heard Ethel say.

I could swear the cow seemed to be reassured, and for a moment, her intense labor subsided. Elmer's concern for the cow was so genuine that tears came to his eyes. We tried to get Mabel up on her feet without success. It was absolutely necessary to raise her hind end in order to clean the uterus and finally re-place it. I attached heavy ropes under her rear legs and figure-eighted them over her back. With a block and tackle attached to an overhead beam and hooked into my rope sling, I was ready to raise her hind end. Before doing so, I gave her a spinal anesthetic to control her contractions, without which the replacement of the uterus would be difficult. Elmer and I began to pull on the block-and-tackle rope, raising the rear end of the cow. As the cow became suspended, the uterus was raised from its guttered resting place. Meanwhile, the organ had further increased in size making its replacement more challenging than ever.

Ethel, followed by Rags, came clanging onto the scene carrying two pails of water, a garden hose over her shoulder and some towels draped around her neck. I had requested the water and towels, but the hose was her idea—and it was a good one. Mabel had stopped straining as a result of the spinal anesthetic. I gently hosed down the uterus with cool water, carefully removing whatever afterbirth was attached.

Rags edged closer, watching the cleansing process with great interest. When a large piece of afterbirth detached and fell into the gutter, he made his move. He grabbed the afterbirth and with stringy pieces dangling from his mouth, scampered toward the barn door with unbelievable alacrity. Ethel bolted after him. I was amazed to see how fast a middle-aged woman and an old dog could run. She soon returned, a bit breathless but smiling.

"I don't know what it is about that stuff that's so irresistible to dogs," she said. "He gulped down most of it before I caught up with him. Now how am I gonna kiss him on the lips again."

Many animals will eat their afterbirths. I had a cow choke to death out in a pasture trying to swallow her afterbirth. The farmer insisted his cow was struck by lightning so as to collect the insurance farmers have for that kind of loss. However, my autopsy revealed a wad of afterbirth jammed in her throat causing the cow to suffocate. He was most unhappy with my finding. Dogs love afterbirth. To them it's the ultimate gourmet food, the riper the better.

After ten minutes of hosing, the uterus looked relatively clean and somewhat smaller but unacceptably large for replacement. There are several methods of reducing its size, but I like a home remedy I learned from that old vet I'd worked for, Tom Swingley. He would sprinkle granulated sugar all over the uterus, and by a process of osmosis, the organ would substantially shrink. Ethel looked at me curiously when I asked for a five-pound bag of sugar. There was humor in her voice when she asked if I would like some coffee or perhaps tea to go with it. I explained what the purpose of the sugar was, and she gave me one of her little smiles.

"I thought that was a lot of sugar for a cup of coffee. I think coffee would go well at this time. No trouble at all to fix a pot."

"I'm afraid we're not going to have time for coffee, but Ethel, I have a big job for you and Elmer in just a little while."

I proceeded to dust the uterus with the sugar. In a short time, the uterus became noticeably smaller. With all my preoccupation with the prolapse, I had forgotten to even glance at my patient. Much to my amazement, even with her hind end slung in the air, Mabel was busily licking up what remained of a scoop of grain that Ethel had given her. You would have expected her to be in shock or toxic as a result of this horrific insult, but she seemed oblivious to her problem. The spinal anesthetic was a factor, but the systemic impact of the prolapse was yet to come. Fortunately nature provides certain species of animals resistance to infection that would have easily overwhelmed a human being.

Farmers are strong, resilient people, toughened by their seven-day work week. I would ask them to do things that would appall a city person. Without hesitation, I asked Ethel and Elmer to sling the uterus in one of the large towels and raise it as high as they comfortably could. To hold this position for fifteen minutes or more would be a challenge for most people, but I was confident two middle-aged farmers would not fail me.

The sugared uterus felt granular and gritty as my fists began pushing the tissue into the vulva. I had to proceed cautiously... slowly. If I punched a hole into the uterus, I either had to repair the hole, which could be difficult, or even amputate, which could be disastrous.

Ethel and Elmer were intently watching my efforts and holding on to their towel corners with grim determination. My clenched fists continued to knead the tissue into the vulva. At one point, I relaxed a bit to catch my breath and folds of uterus began to creep out.

"It's coming back out, Doctor."

That was the first time I noted some tension in her voice.

Until it was all in and hanging over the brim of the pelvis, there was to be no respite for me. Gradually we began to prevail, and it was with a collective sigh of relief that the tail end of the uterus actually sucked into the vulva. My arm entered the uterus and I began to smooth out any folds that had not reassumed their normal positions. Boluses of a sulfonamideurea combination were inserted and large doses of penicillin were administered intramuscularly. And in the event Mabel decided she had a phantom calf in her womb and started to labor again, I temporarily sutured her vulva with heavy umbilical tape, leaving just enough opening for urine to pass. There was no way a cow could cast her withers with the vulva sutured, so I thought. (A year later in a similar case, a cow defied every effort I made to prevent a reprolapse. As soon as her spinal anesthetic wore off, she made violent efforts to expel her uterus. The sheer force of her labor tore out the stitches I had placed in her vulva. In spite of everything I tried to do, I lost that cow.)

We were all caked with dried blood and manure. Ethel insisted I come to the house to clean up, but I knew that everything had to come off. Soaking and scrubbing in several tubs of hot water would be necessary to remove the accumulations. My very guarded prognosis did not diminish Ethel's and Elmer's joy in seeing how well Mabel seemed to be.

The next day I returned to see Mabel. I was pleased she was chewing her cud and nursing her calf. Ethel was so happy to see me that she had tears in her eyes. "You have a rare gift, Doctor. Your hands have a healing touch," she said again.

I wished it were so. In the month of May, 1953, I was to have an unbelievable number of cows cast their withers... nineteen to be exact, four of which died. Some of the survivors never became economically productive.

I did not see Ethel for a couple of months. Occasionally, I would pass her farm and think of my "healing touch." I am sure that had I lost an animal on her farm, she would have a ready explanation for my failure. Faith is rarely shaken even when faced with calamity. I must confess that her belief in me gave me some gratuitous pleasure. It was with some anticipation that I saw her seated in her pickup in front of my house as I returned from a call.

"Good morning, Doctor."

"Good morning, Ethel."

"Rags died this morning. I have him in the back of the pickup."

I looked to see a carefully blanketed bundle.

"If he was sick, why didn't you call me? Maybe I could have helped."

"Oh I'm sure you could have helped. But he was old and suffering. It was time for the Lord to take him, so I helped him die peacefully just as you would have done."

I did not inquire what she did to ease his passing. Tears misted her eyes.

"I plan to bury Rags this afternoon at four o'clock and I would consider it a kindness if you would come to the funeral."

"I'll be there Ethel. Rags was a good friend," I replied.

At four o'clock I was at the Mulvey farm for the funeral. I had expected others to attend, but it was only she and I. A grave had been dug beneath some trees in front of the house. She said she chose the site because "I shall always want to look out and see my Rags." A coffin had been fashioned from old barn planks giving it massive proportions, not to mention weight. We stood beside the grave and in a tremulous voice she said, "When I open the coffin just touch him for one last time. That would mean a lot to him."

A leather handle, fashioned from an old bridle, was used to raise the coffin cover. Rags had been carefully combed and was lying on a satin quilt. I reached into the coffin and patted his head.

"Thank you Doctor. I know he appreciates what you just did. Now just say a few words to him and I'll let you go. I know you must be busy."

She put her rough-hewed hand in mine and I felt its gentleness and silken caress. The dog lay before us, entombed in his barn-planked coffin. Sunlight filtered through the trees, a breeze reached in to brush his golden hair. I sensed her profound sorrow, and for the first time in my life, I began to really understand the feeling of despair upon the loss of a pet.

I stood silently, strangely moved, groping for words. I had to say something. Finally, in a choked voice, I said, "You have had a good life, Rags. Ethel has loved and cared for you. May the good Lord bless you and keep you. Your memory will ever be a comfort to her."

Ethel turned toward me, kissed my cheek and said, "Doctor, Rags and I will never forget you."

"Let me help with the burial, Ethel. The coffin is quite heavy."

"Oh no, Elmer will do that."

She waved to Elmer in the distance and he approached carrying a shovel.

I once thought that Elmer was a hired hand. She always seemed to be so indifferent toward him, except when she had a chore for him. I later learned that they were indeed married, but only Rags was the recipient of her love. With Rags gone, I hoped their relationship would improve. On a call to the farm about two weeks later, I was gratified to see Ethel and Elmer happily chatting with each other.

However, I must confess that I shall always miss Ethel and Rags waiting in her pickup for my "healing touch."

X DISEASE

The boy watched excitedly as I delivered a calf. He had seen many calves born in his eight years, but this one was something special.

"Dad says this calf is to be all mine. I'm going to raise her to be the best ever. Ain't that right, Dad?"

Irwin Albertson looked at his son, unable to contain the pride he felt.

"That's right, Tommy. She's all yours. And a fine little heifer she is."

The black and white calf lay on a bed of straw, brown eyes wide open, assessing her new world. Loud baritone bleats burst from the calf, totally disproportionate to her size. They seemed to say, "Mother, Mother, where are you?" The cow turned anxiously toward her calf, restrained by the stanchion that held her. Tommy had brought some towels from the house and was busy toweling his calf down. I was sure his mother had no idea he was using her best bath towels. His calf was not to know the burlap sacks and feed bags that were commonly used to rub down newborn calves.

"What are you going to name her, Tommy?" I asked.

"Well, we had a cow here called Amy. She was my favorite, but Dad had to ship her to market when she stopped making milk. I felt real bad, but Dad promised to give me the next calf we have and I could name her Amy. Doc, can I tell you a secret?" Tommy whispered.

"Of course you can, Tommy."

"First, what do you think Amy weighs?" asked Tommy.

"Oh, about sixty to seventy pounds."

"Do you think I could lift her, Doc?"

I looked at Tommy. He had all the attributes of a budding lineman on a football team. He was big, hardened by chores on a farm. Early mornings before school, he helped feed livestock, pitched hay and carried pails of milk to the milk house. Farm life demanded physical labor, and on many farms, youngsters were required to do chores very early in life.

"I'm sure you can," I replied.

He bent down, cradled her in his arms, and with some difficulty, raised her to his chest.

"Now here's the secret, Doc. I'm going to lift Amy every morning. Since I'll be doing it everyday, I won't even notice she's getting bigger. I'll stop when she gets with calf cause I wouldn't want to hurt her none."

"Great idea, Tommy. You can depend on me to keep it a secret."

Unfortunately, the way calves were getting sick and dying on this farm, there was a strong possibility that Amy might never survive long enough for Tommy to complete his secret project. Irwin, who had been scooping grain to his cows, called to me.

"Hey, Doc, let's go and look at my sick calves. I lost another one this morning."

It had all started so insidiously. There were the usual calls in the late fall to treat calf scours and pneumonias. The barns had become chilled, drafty places, and farmers were buttoning them up in anticipation of the *Farmer's Almanac* forecast of a severe winter. The corn pickers had done their work and endless rows of stripped corn stalks poked from the earth in crazy disarray, waiting to be interred after the spring thaw. The cows had left their windswept pastures to winter in the barn. Occasionally, some beef cattle were seen gleaning the fields in the icy chill of day.

The calls to treat sick calves were increasing. On some farms, they looked particularly poor—gaunt, coughing with obvious pneumonia. Others had moth-eaten hair coats, thick, leathery skin, and many drooled from sore mouths. This was like no disease I had ever seen. First, I postulated that the calves had been severely chilled, vaguely recalling that some animals had shown these symptoms well before the first autumn frost. Then I speculated that the calves were nutritionally deficient even though they were fed an apparently balanced ration. Maybe a vitamin A deficiency. I prescribed high-potency vitamins without results. Elsewhere I suggested moldy feed to be the culprit and tried sulfonamide and detoxicants.

One thing all these calves had in common was their total unresponsiveness to my many therapies. Finally, they began to die in increasing numbers. Faced with an endemic disease, I was helpless, inadequate. I became extremely depressed as I faced being isolated in this town with nobody to consult, trying to communicate on a five-party-line crank phone with an indifferent county vet, an aloof State University, and colleagues staggering through their own daily workloads. Heartburn was my constant companion. Here, I thought, I had become the ultimate veterinarian, able to surmount the insurmountable. My few years of practice experience had made me unbelievably smug. It did not take too much longer to realize how emotionally fragile I really was. Faced with an apparently insoluble problem, confidence in myself withered. I could not endure my inadequacy.

Harry Ralston called to tell me that another calf had just died, and from the looks of it, all of his twenty-odd calves were goners. It was awful going to a farm to view a disaster that had defied all my healing efforts. I arrived to find that Harry had just started milking. His eyes were downcast.

"Hello, Doc. Be with you as soon as I get this milking machine off this cow."

I stood in the center of the barn breathing the ambrosia scents that make up a cow barn. The soft plop of manure hitting the gutter... the splash of urine... the sweet smell of silage, hay, and grain... the quietude of the cows... the pulsating suction sounds of the milking machines—this is barn ambiance. Cows love to be milked and a stranger in the barn usually disturbs their ruminations. Plop, plop—the splatter of manure hit my pants.

Finally Harry called, "Okay, let's go to the calf pens." We trod along in silence. Beyond a word or two of condolence, there's not much to say at a funeral. The sight of Harry's calves shocked me. They were emaciated, weak, thick skinned, barely able to stand. I felt I was looking into a Nazi concentration camp for calves. The dead calf had been removed to an unused shed and awaited my autopsy. For more than an hour, I knelt over the calf examining every organ, collecting specimens for the university pathologist. I took samples of blood, urine, sputum, manure and skin scrapings for cultures and analysis.

After numerous attempts, I finally got the attention of a toxicologist who suggested that some unknown toxic agent rather than an infectious disease was involved. I talked again with other vets, but the problem seemed to be more common in my area. However, most of them seemed to be inclined toward a nutritional etiology. All other feedback was exasperatingly non-specific. I reviewed literature on calf diseases. If there was any clue to what was wrong, it escaped me.

It took two weeks to decimate Harry Ralston's calves. Yet his neighbors north, south, east and west had no problems. Even Art Ullman nearby reported all was well—and Art was my disaster farm.

When I heard Harry Ralston called in another vet, I could scarcely blame him. But what was I overlooking? I had pinpointed fifteen farms that appeared to have similar problems with their calves. They were spread over the county, not localized to any specific area. If there was an infectious agent, it was contained in individual farms. It had not been introduced by a purchase or transmitted from a neighboring farm. The problem consumed me, preoccupied all my free time.

Even as I delivered a very much prized calf from George Ray's most productive Holstein, I was thinking of its fate. George had lost virtually all his calves and had been very philosophic about his losses.

"Don't take it so hard, Doc. We're not going to let this one die," he said consolingly.

George was a sweet old guy looking toward retirement. A lifetime of farming had tempered his response to disaster. His "this too will pass away" attitude was not reassuring, but it gave him great comfort when things went wrong.

"Tell me, George, why are you having all these calf problems while nobody in this immediate area is having any? You're as good a dairyman as I have seen. What are you doing that is different?"

George shrugged off my question with "Sorry Doc, got to get some hay to those cows."

In despair, I walked to my car. I shivered as a cold northwest wind seeped through my clothes. (I must remember to put on my longjohns.) Hundreds of calves were dying in this area. What was I missing, I kept asking myself over and over. In my mind's eye, I saw calves with necks and withers, wrinkled and leathery. My hands felt sticky from their nasal discharges and slobbering mouths. I watched them slowly die. I opened their bodies, held their diseased organs in my hands and wondered once again what I was doing in this profession. Come on now, I said to myself, there's work to be done.

Again and again, I deluged universities with specimens for cultures and pathology, and they dutifully reported their findings. Sure there was disease in the kidneys, liver, lungs, etc., etc., etc., but where was a diagnosis, a cause, a solution? Even a suggestion would be helpful, but the voices from those ivory towers were muffled.

In desperation, I selected twenty farms, ten that had the disease and ten that were free of the problem. Farmers were questioned about their animal husbandry, the calving, feeding of the calves, conditions under which they were kept, exposure to herbicides, insecticides or any chemical kept on the farm. It was a big chore, but I kept at it every spare moment I had. It was a survey necessitated by not knowing what else to do.

I returned home to find Mary unusually fretful. Mitchell had been rampaging all over the place—throwing his toys with remarkable accuracy, pulling Fang's ears and eliciting serious growls by yanking on his scrotum. The proverbial trip to the wood shed and a good spanking might have been curative, but that was not our way. That was not Benjamin Spock's way.

"Get him out of here. Take him somewhere," Mary implored. "There's nothing urgent waiting."

Okay, I'd give her a break. I'd continue my interviews in the afternoon, but I would really have preferred to take a nap.

"C'mon Mitch, we're going on a call. We'll be at Gene Sommers, Mary. You can reach me there if anything comes up."

Mitchell loved to accompany me on calls. In spite of my cautions, he found animals to be kindred spirits. He was absolutely unafraid of animals, regardless of size. His one consuming fear in this world was elevators. Of course, there were none in our town, but visits to his pediatrician in Rockford with offices on the twelfth floor produced a panic effect. The doctor did not frighten him, but the elevator was his nemesis. Being the permissive parents that we were, I carried him on my shoulders up twelve flights of stairs. We ultimately switched to a doctor with a ground floor office. When I arrived at a farm, I generally put him in the care of the farmer's wife while I was in the barn. In this case, Gene had no wife, only an aged mother. One thing Mitchell could always bank on was milk and cookies and, if he was really lucky, homemade pie.

I interviewed Gene in the barn at length, taking notes as we went along. This farm had no problem. Outside I could hear the cackling and shrill screams of chickens being chased by Mitchell. When he visited a farm, I'll bet egg production was set back a week. No one seemed to mind. In fact, he was repeatedly invited to come back, and they seemed to mean it.

Suddenly all was silent. I figured that Mitchell had stopped to catch his breath. Maybe the milk and cookies had arrived. It could not have been more than five minutes when I exited the barn. Mitchell was nowhere to be seen. The chickens were restless, wary. I'm sure they would have liked to have eaten him, but I deemed that most unlikely. I checked with Gene's mother, called and called, and finally beeped the horn on my car, which brought Gene out from the barn. After exploring every nook and cranny, and there are lots of them on a farm, I felt my anxiety escalating to panic.

"Maybe he went up this cow path beside the barn," Gene said.

He had barely completed the sentence before I started running up the path. My right shoe slid in a cow pie but I gave it no mind. In the distance, I could see a bull tethered to a lone tree placidly grazing on some sparse grass. As I got closer, I saw Mitchell seated at the base of the tree, a stem of timothy dangling from his mouth just as he had seen me do on occasion. Gene was right behind me. I sensed his tension.

"Easy Doc, Homer can be pretty moody at times. I wouldn't just dash in there and grab the kid. Let me see if I can tempt him with some clover growing over there."

Gene ran to get a few handfuls of clover. The bull, apparently oblivious to Mitchell, stopped grazing and looked at me warily.

"Just stay where you are, Mitchell, and don't move. Don't move," I yelled.

I knew the bull was tethered with a rope, but I also knew he could snap that old rope in an instant. A year ago, I'd passed a brass ring through his nose to help control him. Even with his head locked in a steel stanchion, I could feel his enormous power. Farmers were being maimed and killed by bulls, so why keep a monster like this around when artificial insemination would serve so much better? Gene said he had sired great calves and was no bother, even though he was a bit spooky at times. Two handfuls of clover were enough to lure Homer to the other side of the tree. As Homer bent to eat the clover, I slowly approached Mitchell, picked him up and walked down the cow path, glad to have him safely in my arms.

"But I didn't get my milk and cookies," Mitchell complained. My anger hissed out of me like steam from a safety valve on a pressure cooker. Perhaps it was Gene... or was it Mitchell's innocent, happy face that made me contain my scolding, harsh words? Here was a free spirit, unafraid, a joyous child, rambunctious at times, a delight to his parents most of the time. To scold him would be equivalent to spanking a puppy for chewing on a shoe. I couldn't do it in either case. Perhaps he and I could discuss it the next morning.

I knew it meant a twenty miles round trip, but I said, "How about a black and white ice cream soda?" My anger needed expiation.

He was all smiles. "You mean the one with vanilla ice cream, chocolate syrup and bubbling over with soda?"

"That's it exactly," I said.

From a remnant out of my army days, I said, "Let's move it out, Mitch."

He knew the expression well. "Let's move it out, Daddy."

Two weeks had elapsed; calf losses continued unabated. I had interviewed the involved and the uninvolved. It was late evening as I sat at my desk mulling over and over the information I had gathered. I could find nothing unusual. Everything seemed so proper and routine... except that calves were dying without any apparent reason.

Mary came into the little room I called my office.

"Time for bed," she announced. "It's 10 o'clock and you have an early appointment to vaccinate some pigs for hog cholera."

"I've gone over my notes repeatedly and nothing seems to suggest anything."

"Here, let me take a look at them."

She bent over my shoulder, and I could smell the vanilla scent of an angel food cake she had just removed from the oven.

"I love that new perfume you're wearing."

"But I'm not wearing any perfume."

"You are and I'll tell you its name, Parfume D'Angel."

"Okay, you want a piece of angel food cake. You've got it. First let me look over your summary."

She looked at my chart long and hard.

"There is one difference I see but I don't know how significant it is. All the farms having a problem are feeding Perfection Calf Pellets—the others are not. Could there be something wrong with those pellets?"

"I noticed that too, but that's an international feed company, been around a long time, has all kinds of quality controls."

Mary smiled, "I see you have that silly notion that the bigger they are, the more integrity and responsibility they have. It's the big ones that perpetrate the worst disasters. You must remember that my baby books were written by fellows like Lincoln Steffens and Upton Sinclair. These writers taught me how inhumane big business can be and how far they would go to enhance their profits."

I turned... her cheeks were flushed and her eyes had that missionary glow. Once again I asked myself—how could I have lured this exciting, dynamic woman out of her environment and exiled her to this blip on a map?

Maybe she has a point about those calf pellets. I must admit there was a statistical coincidence probably worth looking into. It was a slim possibility, but I had no choice. I had to follow it up. It was the only thing I had going. I would ask five of the ten farms feeding Perfection Calf Pellets to discontinue their use; the other five would continue as they had.

The next morning I drove to each of the five farms, described the purpose of the experiment and had no problem persuading them to stop feeding Perfection Calf Pellets. I explained that five other farms would continue their use of the calf pellets.

I called the a major university to see if they would get involved, but they questioned the validity of the study. Much to my pleasure, the School of Agriculture at the University of Wisconsin showed an interest. They wanted a supply of the suspect pellets from the affected farms sent to them, which I immediately arranged to do. They agreed to set up a study using two groups of calves, one group being fed the suspect pellets and the other group as a control.

A week had gone by and I soon became aware that my project had gone awry. The word was out that Perfection Calf Pellets contained a poison and just about everyone stopped its use. The five farms that were to continue feeding discontinued as well. This became a dry county for Perfection Calf Pellets.

In town, I was accosted by Jess Waggoner, the manager of the feed mill that distributed Perfection Calf Pellets.

"What are you trying to do—drive me out of business, Doc? I ain't sold a bag of calf pellets since you started telling everyone how bad they were."

"Well Jess, that's not exactly so. I don't really know for sure if your calf pellets are causing the calf losses we're experiencing."

"I've been here all my life, and I am not going to have a smartass city boy put me out of business."

I was unprepared for his hostility and certainly unaware that I had hurt his business.

"Now listen, Jess, can I explain to you what I'm trying to do?"

"You can go to hell." And with that he strode off. My heartburn returned with a vengeance. This was a very little town, and it was unthinkable to antagonize an important member of the community. I recognized that events had proceeded beyond my control and my relationship with some town residents would be irrevocably changed. Even if I ended up a hero, I would be affected socially—and possibly economically. I knew my name would be subjected to abuse at the feed store where almost everyone came at one time or another.

In the interim, Jess' anger toward me never mitigated. Whenever he heard I lost a patient, he would never fail to put in some unkind words as to my competence. Although I was not wanting for clients, his criticism did annoy me.

Two weeks had gone by and no calf pellets of any kind were being fed to calves. Sick calves continued to die, but many seemed more responsive to medication. More importantly, no new cases were seen or reported. I began to think I was on to something. I heard nothing from the University of Wisconsin and my calls to them were answered with, "Too soon to make a judgment. Don't worry, we'll contact you as soon as we know something."

My impulse was to drive up to Madison and see for myself. However, the practice was extremely busy, and I just could not spare the loss of a whole day. Three weeks had elapsed since everybody stopped feeding calf pellets, and I must confess all was going well. There was no doubt that Perfection Calf Pellets contained a lethal substance. But what was it?

I returned home late afternoon to find a dream car—a beautiful blue Oldsmobile 98 no less—parked in front of my house... glistening in the setting sun. It was apparently new and had never been humiliated by washboard gravel and dirt roads. For one heart stopping moment, I thought maybe this was a prize Mary had won in one of those contests she had entered, but alas it was not so.

Seated in my living room were three gentleman appropriately dressed to ride in an Olds 98—shirted, tied and with nicely combed hair.

"We're from Perfect Feed Company. This is Bill Watson, Tom Evert, and I'm Albert Thompson."

We shook hands and I asked everyone to be seated. They declined my offer of cold lemonade, probably preferring something stronger.

"What brings you gentlemen here?" I said as if I didn't know. Apparently Albert was to be my chief inquisitor.

"How come you're telling farmers not to feed Perfection Calf Pellets? It's been a boon to farmers for ten years."

"You may or may not be aware that virtually thousands of calves are dead or dying from a mysterious illness in the last four or five months. The disease is present only on those farms feeding your calf pellets. I only requested five farms to discontinue their use, but the word got out and it seems that most farms have stopped using your pellets. I have no control over that."

"You have caused our company irreparable harm, not to mention the local feed supply stores," Albert said.

"Perhaps I had better show you gentlemen what information I have gathered."

I provided them with a summary of the disease and items from my notebooks and charts. It was Bill Watson's turn to say something.

"I can't see where you have made a convincing case against Perfection Calf Pellets. In your anxiety to solve what you consider a problem, you have made an arbitrary decision that this disease is caused by feeding Perfection

Calf Pellets. You have gotten yourself into a lot of trouble—expensive trouble. If you persist in doing what you are doing, you are inviting serious litigation. Our company can't stand by while one of their major products is being unfairly attacked."

Well this must be the lawyer in the bunch and he's really trying to intimidate me. "Expensive trouble" did he say? My legal innocence burst out of my face and I smiled at them.

"Do you guys really think that one little vet can be a threat to your large corporation? Let me tell you what else is happening. In the last three weeks, the death rate among calves has markedly declined, and no new cases have appeared. In about a week or so, I should have results of the calf feeding study from the University of Wisconsin and that should settle the matter. Meanwhile, you should go back, thoroughly analyze the ingredients that make up the calf pellets and the machines that make them. Something is radically wrong. You must find it. Meanwhile, pending the University of Wisconsin report, I suggest you recall every bag of Perfection Calf Pellets sold in the last six months. See that pretty girl peeking out from that doorway—she made the diagnosis."

Mary entered the room. "There's an urgent milk fever waiting for you at the Simon farm."

"Gentlemen, I'm afraid I have to leave."

I was glad to have some excuse to break up the meeting. We all rose, and with some muted goodbyes, they left.

"You don't have a milk fever," Mary informed me, "but the way you were telling them off, I thought you had better escape while you had your head. These fellows can cause you lots of trouble."

It was four weeks into the mission when I saw notices all over town, tacked to just about everything that wasn't breathing. The Perfect Feed Company was hosting a gala affair at a nearby American Legion Hall with a Professor from the university that had previously questioned the validity of my study as guest speaker. There would be free food, drink, entertainment and important information on Perfect Feed Company products. I knew that every farmer that was ambulatory would be there. When they ran an affair, it might not be the most elegant, but it was sumptuous. Of course, they would tout their products, emphasizing their effectiveness and safety.

The call that I was anxiously awaiting finally came. The University of Wisconsin had duplicated the symptoms I had seen by feeding Perfection Calf Pellets. The control group that had not been fed the pellets were perfectly healthy. Furthermore, they had subjected the pellets to a chemical analysis and found they had been contaminated with a lubricant containing chlorinated naphthalene, a highly toxic substance. They assumed that somewhere during the manufacturing process, the Perfection Calf Pellets were contaminated. The symptoms had been seen before, and it was called X Disease since nobody knew its cause. Finally, it was called Hyperkeratosis to describe the marked thickening of the skin.

I called Perfect Feed Company to advise them of the results of the study. They scoffed at what I said, but I felt sure they would look into the problem. They could not afford to ignore the situation.

I called the university I had originally notified and spoke to the Dean of the School of Veterinary Medicine, relating to him the findings at the University of Wisconsin. I also said that I deemed it inappropriate for one of the school's professors to plug Perfect Feed Company products, especially in view of the fact that their calf pellets had produced Hyperkeratosis in thousands of calves. He thanked me for the information and hung up.

Needless to say, the Perfect Feed Company held their gala affair—and the guest speaker endorsed their products enthusiastically. A good time was had by all.

Eight weeks had passed and Tommy had given up trying to lift Amy some time ago. The calf's growth had been phenomenal, and I advised him to switch his efforts to his Golden Retriever's puppies that were just whelped.

In retrospect, I must confess that Tommy's calf provided a clue to the cause of all these calf losses. All of Irwin Albertson's calves sickened at one time or another, but Amy remained remarkably well in spite of the fact that she was raised with calves that sickened and died. At first, I thought her good health was a result of the individual loving care Tommy had given her. However, upon questioning Tommy, I discovered that he did not feed Amy Perfection Calf Pellets, preferring, with his father's approval, to make a calf supplement he learned about at the 4-H Club. Unfortunately, I failed to immediately see what later became quite obvious.

Meanwhile, Hyperkeratosis faded from the scene. I did not see any new cases, and it was reliably rumored that Perfect Feed had discovered a gear in a pelleting machine leaking a lubricant. Undoubtedly this lubricant contained chlorinated naphthalene. I was sure the problem was hastily corrected.

Jess said the company had come out with a new improved calf pellet—"not that anything was wrong with their original product, mind you." To promote the new pellet, buyers would receive a free bag of pellets for each one purchased. The farmers flocked to buy the new product.

I remained *persona non grata* at the feed store, insofar as I had engineered a problem that never existed. What bothered me most was that a company can inflict so much damage on their customers and walk away unscathed. There had to be a remedy. It occurred to me that many farmers included in their farm insurance policies a livestock poisoning clause that would reimburse them for animals that died as a result of being poisoned. Here was a case of documented livestock poisoning if I ever saw one, and I would so testify. With a little coaxing from me, farmers began to submit claims. The insurance companies were overwhelmed with claims and, of course, went to the perpetrator—The Perfect Feed Company and finally to me. I presented the case for the farmers. If I had possessed a little less naiveté, I would have persuaded the farmers to retain a lawyer. A watered-down settlement was agreed upon. The Perfect Feed Company, neither denying nor admitting their guilt, assumed half the expense of the settlement and the insurance companies the other half. The farmers did not get what they should have gotten, but I never heard a word of complaint.

MISSY

We had seated ourselves for dinner and were startled by a pounding on our side door.

"Doc, Doc, open the god damn door," a voice demanded.

Mary gave a look that said, 'Why always at dinner time?'

I bolted from the table stumbling over Nicky who had begun to howl in response to the banging. Fang had already placed himself at the door as if to say 'Nobody gets past me.' I opened the unlocked door to find Roy Latt clutching a bloody feed sack in his arms.

"Caught her in the mower. She's bleeding somethin' fierce."

Indeed, blood dripped from the feed sack to the kitchen floor.

"Put the feed sack on the floor, Roy. Mary, you get my surgical kit from the car as fast as you can—and get the dogs outside."

The sack began to heave a bit as the creature inside stirred.

"What's in the sack, Roy?"

"Just my life, Doc. If she dies, I have no reason to live."

I looked at Roy's face. Ordinarily, he had a weather burnt complexion, but now it had turned to white ash.

With a hint of exasperation, he turned toward me and said, "Don't you remember? It's Missy. You spayed her two years ago."

I recalled the event—Roy pacing our living room during the surgery, dropping to his knees in prayer while Mary tried to reassure him that everything was going well. He was worse than any expectant father.

Mary returned with my kit and I groped into the blood-soaked bag in search of Missy. I felt teeth sink into my finger, but, weakened by blood loss, the effort was perfunctory. I located the scruff of her neck and raised her from the bag. She made a feeble effort to grasp the burlap in her claws, but Mary quickly released her grip. Shoving our dinner dishes away, one fell to the floor shattering. I saw Mary wince—it was her good china. It was immediately obvious that Missy had severed her right front leg above its elbow and it dangled grotesquely, held by a piece of skin. To add to Missy's problems, the skin along her back had been neatly sliced open as if she was about to be skinned. The surgery should not be a serious challenge, but the considerable blood loss had definitely put Missy's life in jeopardy.

Behind my back, I heard Roy sob.

"God, I just about butchered her. I shouldn't have mowed that field. It was too close to the house. I knew she liked to hunt in that field—often brought me home a mouse as a present. She was a sharing cat—Missy was. Save her, Doc. It's no matter of what she's gonna look like."

Snip, snip and the severed leg lay on the table. We all stared fixedly at the shattered limb until Mary removed it, placing it back in the burlap sack. Somehow, she felt Roy would want to bury it on the farm. Missy was Roy's Buddha and every part of her would be holy to him.

I had placed a tourniquet on the leg, effectively controlling all bleeding. With Mary feeding me hemostats, I clamped every bleeder I could find. Mary had sponged away the blood with kitchen towels and I began to tie off all the bleeding vessels with catgut. Bleeding from the laceration on her back was surprisingly insignificant.

Missy was probably a Silver Tabby. Her hair was silver with black marking—her eyes were jade green. She was a fat cat, weighing more than fifteen pounds. Roy fed her obsessively and obviously she was a good eater. Missy was not a barn cat that had to survive hunting mice and rats and getting hand-me-down skim milk from the milk separator. She was a queen and her one and only subject was Roy. Despite the fact she was fed a diet that could sustain three or four cats, Missy was a compulsive hunter. The joy of the hunt was in her genes.

It was obvious that Missy would need immediate surgical repair. Anesthesia was not an option, nor was it necessary. The cat lay on the table, mucous membranes blanched—comatose. Her survival was very much in doubt. She needed a massive blood transfusion—and quickly.

"Mary, go to my office and bring back some saline and dextrose 5% with a 50 cc syringe. Perhaps some subcutaneous fluids will help. Bring the small animal clipper."

I turned to Roy, "How about going to the farm and bringing back a couple of cats? Missy's survival may depend upon a blood transfusion. You have lots of cats around the barn. Being blood donors won't hurt them."

Roy was out of the house like a shot. I could hear his pickup wheels spinning in our gravel driveway as he got underway. Meanwhile I injected the saline dextrose under Missy's skin and Mary began to clip hair from the leg stump area. The bloodied hair once so beautiful fell in clumps to the kitchen floor. I knew how fastidious Mary was about her kitchen, but she would never complain under these circumstances. She meticulously clipped the hair from the extensive wound on the back while I threaded sutures for the closure.

Missy was still hanging on, but barely, when I heard Roy's pickup screech to a halt in our driveway. He rushed into the house carrying two feed sacks.

"Is she still alive? What did you do to her hair?" he said obviously disturbed by her appearance.

"I clipped it off so Doc can sew the wound closed. It'll all grow back, Roy," Mary explained.

'That's if she lives,' I thought to myself.

I untied one of the bags Roy had closed with baling twine, reached in… only to be greeted by claws and hisses. These were wild or feral cats Roy had brought back. Sure they lived in a barn, but they had minimal human contact. They recognized Roy and only Roy. I was amazed he was able to bag them. I looked toward him and saw that he had paid a price. His hands and arms were bitten and scratched, but he seemed to relish his pain. This was the first phase in his penance and atonement for what he had done to Missy. I dreaded to think how he would punish himself if she died.

It was immediately obvious that I would not be able to handle these cats in any normal way. Roy was willing to reach into the bag and drag one out, but I would not permit it. The damage to his hands might be irreparable. Time was of the essence if I was to save Missy's life. I loaded a syringe with 2cc of Nembutal, had Roy raise the sack off the floor, palpitated till I found what I thought to be the abdomen and plunged the needle through the sack into the abdomen, injecting the anesthetic. Roy and I repeated the procedure with the other cat.

I frequently examined Missy to see if she was still alive. Her wounds had not been surgically closed, but there was no bleeding. I doubted whether she had sufficient blood pressure to bleed significantly. Her heart rate had slowed and her breathing was exasperatingly infrequent—death was imminent.

Had to get whole blood into her immediately. I reached into one of the sacks and extracted a cat that appeared to be more in a drunken stupor than under anesthesia. I had prepared a large syringe containing an anticoagulant. The plan was to insert a needle into the heart and aspirate a syringeful of blood. The problem, which I hardly dared think about, was how the hell was I going to find an open vein to tranfuse the blood into Missy. With Mary assisting, we could find no blood vessel with sufficient blood pressure to accept a needle.

"Mary, clip the hair from Missy's neck. I am going to try a cut-down and expose the jugular vein."

I quickly incised the area. It was a simple dissection to expose the vein. Mary's finger pressing below the incision caused the vein to balloon a bit—enough to insert the needle and slowly inject the blood. Leaving the needle in the jugular vein, I was able to inject the second cat's blood into Missy.

To add to my frustration and exasperation, Roy had sunk to his knees and began to pray.

"Save her Lord. I shall ever be beholden."

He kept repeating his prayer over and over. His deep voice resonated in the room like a mantra, and for some strange reason, I began to find it comforting.

The ugly gaping wound on her back was more distressing to look at than the amputated leg, so I elected to close that first. I shall never know what was keeping Missy alive. It could only have been his prayers.

There was no way Missy would need a prosthesis, so rather that leave a dangling stump that would always impede her, I sawed off additional bone close to her shoulder. I padded the stump with muscle and connective tissue and flapped it closed with skin.

"Looks pretty good, Irv. You did a nice job. Come on Roy, look at Missy. See how well the surgery went," Mary said.

A look at Missy brought no comfort to Roy. He ran out the door nauseated.

"I should have known better," Mary said.

It was a terrible scene: Missy lying on a bloody table, most her beautiful silver hair sheared off and clumped about the kitchen floor, bloodied instruments and towels scattered everywhere and Mary and I standing over Missy with bloodied hands. It was no wonder Roy ran out of the house.

I gave Missy additional penicillin and dextrose and was happy to see a blush of color to her mucous membranes. The blood transfusions might have been a lifesaver. Fortunately, I did not have to worry about a transfusion reaction. Blood types are not as distinct in animals as they are in humans.

Meanwhile, Roy returned to the scene somewhat recovered.

"Is she gonna make it, Doc?" he asked looking at me intently.

"I really don't know, Roy. It'll take a couple of days."

I looked up at this man. He was six feet four, about forty years old, unmarried, lean, taciturn, stoic. Who could believe that his whole life revolved around a cat. His love for her consumed him. Meanwhile Mary had wrapped Missy in towels, placed her in a corner of the kitchen, and set about cleaning up. Roy sat on a kitchen chair immersed in his own thoughts, looking frequently toward Missy.

"Join us for dinner Roy," Mary said.

"That's very kind of you, but I had best go back to the farm and milk the cows."

I was glad to see that he had not given up on his other responsibilities.

"Roy, Missy will spend the night with us. She'll need some care," I said.

I saw him hesitate. "She's never been off the farm. She'll be very lonely."

"I don't want to upset you Roy, but her life is very much in danger. She'll be sleeping most of the time anyway. Call me first thing in the morning."

Roy approached Mary and myself, clenched my hand in his and startled Mary by kissing her on the cheek. A few whispered regrets to Mary about interrupting our dinner and he was on his way.

I bedded Missy down in a laundry basket and placed her alongside our bed. During the night, I would awaken to check her vital signs, and administer some 5% glucose and penicillin.

It was 2:00 a.m. when I was awakened by Missy stirring in the basket—she was making a vain effort to climb out. I slept intermittently after that, frequently awakening to check on her. Missy's condition remained extremely critical. I repositioned her body to improve circulation and stroked her gently to reassure her that she was not alone. I found her disturbingly cool to my touch.

"Is she all right?" I heard Mary ask.

"She's still alive, but feels very cold."

"Wrap her in a towel and place her alongside me in bed. How many times have I defrosted you after one of your winter night calls?"

I recalled those nights, shivering and chilled on my way home. The thought of lying beside Mary was always a big impetus to get home quickly. I had heard of women placing chilled, hypothermic puppies and kittens in their bras where the warmth and caressing motion of their breasts made a life or death difference. Perhaps Mary's body warmth would revive Missy.

I spent the next couple of hours in a deep sleep while Missy lay snugly against Mary's body. I awoke at dawn to find Mary and Missy asleep. An examination of Missy revealed her to be warm and comfortable. Now for the first time, I thought she had a chance.

At 5:00 a.m., I heard a vehicle enter our driveway. I knew it had to be Roy, but there was no knock on the door. In about ten minutes, Missy and I were down in the kitchen, and when the yard lights were turned on, Roy knocked on the door.

"Come on in, Roy," I called.

He quickly entered carrying a package.

"Is she alive, Doc?" he asked in a trembling voice.

"Come see for yourself. She's right here in the basket."

He slowly approached the basket.

"Missy baby, are you okay?" he murmured. "I'm so sorry I had to leave you last night, Doc said I had to for your sake. Don't worry about your hair. It'll grow back real quick."

He reached into the basket and began to stroke her gently. Missy made an effort to stand but the absence of her right front leg and general weakness made it difficult.

Mary was now in the kitchen and had begun her breakfast preparations.

"Roy, I insist you have breakfast with us—scrambled eggs, pancakes and hot coffee are on the menu. It's normal hospital food here," Mary said.

"I brought some food for Missy. Can I give it to her, Doc?"

"Sure thing, but hold her head and body up so she can eat it."

I was delighted to see Missy make an effort to eat and actually swallow a couple of spoonfuls.

Mitchell came down for breakfast and actually succeeded in getting Missy to eat some scrambled eggs and sip some milk. It was a happy breakfast and Roy, released from all his inhibitions, chattered incessantly. Roy had Mitch laughing uproariously with his funny stories about Missy and a cow whose back she liked to sit on.

"Well, Doc, gotta go milk my cows. When can I take Missy home?"

"Maybe tonight. She's not out of the woods yet. I see she can eat and drink, but I'll have to stop by to give her shots of penicillin for a few days."

Roy came over to Mary saying, "Thanks for the best breakfast I have ever had," and once again kissed her on the cheek.

I immediately detected that these 'good bye' kisses were causing Mary considerable embarrassment. Why is it that everybody wanted to kiss Mary? I think I understand why.

"I'll be back tonight for Missy," Roy called out as he left.

Mary, still blushing from the kiss, turned to me and said, "He's quite a lonely guy. I wonder if we couldn't have him meet Alma. She's a wonderful girl—lost her husband a year ago in that tractor accident. Wouldn't it be nice if they could get together."

Three months later, I received a call from Roy Latt to see an ailing cow. As I drove past Rod's pickup, I noticed Missy perched on the roof, tail tucked around her body, her left paw folded under her chest, surveying her domain—a world of fields, barns, sheds and outbuildings. Her hair had regrown and if she had a disability you never would have guessed it. Two other cats were basking on the hood of the pickup. I later learned they were Missy's blood donors—Roy had given them access to the house out of gratitude. After all, their blood flowed in Missy, and he was beholden to them as well as to the Lord.

INCIDENTS AT CHRISTMAS

It was late December, but the weather belied it. There were frost-tinged mornings and the rising sun in a clear blue sky warmed the shadows. The fields became soft and receptive before their time. The shroud of winter had not completely enveloped the landscape. Christmas was almost upon us and my hibernating town was bustling. Cars and pickups were returning laden with Christmas trees and colorfully packaged gifts. Residents were strolling through the town's abbreviated streets—it felt so good to be out and about in the balm of Christmas cheer.

I returned from farm calls in the early dusk of evening to see the flickering lights of Christmas trees decorating the front windows of almost every home. I entered the house still very much enthused by the Christmas spirit, to hear Mary say in an exasperated voice, "You only had three calls. Where have you been? You know I have to get the turkey roaster over to Tony at the school before he leaves for home."

The charm, the delight and the happiness of the moment sped from me with the speed of light. Her tone of voice irritated me.

"Where the hell do you think I've been—consorting with some farmer's daughter?"

That was a favorite tease of mine lately. I saw her flush, eyes opened wide with the glisten of tears to come. She was momentarily aghast by my angry response. I had hurt her and I wondered why I exploded in this uncalled-for manner.

"What's eating you?" she said softly. "You know I promised Virginia Van Larhoven my turkey roaster. All I want is to drop it off at the school so Tony can take it home. I needed you to stay with Mitch."

Tony Van Larhoven was the grade school principal, an amiable young man, and a disturbingly good chess player.

"Sorry," I muttered.

Even when I was dead wrong, I found it difficult to apologize. That was one of my father's hand-me-downs. Nothing more was said.

Mary grabbed the roaster and was on her way to the school, four blocks south on Main Street. I knew the Christmas decorations would capture her fancy, and the Merry Christmas greetings from everybody she encountered would be pleasant indeed. I was sure she would never for one moment forget she was on the outside looking in. At times I know she longed for the intimacy of her family and friends in Chicago. Sometimes when she seemed to be in a pensive mood, I wondered if she was dreaming of her life there. Was she unhappy here? No, I really believed she enjoyed being a vet's wife and raising Mitch. But there was the problem. He was almost four now, and I know it disturbed her to think of how few friends he had in town. Most of his social contacts were with Jewish children from the Rockford Jewish Community Center, where Mary and some friends volunteered to supervise a pre-school class on Sundays. There were no children playing in the streets—there were no small children in town—they all lived on farms. The homes in our town were mostly inhabited by retired farmers whose children were now working the farms and raising families of their own. Everyone, farmers and townspeople alike, were very friendly, but being Jewish in a community of non-Jews often made her feel isolated and lonely. The poignant Christmas atmosphere accentuated her moodiness. It was difficult to be aloof from the passion of the holiday.

Mary was gone at least an hour on an errand that should have taken fifteen to twenty minutes—tops. Just as I was beginning to develop some concern, she entered the house.

"What delayed you? I was getting worried," I said.

"Well, if you really want to know, I have been consorting with Pastor Winkler," she said mischievously.

"I don't believe a word of it. After all, the blood of Jesus does not flow in his veins and I know that would be a definite deterrent for you," I said.

"Funny you should say that. That's just about what he said to me. We had our rendezvous near the school. He said how delighted he was to have a Jewish family in town and how the blood of Jesus flowed in our veins. We chatted a bit and he wished us a Happy Hanukkah," Mary said smiling.

"According to Morgan, he's always saying that. I see no problem so far," I said, urging her to continue.

"He was about to walk on, but hesitated and turned to me, saying 'You know Mary, Jesus was a Jewish Rabbi and his blood flows in all Jews. You are a chosen sacred people. I cannot understand the hatred that lurks throughout the world.' Suddenly he came closer to me, face flushed, and blurted out, 'Mary, would you mind if I embrace you? It would bring me closer to Jesus.'"

"It's a good line and I hope you didn't fall for it," I said, shaking my head as Mary continued her dialogue.

"I looked at the Pastor intently. It seemed that in a moment, our entire relationship had changed. Was he making a pass at me? There was a fervor and excitement in his face. A red flag began to flutter in my mind, but his eyes signaled no amorous intent. Perhaps this man was indeed imbued with a Holy Spirit. I thought to myself, here we are in public, so what could be the harm? I turned to the Pastor and said 'Sure, but strictly in the interest of Christmas.'"

"You mean you actually acceded to his wishes?" I said, in disbelief.

"I'm afraid I did. The Pastor's arms encircled me. I could feel his open hands pressed against my back. He held me for a few seconds and the he released me with a sigh. Looking up at the night sky—almost ecstatic, he said breathlessly, 'Mary, this is the closest in my life that I have ever been to our Savior, thank you. It's wonderful that you are called Mary. May the good Lord keep and protect you and your family.'"

"Irv, I want you to know I was a bit flustered by this turn of events. Perhaps I had been indiscreet. I had permitted myself to be embraced and hoped this would end the matter, but the good Lord had other plans for me. Are you ready Irv, for what happened next?"

"I wouldn't want to miss a word of this Mary."

"Okay, you got it. I continued on to our little red schoolhouse where, much to my surprise, I found the walls in the corridors papered with posters dealing with the Nativity Scene, the Star of Bethlehem and the Three Wise Men. A beautifully decorated Christmas tree stood at the end of the hall. On another wall was a selection of drawings by children from grades one to four. It was interesting to note their emphasis on rural life—farmhouses, farm animals, landscapes, barns and silos reaching to the sky. One child's drawing of city skyscrapers piercing the clouds shows that even in this town there was a dreamer. In fact, Mitchell's drawings at home, show the rural influence."

"I then knocked on Tony's office door and entered. 'Merry Christmas, Mary.' Was his greeting, as he rose to kiss my cheek."

"I don't want to guess what happened next, but is another embrace coming up?" I kidded. "But go ahead with your story."

Mary blushed a bit and continued, "'Merry Christmas to you and your family, Tony' I replied."

"I couldn't wait to get to what was bothering me. 'Tony, how come you have religious posters and a Christmas tree in the hallway?'"

"'Why? What's wrong with that? Nobody objects.' he replied."

"'Well, Tony, I object,' I told him. 'Haven't you heard of the separation of church and state? You're the principal of a public school and receive funds from the state. Our Constitution, the Bill of Rights and the Supreme Court makes this very clear.'"

"Tony looked at me closely, the smile on his face quite diminished."

"'You're kidding aren't you? The children would be very upset if we did away with our Christmas celebrations?'"

"'You're missing the point, Tony. I'm not Scrooge, this is the law of the land. It was enacted to free people from religious persecution. Why do you think the Pilgrims came to this land? You cannot have a public school sponsor or celebrate a religious event, and Christmas is a religious event,' I told him."

"Tony was no longer smiling, but there was a twinkle in his eye. 'Tell you what I'm going to do,' he said, 'When Mitchell attends this school, I'll do my best to remove all the symbols of Christmas except 'peace and good will to all men.' Of course, we'll have to bring it up before the school board for their approval.'"

"'You're still missing the point, Tony,' I said to him."

"'I know exactly what you are saying, Mary. It's just that I have never confronted this issue before. Let me broach the subject at our next school board meeting—I don't plan to mention your name. They're wiser than I once thought. Maybe they'll regard this as heresy, and want my head. And maybe, just maybe, they will understand the issues you are presenting, and be sympathetic. In any event, I want you to know that I am on your side.' Then, as if to change the subject he said, 'Mary, Virginia called to remind you, Doc and Mitch that you're expected for Christmas day dinner. You're going to come, right?'"

"'As long as it is not at the school, we'll be there. Here's the roasting pan for the turkey I promised Virginia,' I replied."

"He rose, kissed me warmly on the cheek and said, 'Don't worry, Mary, I'll do what I can.'"

"I left his office with thoughts that only the future would sort out. To tell the truth, I'm worried about how Mitch will accommodate to life here. How will he feel to be the only Jew among these Christian children? What will school be like, especially where children have none of the inhibitions of their parents?"

The school only went to the fourth grade and we wondered where Mitchell would continue his schooling. There was talk about building a consolidated grade and high school on some already acquired farm land two miles north. In fact, Mary was on one of the committees, but that was years away.

We were worried about how Mitch would accommodate to life here. Would he be singled out as being different? Hell, it would be no different here than anywhere else. Jews are singled out everywhere they live—perhaps not in Israel though.

"Tomorrow, you, I and Mitch are going to pay our respects to Mrs. Hayden," Mary announced.

"But she gave us such a hard time when we first came to town. The woman was downright hostile. What prompted you to want to do this?"

"Well, I walked past her house this evening. There was a Christmas wreath on the door, but no tree in her front window. The lights were on in her living room and I could be see her stirring about through the lace curtains. I don't know if she has family to share the holiday season. Her neighbors say that she's always alone and wants it that way. We're paying a visit tomorrow—after you finish calls. She had disconnected her phone so I can't even call her."

"Are we just going to barge in, Mary."

"There's no other way. I really think she'll be happy to see us. I don't believe she'll see us as interlopers after all these years."

The following evening after my calls had been completed and we had finished dinner, Mary wrapped in foil angel food cake she had baked earlier, and we were on our way. It was a three-block stroll, the weather continued mild and Mitch was in good spirits.

I knocked at the side door and waited a full two minutes before a cautious voice asked, "Who is it, please?"

"It's the new vet and his family coming to wish you a Merry Christmas," I replied. Although it was four years since I opened practice, I was sure she would still think of me as the new vet.

"Why you're the new vet and you're Mary. And this handsome young man must be your son." She smiled broadly, her uppers shifting a bit.

"Won't you all come in?" The hinges creaked loudly as she opened the door wide, suggesting its infrequent use.

"I'm glad you remember us," Mary said. "I brought you a freshly baked angel food cake. Please accept it with our best wishes for a happy holiday."

"How very thoughtful and kind of you. Won't you come in?" Mrs. Hayden asked. Her demeanor was warm and friendly, in sharp contrast to our first encounter.

"And this must be your son... a lovely boy," she said, patting him on the head.

"How are you getting along?" she asked Mary.

"Just as you said when we first met—it's a difficult life, but we have adjusted. Doc loves it."

"When we first met, I was very rude to you young people and I apologize for it. At that time I lived in the past, not in the present. I think I see things more clearly now."

"Mrs. Hayden, who made that beautiful hutch? I can't stop admiring it," Mary said.

"That hutch was made by Dr. Hayden in his basement workshop. Would you all like to see where he worked? And by the way, Mary, please call me Norma."

"We'd all love to see his work shop, Norma," Mary replied.

"Well then, follow me."

We descended on a well constructed stairway to a basement designed and crafted by a master carpenter. The walls were covered with wormy cypress paneling, and finished with exquisitely carved moldings. Occupying a basement corner was a large workbench with all kinds of tools and drills hanging from the walls. Everything was in immaculate condition. Norma was doing a good job preserving his memory. In another part of the basement was an assortment of labeled kits for every possible veterinary procedure: obstetrical, bloat, colic, autopsy kits, all stacked on shelves at the ready. Wonderfully designed shelves supported all his medications. He had a treasury of antique glass bottles containing liquids with a rainbow of colors.

"What are all those colored liquids?" I asked.

"The doctor added color to all his liquid medications. A farmer need only identify the color for me to fill his prescription when he came to the house.".

"Absolutely remarkable," Mary exclaimed.

"It would take a vet and his wife to fully appreciate this place. When I'm feeling lonely, I come down here. I can feel his presence—it helps me to sleep. The nights are so long and I have never stopped bemoaning his departure. Tell me, what made you stop by?"

"To tell the truth, Norma, I was walking back from the school after I had completed an errand and was feeling terribly lonely. As I passed your house, I thought you must be lonely as well. I could not resist stopping in. Perhaps we could be of some comfort to each other. Merry Christmas, Norma, I'm sorry we can't stay any longer, it's already past Mitchell's bedtime."

"Please come back soon, so we can talk about what our doctors are doing—share their adventures, so to speak," she said with a smile.

I noted that Norma was speaking in the present tense. The reality of his death only reached her in the insomniac darkness of night. This house was his shrine, and she was the caretaker. The thought almost brought Mary to tears. Maybe she was thinking that this could be the scenario of her life.

Norma took Mary's hand in hers and gently stroked it. The contact seemed to bond them in some strange way. These women were the wives of veterinarians and had experienced the trials, achievements and frustrations that accompanied them on their daily rounds. They saw in each other's eyes an unshakable loyalty to the men they loved. I immediately discerned that this was the beginning of a very special relationship. It would be therapeutic for both of them.

"I can't tell you how special you have made my Christmas," Norma said. "You're an Angel, Mary, and how appropriate to bring an angel food cake. I can't wait to taste it. Next time you visit, I would like to show you what Dr. Hayden built for our bedroom upstairs. I'd ask you to take a look, but I'm afraid there's a bit of disorder up there now."

"So sorry you can't stay for tea. Go home, Mary. Try to be with your doctor as much as you can. Please come again and bring Mitchell with you. I once had a boy just like him."

As we left, we once noted the wedding photo of Norma and Dr. Hayden. What a handsome couple they made.

SUPPER ON THE PRAIRIE

I often gazed out at the landscape beyond my house and tried to visualize what the early settlers saw when they came to this land. It was hard to believe that it was once a countryside of long-bladed prairie grass, hardwood forests, conifers, and profusions of wild flowers such as geraniums, bluebells, bellworts, ironweeds, black-eyed Susans—remnants of which still remain. Buffalo, elk, bear are all gone, but white-tailed deer, pheasant, and quail still roam around.

The forty-acre field in back of our house was finally being put into corn. It had lain fallow for three years and used only as pasture for some Angus steers. Between calls, I would watch farmers' plows incise the soil, billowing earthen waves. Rows of sharp-bladed discs followed, slicing clods and clumps of soil into a lumpy, granular carpet. Finally, harrows raked the land into golf-course smoothness.

I marveled at the precision of the planting, the unerring straightness of the rows. There could be no random planting of seed. Tractors would soon thread through this field dragging cultivators that would spare the young corn shoots yet uproot the inevitable weeds. When the corn was ripe for picking, tractors tugging mechanical corn pickers had designated pathways through a field that had exploded with a hundred bushels of corn to the acre.

The corn planted in this field was a hybrid developed by inbreeding different varieties. Hybrids substantially increase yield per acre and tend to be more resistant to disease. The corn planted was field or dent corn—each kernel having a characteristic dent. Half of the corn grown was fed to hogs, cattle, sheep and poultry. Hogs probably eat half of this. Corn in one form or another makes up more of our diet than any other farm product.

As the days sped by, the corn grew with adolescent energy. "Knee high by the Fourth of July" was a popular way to describe corn's growth. The corn easily passed that goal, and by the end of August, it was "high as an elephant's eye." It towered above me, green and sturdy. From my upstairs bedroom window, I could look out at a Sargasso Sea of corn rippling in the breeze, its genitalia tasseling forth. The tide of corn swept onto the horizon and then scrolled beyond. On nights when the wind slumbered, Mary and I would stand quietly at the edge of the field hoping to hear the corn's sighs and whispers, its snaps and crackles. Farmers are taciturn, reluctant to tell you they hear voices within their corn fields, but after a few beers, they readily confess. Now after three years, I hear their voices. It made me feel that this is where I belong... this is home.

On moonlit nights, Nicky, our beagle, would entice our German Shepherd, Fang, to enter the corn field. They would disappear for hours. I could hear Nicky baying as he followed the scent of some creature. My dogs knew that wildlife were using this field as a temporary sanctuary and they did their best to make them unwelcome. Thankfully they soon would lose interest and their forays into the field would end.

One cloudy, windy day I stood at the rim of the corn field looking at the swirling leaves. I don't know what possessed me, but I entered the corn field and found myself gulped into its shadowy recesses. A canopy of broad leaves permitted slivers of light to penetrate as wind rustled through them. The ground was furrowed and the black, dank smell of trapped moisture from a previous rain pervaded the air. My shoes were muddied, but I squished along, turning in the direction of whatever caught my fancy. By the time I asked myself what I was doing there, I was completely lost. For a child, being lost in this jungle of corn could be a high-anxiety experience. An adult without claustrophobic tendencies should have no problem following a furrow and finally emerging.... After what seemed to be hours of wandering about, a bit bedraggled, I finally made my way out. If my neighbor Morgan had seen me, I would never live it down.

Some farmers had extensive plots of sweet corn and popcorn—totally different varieties of corn. They would call to tell us that their sweet corn was ready to be eaten. We would invite the corn aficionados among our friends—and that was all of them—to a sweet corn orgy. We never had a refusal or a no-show. Mary began to boil water in two monstrous pots, gifted us by a junk-dealer friend who lived in a nearby town. His capacity to consume corn was astounding, and I would say that those big pots were mostly for his benefit. While the water was coming to a boil, we would invade the corn field, pick a few bushels and hasten back home. This land was so bountiful and the crop so plentiful that farmers encouraged me to take all I wanted. After shucking the corn, the gleaming yellow ears were placed in boiling water. When fully cooked and baptized with a bit of farm-churned butter and a twang of salt, it was ready to be eaten. The ineffable taste of that corn is a residue of my life in the countryside.

Most of what we ate, whether it be fruit, vegetable or meat, was grown locally. Bushels of vegetables, apples, pears, strawberries and cakes and pies were brought to our house by many of my clients. The earth was generous to extreme, and so were the farmers. Those were the days when the palate was young and uninhibited by the admonishments of age.

Church suppers were sumptuous affairs. They were a joyous extravaganza of home-grown foods prepared with missionary zeal. The delight and animation with which these suppers were served made them a not-to-be-missed occasion. For two dollars you could indulge in the most munificent feast imaginable.

Most of what was served were from generational recipes imported from the old country—be it Sweden, Norway, England, Scotland, Ireland or Germany. There were gargantuan platters of variegated beans, diamond-branded roast hams dotted with cloves and pineapple and glazed with brown sugar and honey, mountains of Swedish meatballs in fjords of brown gravy, chicken with mushrooms in a delectable white sauce, pot roast, leg of lamb burnished with coarse salt and spiced with mustard and garlic—all delightfully succulent. Potatoes—scalloped, mashed, stuffed, roasted, fried and baked—were accompanied by farm-brewed sour cream and chives. Heaping chilled salads, tangy cole slaw, assorted farm baked breads, baking powder biscuits and sour dough rolls perfumed the palate. The inevitable bowls of steaming corn and the gallons of full-bodied, sensuous coffee blended with shattered eggs and shells, served piping hot in tall, spouted green-enameled coffee pots caused the table to sag. How did they coax that flavor out of Maxwell House coffee? The burnt sugar pound cake, pyramids of cookies precariously structured, assorted fruit pies—the rhubarb being exceptional—luscious rice pudding swaddled in whipped cream from Jersey cows, strudel bulging with slivered apple and golden raisins, gelatin molds with fruits and nut meats, and fruit cake crowded with colorful dried fruits culminated the feast.

"And what can we expect from you, Mary? We understand you're a good cook."

The church ladies had pressed Mary to make a culinary contribution to the church supper.

"We understand you make a caviar dish that's very unusual. Most of us have never tasted caviar; many don't even know what it is. Can we count on you?"

"Of course you can. I can't just come and eat your wonderful food and not contribute one of my recipes. If it's caviar you want, it's caviar you'll get."

"Mary, you want me to get caviar for maybe a hundred and fifty to two hundred people? I know those ladies have no idea what that might cost, but you do."

"Look dear, I'm not asking you to get Russian Beluga, just pick up some red and black caviar from Holland or Sweden. They sell it at the A & P in Rockford, and you'll find that it's very reasonable. Now I'm committed to do this, so please don't give me a hard time. It might cost fifty dollars, but maybe I can sneak you into the church supper without paying two dollars." She laughed happily.

I knew how much she loved making her caviar "pin wheels," as she called them. On milk-dampened bread, sliced lengthwise and flattened with a rolling pin, she placed a long row of green olives stuffed with either pimentos, capers or almonds, as the center for her pinwheels. She then placed chopped onions alongside the olives followed by black caviar. Next came separate strips of chopped egg yolks, red caviar and chopped egg whites. A last row of green colored cottage cheese, blended with anchovy paste, completed the marriage. Consummation occurred when the bread was rolled, jelly-roll fashion, starting with the olives and ending with the green colored cottage cheese. A long sheet of wax paper extending at least two inches on either end was used to snugly wrap the roll. After twelve hours of refrigeration, this special treat was ready to be sliced and placed on a serving platter. There were variations on this theme, but you have to know Mary's many-faceted imagination to appreciate them.

Off in a corner, I saw a few farmers, cups in hand, sipping something that didn't exactly look like coffee.

"What are you guys drinking?" I asked.

"Oh, this ain't for boys like you, Doc," Jim Cleary said, grinning broadly. It was said that Cleary had a still on his farm and his moonshine was much prized in town. He was a balding, square-built man with a booming voice.

"C'mon, what are you drinking?"

"Well, I'd like to give you a taste, but I'm not sure you're old enough. Maybe a sip would be legal, but first you ought to know what you're sipping. This here is dandelion wine, Doc."

"You're kidding me. You mean those plants I'm trying to get rid of, you're making wine out of them?"

"Not only that. See that salad my missus brought in—it's loaded with young dandelion leaves. They taste good when she cooks them, too."

"How do you make the wine?" I asked.

"Right away he wants to know my secret. All I'm going to tell you is that I make it from dandelion flowers. Here, take your sip."

I accepted the liberally filled cup and took my sip. It was very different from any wine I had ever had: It was dark, earth colored, with a wonderful full-bodied flavor. I drained the cup and pretended to stagger as I left.

I was making my third trip to the buffet and was standing admiring Mary's pinwheels when I heard a voice behind me say, "Those pinwheels are wonderful. I never knew what caviar was before tonight."

I turned to see Jess Waggoner extending a hand toward me. "You're okay Doc. What I did was not right. I know Perfect Feed would not have paid off if what you said was not true. I apologize. Come down to the store and we can talk about it a little more." He released my hand. "Gotta get some more of this great food before guys like you eat it all. See you soon." Plate in hand, he strolled off.

I felt I had consumed a liter of champagne. I was tipsy, exhilarated and couldn't wait to tell Mary what had happened. That disquiet I always experienced when I drove past the feed mill would be gone. The averting of eyes when I met Jess Waggoner in town would be gone. And maybe my heartburn would subside. It was fairly constant these days, and in fact, I was growing accustomed to it. Maybe I'd discuss it when I play poker with those doctors. I know one of the doctors has a similar problem. Perhaps he has a good treatment.

OF BLOAT AND MEN

It was a delightful October day. Everybody was busy except me. Farmers were harvesting crops, mowing, baling hay, repairing barns, sheds, equipment and doing other muscular chores. Except for Mary's personal calls, which came as regularly as the tides, I had that rare opportunity to be a forgotten man.

Adrift in thought, my mind wandered out to that world beyond this country. I gleaned a bit of what was going on after reading the scanty reporting in our local paper. *Time* magazine kept me better informed. When I think of 1953, I identify that year with Jonas Salk. What a thrill it was to learn that the Salk vaccine was successful against polio. I remembered my mother placing camphor around my neck to ward off infantile paralysis, as it was then called.

"Everest Conquered," read a recent headline. The height of that mountain, 29,028 feet, was indelibly imprinted in my brain. I had many times fantasized climbing Everest as a youngster. The Tibetans called it "The Mother Goddess of the World," and now it was finally scaled by Sir Edmund Hillary of New Zealand and Sherpa Tenzing Norgay of Nepal.

The Korean War had fizzled out and an armistice was signed at Pannmunjon. The guns were scarcely silent when the rumbles of a new conflict began. The North Vietnamese, under their charismatic leader Ho Chi Minh, were making life difficult for the French. Stalin died—a six-mile queue of people came to pay their last respects to the tyrant's corpse. Roger Bannister ran the mile in under four minutes. Impossible. My brother sent me J.R.R. Tolkien's fantasy *"The Lord of the Rings"*—wonderful reading in my spare time. A Boeing 707 had its maiden flight—I promised myself I'd visit the world in that plane someday.

Dream, dream, dream. I thought I'd read some vet journals, maybe listen to music or, better yet, have a catch with Mitchell. Where was he anyhow? The ringing of my phone startled me, even though I listen to it day and night and sometimes hear it when it doesn't ring.

"Hello, Doc. This is Laura Clifton. I'm looking out of my window and I see your little boy doing something real strange to your dog. I think you better look into it."

"Thanks a lot, Laura. I'll get right out there."

I wondered what had prompted that little old arthritic lady to rise from her rocking chair, descend a flight of stairs to place a call to me. It was obviously something very disturbing to her.

I hastened out of the house to find Mitchell doing something he had seen me do dozens of times—to cows. He had raised Fang's tail and was trying to perform a rectal exam, unsuccessfully I would say. The dog was standing perfectly still enduring another insult perpetrated by my son. What was truly amazing is how many dogs submit to these indignities without serious protest. I've seen toddlers pluck fistfuls of hair, pull ears, gouge eyes, ram fingers into mouths and hang onto tails as if they were water skiing. Fortunately, most animals are forgiving of these childhood antics. My animals were saints in that respect.

I had a serious conversation with Mitchell regarding his inappropriate behavior and warned that he needed a license to practice veterinary medicine if he were to further torture Fang. He said he would get a license next week. He did get a license, but it was twenty two years later.

"Hi boys, I'm back."

Mary had become, much to my amazement, the secretary-treasurer of our local credit union. She had just returned from a meeting carrying those enormous ledgers that she and the state auditor submerged themselves in twice a year.

"I can't understand these farmers. Why would they go to a bank for a loan at six percent interest when the credit union charges five percent? We have money for loans available, but nobody wants it."

"Mary, you must realize that farmers are pretty private people. I think a credit union loan tends to make their financial needs more public than they would like. But it's comforting to know you're so solvent. At least you'll be able to pay the three percent interest on the money I have with you people."

"Okay. I know you and Mitch must be hungry. It's way past lunch time.

How about a tossed salad and some tuna sandwiches? I'll be in the kitchen. Mitch, give me a hand. I know how good you are at making salads."

Mitchell smiled happily and in a moment they were off to the kitchen.

"Be sure to have him wash his hands!" I shouted after them.

They had no sooner left when I heard the phone ring.

"It's Edgar Crossman on the phone," I heard Mary call, "and he's quite excited."

"He always is," I replied.

Edgar Crossman farmed just across the Wisconsin state line. Although I did not have a Wisconsin license to practice veterinary medicine, I would foray across the border when called in an emergency, determining it to be legally permissible. Edgar was a blustery, irascible sort of man, pleasant when he called you but unpleasant when you completed your call. He had not paid his bill for the last call I made six months ago. In fact, I told Mary not to send him anymore bills, hoping he would never call me again. It was a cheap price to pay. He did have his own vet in Wisconsin who I am sure found Edgar as unendurable as I did.

"Hello, Edgar. What can I do for you?"

"My God, I'm glad I caught you. My cows broke through a fence and got into the apple orchard. They're bloated somethin' terrible. One's about dead and the others are gonna be unless you get here real fast. My vet is away at a meeting."

I knew there wasn't a meeting within five hundred miles. Edgar was a louse, but I couldn't slough him off. One thing I knew for sure, that no matter what happened on this call, I would come out looking bad.

"Okay Edgar, I'm on my way. Get them into stanchions if you can."

I forgot to ask him how many cows had bloated, but I knew he had a large herd. I flew out of the house and started on a high-speed drive due north on a gravel road. The road was good, the weather fine, and I was able to maintain a speed of seventy miles per hour, leaving a rooster plume of dust to settle on the bedraggled vegetation beside the road. It should take ten to twelve minutes to reach Edgar's farm.

Cows have a remarkable digestive process that enables them to convert large amounts of roughage into simpler compounds that can be absorbed.

They are ruminants (animals that chew their cud) with stomachs divided into four distinct compartments, having a total thirty to forty gallon capacity. The paunch, or rumen, is by far the largest. These animals consume their feed with minimal chewing. The food descends to the rumen to undergo mixing, maceration and fermentation. Portions are regurgitated for more serious mastication. "Chewing of the cud" is the term given to this process. After the food is processed through the second and third compartments, it enters the true stomach where gastric juices and enzymes complete the digestive process.

Hungry cattle placed in new pastures are good candidates for bloat. I had seen cows bloat on apples and knew that the fermentation produced enormous amounts of methane and carbon dioxide that animals cannot adequately belch. Often the passage of a stomach tube would release the gas, or a puncture of the bloated area with a sleeved, pointed instrument called a trochar and cannula. The trochar is removed leaving the cannula or sleeve, to permit escape of the gas.

In the distance, I saw Edgar frantically waving to me. When he determined that I had seen him, he started running toward a pen where he had herded the cows. It was a startling sight. At least twenty cows were staggering about, their left flanks terribly distended by the bloat. Saliva was stringing from their open mouths as they labored to breathe. Some stood like straw horses, feet wide apart, faces distressed. One cow had fallen down and was convulsing. The asphyxiating pressure these cows were enduring would soon be fatal. There was no way I could entertain passing a stomach tube or using my trochar and cannula. By the time I treated a couple of cows, the others might be dead. There was no other feasible option. I knew what I had to do. I reached into my autopsy kit and removed a knife that I kept incredibly sharp.

"Edgar, where the hell are you? I need your help." Nearby I saw him tying a short stick, using it like a horse bit in the mouth of a cow in the hope it would encourage belching.

"What do you want me to do?" he screamed, wild eyed.

"Edgar, I'm going to go from cow to cow and make a cut into the paunch to relieve the bloat. We don't have time for anything else." I could feel the tension seething within me.

"You try and steady the cows for me, but I don't think they will move in the condition they're in."

Edgar grabbed the head of a cow and I thrust my knife into the bloat area with as much force as I could muster. I knew it had to penetrate a tough hide and finally the wall of the rumen.

A geyser of feed and fermented apples propelled by the gas exploded from the opening. It shot up four or five feet and showered Edgar and myself. The bloated abdomen collapsed like a stuck balloon. We were completely drenched with this sour sickening material, and that was only from one cow.

"Let's get the next one, Edgar. We have to move fast or we'll lose some of these cows."

He immediately grabbed another and I repeated the procedure. In one case, the cow shifted and I got caught in the face with some of the exiting material. But I was totally undeterred. I had a mission and nothing could stop me. I wielded that knife like a crazy man going from cow to cow, occasionally slipping on the fermented mush that covered the ground. I thanked the good Lord for my razor-sharp knife and that miserable month I worked in a slaughter house where they taught me how to sharpen a knife.

It was over. Edgar and I stood back to view our handiwork. The cows were milling about ostensibly relieved. At the site where they had been stabbed, a fermentable discharge oozed out. It flowed down their left flanks like molten lava from an erupting volcano. I knew I would have to surgically close most of those openings. Certainly some localized peritonitis would develop, but cows tolerated these insults quite well.

"Let's get them into the barn, Edgar. Looks like they can walk fairly well. I want to get some anti-bloat medication into each of them."

Edgar opened the barn doors and cows filed unsteadily into the barn. Some of the cows staggered precariously, and Edgar and I rushed to support those that might fall. Usually a scoop or two of grain would await them, but eating was not their prime concern, survival was.

"Hell, Doc. I hope you didn't kill off all my cows. I never heard or saw the likes of what you done. I don't even know if I'll ever get milk from any of them, that's if they live."

"God damn it, Edgar, you have to know that most of those cows would be dead if I didn't do what I did. You're lucky just to have lost that one down cow. Instead of being grateful you're criticizing me?" I looked at him in disbelief. "Get me a couple of buckets of warm water with soap and a towel. I have to clean up."

His face was set in a scowl as he headed for the milk house to get the hot water. I knew that he felt he had lost twenty prime milking cows and that was an awful economic blow. I believe I had saved most of his cows—there could be some developing complications, of course, but all in all, these cows should be back in production in a few days.

Edgar returned with hot water, soap and a towel. The scowl on his face was now set in stone. I had my anti-bloat medication and drenching bottle ready to go. Drenching is the forced administration of medication. I like to use a long necked wine bottle, and I have often confused a wine merchant by requesting a long necked bottle rather than a wine. Being an intermittent tea-totaler in my early days, I discarded the wine in the sewers of Rockford. Perish the thought that my wife, who had been known to sip a martini or two, should imbibe the stuff.

Holding my drenching bottle in one hand, I grasped the cow's head and inserted the neck of the bottle inside her mouth. A cow, unlike a horse, has no upper incisor teeth. With the head tilted, the medication was easily swallowed. I gave each of the cows an intravenous sulfonamide and packed up to leave.

"Edgar, I'm going to leave those openings to drain overnight. I would not want any of these cows to rebloat. I'll be back tomorrow afternoon to close some of those openings. Feed them only dry hay and water—nothing else."

His fuse was lit; he was about to explode. He had not cleaned up and looked like a monster just arisen from a swamp. His eyes glowed. I cannot recall anyone looking at me with such obvious hate.

"You ruined me good," he hissed.

"It'll all work out Edgar. You'll see."

"A lot you care. Once you cross that state line you'll forget the devilish thing you done."

Now why was he bringing up the state line? This guy was insidious. I was certain he had formulated a plan to attack me in some way. He was sure I had mistreated his cows and had done irreparable damage.

Oh well, I'll give him one final bit of advice before I leave—just a little more coal on the fire.

"Edgar, do you know the first thing you must do after I leave? You should get out there and repair that fence to your apple orchard. I wouldn't want to do this all over again."

His fury reached a new height. I saw his face redden beneath his mask of fermented apples.

"I'll be back tomorrow afternoon," I said with some reluctance.

These cows needed more care, and I couldn't abandon them in spite of his hostility. Who knows how he would greet me when I returned. He might be waiting for me with a shotgun. I could just hear him say, "Git off my land or else."

I headed home for a major cleansing of the body and spirit, to restock my car with medications, and to confess my misdeeds to Mary. She had learned to view my besmeared arrivals without comment, but this time she looked concerned and said, "What happened?" I gave her the details and her response was 'I wouldn't go back if I were you. He has his own vet and he won't pay your fee anyway.'"

"I'm involved in this case and I can't ignore my obligations to these animals just because he is such a louse," I replied.

The next day I completed my morning calls, and after a superb lunch with Mary and Mitch, I headed for the Edgar Crossman farm. I approached nervously. No one was about. I had never seen dogs on this farm, so there were no barks to announce my arrival. Even dogs must find this guy unpleasant. I entered the barn and was pleased to see his cows eating hay. My presence caused some of them to pass manure and urinate—a very good sign. I immediately saw that someone had been here and had made repairs on my "surgical" handiwork.

"What the hell are you doing here?" His voice boomed through the barn. "Sneakin' in, are you? Afraid to face me after what you done to my best cows. I had a proper vet come and fix the mess you made."

"I told you I would be back today to close some of those openings."

"Well git goin'. I don't need you. I don't want you. Out, out, out," he yelled. The cows shifted nervously in their stanchions.

Mary was so right when she said not to go back. His behavior was not entirely unexpected, but it was a lot more than I could have imagined. I was not going to leave without a parting shot.

"Mr. Crossman, did you not call me yesterday to come as quickly as possible to treat some bloated cows?"

"That I did. But I didn't call you here to put me out of business. You ruined my cows. They're not giving any milk at all. My vet says he's never seen anything the likes of what you done. You botched the job."

"Is that what he said?"

"No, but that's what he meant. You boys always stick together, don't cha? Now, I ain't goin' to tell you agin. Git off my land—now!"

I was angry—very angry. I looked at him intently as if to say "make your move," but he avoided my eye contact.

"There's one thing I'm going to ask of you, Mr. Crossman. Would you be so kind as to pay my fees for yesterday and for that cow I treated six months ago?"

"You got a lot of guts, Doc. You botched that one good, ruined my best milker. After I'm done with you, it'll be you who'll be payin' me. You ain't got no business vetting in Wisconsin."

He had played his trump card to further intimidate me.

"Mr. Crossman, see that cow behind you. She's the cow that tore open her bag on barbed wire six months ago. See how nicely I sewed her up."

"Hell, she ain't worth a damn since."

"I'll wait while you go write me a check." I was fearful I was pushing this guy a bit too far, but I didn't feel I could walk away from his barrage of threats and insults without a parting shot or two.

"God damn it, git off this farm. Do I need my shotgun to make you move?" Well, he did make the shotgun threat.

I could just see the headlines: "Farmer Shoots Vet." I could not contain one final remark before I left—"Mr. Crossman, I'm going to notify every vet in the area what happened here. You'll be lucky to get a vet to come out, probably beg to have me come. If your bill is not paid in thirty days, I'll see you in court."

He stared at me, mouth ajar, unaccustomed to such anger. I was furious. Nobody had ever riled me up this way before. I turned abruptly and left. On my drive home, I wondered why I had subjected myself to so much stress. I knew it was a losing proposition and just should have let it go. When will I learn to follow Mary's advice?

"Hi Mary, I'm home. The guy threatened to shoot me if I didn't get off his farm," I blurted out.

"I'm glad to see that you didn't challenge him to a duel."

She seemed remarkably nonchalant about the threat to my life. Probably didn't believe a word of it.

"Almost forgot, Edgar's vet from Wisconsin called. He said you did a remarkable job saving that bastard's cows. His words, not mine. Doesn't know what he might have done in similar circumstances. He wonders why he called you instead of him. Says he was home. Probably figured he'd have to pay him and could get away stiffing you. Wants to get together with us some evening. He wants to meet the person that put Edgar Crossman into shock."

Then, as if the reality of what I had said penetrated her consciousness, she said, "Did he really threaten to shoot you? It's like going off to war when you make a call. If the animals don't get you, your reckless driving will. Now I have a third worry—some unhappy farmer may shoot you."

Mary was visibly upset. I never realized she had these concerns. For myself, I never gave it a thought. She was still a city girl at heart. Her husband was supposed to work in an office forty hours a week and spend the rest of his time with family and friends. I had never seen her quite so forlorn. I had to make more time for her, take time off, travel. Other vets did, so why shouldn't I?

"How would you like to go to Chicago next weekend? We'll visit your sister, take in some theater and eat at some of your favorite bistros. Mitchell will love it."

"Come on, don't feel so guilty. I really love it here."

"Mary, we're going to Chicago—no ifs, ands, or buts."

"Who will cover the practice?"

"Maybe the vet from Wisconsin," I grinned.

The smile returned to her lovely face.

"I must call Lilly to tell her we're coming, but before I do, I want to ask one question. If Edgar Crossman calls next week and says he has twenty bloated cows, what will your response be?"

"I have no problem with that question. Of course, I'll make the call."

"I knew you would. You're incorrigible," she said, and proceeded to kiss me hard on the lips.

"You stink of sour apples, but I love you anyway."

DR. MOM

My head ached and I felt flushed. It was 7:00 a.m. and I was still in bed, reluctant to move. Mary, Mitch and the dogs were downstairs and I heard their stirrings and chatter. The aroma of coffee had ascended the stairs and that was my incentive to get moving. There must be some calls to make—Mary would know. I would have loved to take a day off, but I never would consider that a possibility. I had to be available. That was my obsession.

I plodded down the stairs. My usual buoyancy had escaped me.

"Hi family. How's everybody today?"

The table was set for breakfast and the dogs were immersed in their feeding bowls too busy for even a minimal greeting. Mitchell was busily eating his Cheerios while looking at "Tubby the Tugboat" alongside his bowl. I patted his head, but his attention was unruffled. He was doing exactly what I do at the breakfast table, read. Mary was stirring some oatmeal on the stove. She turned and examined me with a clinical eye.

"Slept late this morning. You look tired—a bit flushed. Do you feel okay?"

"A slight headache, but I'm fine," I replied. "What do you have on tap for me today?"

"Well, let's see. You have a light day. Ernie Weber called. Says he got some stiff-gaited hogs—probably swine erysipelas. Jason Fuller called. Says he has heifers with some round crusty spots on their faces and necks—probably ringworm. Mike Stover called. Says his cows got blisters and sores on their teats and udders, and his cows are kicking him all over the place when he puts the milking machines on them—sounds like cowpox. That's it. It's a piece of cake. Take some swine erysipelas antiserum with you for your call to Ernie's."

I listened to this city girl rattle off these symptoms, make a diagnosis, even advise a treatment. She had come a long way. I had come a long way as well. I could not help smiling.

She turned and said, "What's so amusing?"

"I think you are ready to practice veterinary medicine. In fact, I want you to make these calls for me today. I need a day off."

"I know you're kidding, but I'd make them if only I hadn't promised to take Mitch shopping today."

"You win. I'll make the calls. Anything's better than shopping," I replied.

I had taken Mary on many calls to acquaint her with the countryside I loved, and the farmers and their livestock. She developed an interest in animal nutrition and I often had to go to Morrison's Feeds and Feeding, a virtual nutrition encyclopedia, for answers to some of her questions. I was often amazed to return from calls to hear her discuss something like the curing of hay with a waiting farmer. She had developed a consuming interest in all aspects of farming. I took her out to see large fields of alfalfa, explaining how it was cured. If it was cured when it was bright pea-green, it had its highest feeding value. She understood that exposure to rain during the curing period will leach out a considerable part of the most soluble nutrients. Occasionally, cattle or sheep that are fed good quality alfalfa as the only roughage will tend to bloat. She absorbed all this information and was eager for more.

The revelation that farming was such a labor-intensive business made her wonder whether some alternatives to relieving the seven-day workweek could be found. A wisp of a newspaper from a nearby town with its one and only reporter—editor, publisher and local postmaster to boot—excited her interest. Outside of a couple pages on local happenings, there was always an editorial on the positive aspects of the cooperative movement. Once the editor, Bill Boyd, learned of her interest, he was a frequent caller at our home. He was an indefatigable man, bursting with ideas... bubbling with words. To have a convert to his ideas was indeed a coup. The farm community ever respectful, generally ignored his message, often equating it with socialism or worse yet, communism. In this politically-staid community he was considered an eccentric, but to Mary and myself he was a visionary.

Nevertheless, his paper flourished. He knew his readers, and his newspaper always had items of interest that involved the community in many personal ways. There were the comings and goings, births, birthdays, anniversaries, deaths, news of sons and daughters away at colleges or in the armed forces, with special mention for their achievements, whatever they may be. In our small town everybody's name was mentioned as often as possible.

After a breakfast with frequent yawnings, followed by a two-aspirin chaser, I made my way to my car for my visit to the Weber farm. Arriving at the farm, I stifled a yawn as I shook hands with Ernie.

"Let's get out to the hog pens so you can see my hogs before you fall asleep, Doc. Had a big night, did you now? Now to these hogs. I noticed that some of them seem out of sorts—off feed, sleepy, a little diarrhea and stiff in the hind end just like me. Found one dead this morning. I got her over here," he said, pointing to a dead pig in the corner of the hog lot.

Sure enough his description of their symptoms was quite accurate. In addition, I noted that some had irregular red patches on their skins, especially on ears and the inner aspect of their thighs and groins. I took a few temperatures and was not surprised to find fevers between 105 degrees and 110 degrees Fahrenheit. Mary's diagnosis was probably correct, but I better do a post mortem on that dead hog for confirmation. I had to be sure I was not dealing with hog cholera where there is a very sudden onset, and often with very similar symptoms. My autopsy revealed a swollen spleen free of hemorrhage; the kidneys lacked the turkey egg spots seen in cholera, nor were there significant lung lesions. I reached into the abdomen to remove the stomach and in doing so nicked my thumb on the split-open rib cage. I stopped to wash my bloody hands in an antiseptic solution. I was not only careless but indifferent to any exposure to disease. This was the way the vets I knew were handling these situations and the "ignorance is bliss" syndrome was my lifestyle. I proceeded to open the stomach to find the typical paintbrush hemorrhage inside.

"Okay Ernie, looks like swine erysipelas. I'll give all your hogs some antiserum and if all goes the way I think it should, there will be a definite improvement by tomorrow. Get your boy out here to give us a hand and I'll start giving them their shots. Meanwhile, I suggest we separate the sick from the well."

I proceeded to give every pig a shot of swine erysipelas antiserum.

"Will stop by tomorrow, Ernie." I scrubbed up, disinfected my boots and was on my way.

My car now bumped along a lumpy terrain. You had the feeling that someone or something had dissipated the fertility of the fields. Every hilly area had those tell-tale wrinkles of erosion. The noxious weed, Canadian thistle, had invaded the soil, but no one seemed to care. I knew I was approaching Jason Fuller's rented farm.

Jason Fuller rented his farm from a retired farmer. He never had the money to buy a farm and did not have the good fortune to inherit one. From what I saw of his farming practices, profitability would be very elusive. Jason was in his thirties, a small, skinny, overworked man with an equally skinny wife. There was hardly a visit I made that I did not hear one of his four kids howling from the house. I had the impression that this family lived a troubled lifestyle.

A scrawny dog walked toward me as I got out of my car. The animal proceeded to make a few obligatory barks and then got down to the business of intense scratching and biting at a denuded, excoriated dry scabby skin. The dog was a dermatological mess from head to toe. The vicious intense itch of the mange mite burrowing within the layers of skin was probably the cause.

"Used to be a great dog. Not much good these days. I was gonna shoot him, but the kids like him even the way he looks. Heck, he got them itching too. C'mon Doc, I want you to look at these heifers. They got these awful round scabs on their faces and necks. Probably catched it from that damn dog."

Mary had made the diagnosis once again.

"They have ringworm, Jason, and they didn't catch it from your dog."

The heifers were in a cow pen munching hay. Large round asbestos-like patches involved areas around the eyes, ears, muzzles and necks of about all the animals. Daily applications of an iodine-glycerin mixture was usually effective, and Mary had seen to it that I had a supply in my car.

"Now getting back to your dog, Jason. He's got mange, and your kids probably picked it up from him."

"Damn him, I'm gonna shoot him sure as the sun comes up in the morning. Making my kids scratch and scratch—he was never good for anything."

"Take it easy, Jason. Come down to my office and I'll give you a lime-sulfur dip that should kill the mange mite. As for the kids, these mites don't like the taste of humans—the problem will go away by itself."

Jason, in spite of all his bluster, was relieved by what I said. He knew his kids loved this dog and disposing of it would demean him in their eyes. He cherished his children more than I imagined.

"Doc, I got a little problem with my chickens. Just take a quick look."

I was never going to be let out of this place.

Chickens were my weak subject, and I always felt somewhat quackish when asked to treat them. Okay, I'll take that "quick look."

His chickens were in a small enclosed area adjoining a chicken house.

"Now look at those chickens. Hell, they can hardly take in air. Damn, there's another dead one."

The symptoms were obvious. Some were choking, gasping and shaking their heads. The diagnosis was not so obvious. My first inclination was to dispense a sulfonamide to add to the drinking water and be on my way. However, I kept eyeing the dead chicken knowing in my heart that I should at least do an autopsy. It will only take a few minutes. That hang-dog expression on Jason's face suddenly made me feel very sorry for this man—four kids, one or two of them were always sick. How could a man like this extricate himself from his burdens... his poverty. Other than winning an Irish sweepstakes, his future was his children. Hopefully they would provide for him and perhaps he could bask in the joy of their accomplishments if he could survive that long.

"Jason, bring that dead chicken out of the pen and I'll open her up."

He quickly brought her out, set up a table with a couple of boards on two sawhorses and was off to fetch water, soap and a towel for my cleanup.

I slit the chicken wide open and began my dissection in the upper respiratory passages expecting to discover a bronchial pneumonia. As I opened the windpipe I braked to a halt. A pair of attached worms, male and female, "Y" shape in appearance, blood red in color were residing in the trachea. I had never seen this parasite before but I knew what it was—gapeworm. Blitzing through a book on poultry diseases, this parasite for some strange reason had caught my attention. Perhaps it was their life together in a perpetual sexual embrace.

Jason returned and I showed him the cause of the problem, but I had no idea how to treat the disease. I promised to call with a possible treatment. However, one thing he had to do was get his young, uninfected birds onto soil uncontaminated by the droppings of older birds. Curiously, infection is acquired by eating infected earthworms. Larvae can live in earthworms from one year to the next. Even young robins are susceptible by eating infected earthworms. The early bird doesn't always get a healthy worm.

This turned out to be an interesting call. Seeing those gapeworms was fascinating. Maybe there was something to this chicken business after all. I must remember to tell Mary to charge this farmer a minimal fee.

It was a bright, cool, sunny day as I drove through a gently undulating landscape to Mike Stover's farm to see what Mary had diagnosed as cowpox. I always looked at cowpox lesions with a certain degree of awe. To think that these pustules had the capacity to protect our civilization from a disease that terrorized, mutilated and killed untold millions. In the 1700s, forty million died of smallpox—two hundred thousand Europeans in a single year. In one devastating year two million Russians were decimated by smallpox.

Fortunately toward the end of the eighteenth century an English physician, Edward Jenner, observed a link between smallpox and cowpox. Jenner noted that many milk maids were apparently immune to smallpox, especially those who had previously contracted cowpox on their hands during the milking of infected cows. He observed with great excitement that a young milk maid who previously had cowpox did not contract smallpox after caring for a smallpox patient. Ridiculed by the medical profession, efforts were made to discredit his observations.

An outbreak of smallpox in his area prompted him to vaccinate his own child with cowpox, but cowpox, having only an occasional incidence, was not to be found at this time. Instead he used swinepox which was present, reasoning that it would be just as effective. Weeks later, he inoculated his child with smallpox and the child withstood the challenge.

The culmination of his work came on May 14, 1796, when a mother persuaded him to vaccinate her eight-year-old son with cowpox. On July 1, 1796 the boy showed no evidence of smallpox after being inoculated with material from a smallpox pustule.

This dramatic proof of cowpox to protect against smallpox was received with disdain and harassment. A leaflet was circulated, "Attention all residents! Do you wish your innocent offspring to take on the physical and mental attributes of a cow?" He was accused of spreading a "foul and loathsome" disease from cows. Jenner was not deterred. Further efforts were made to expel him from his medical society, but nothing could diminish the fact that he had discovered an effective vaccination against smallpox. He was on an inexorable path to medical immortality.

"Cowpox, isn't it?" Mike Stover said as I looked at some of the pustular eruptions on the teats and udders of some of his cows.

"Sure looks like it, Mike. How long has this been going on?"

"About a week I guess. It seems to be spreading around. Milk production has dropped off a bit and some of these cows are tough to milk. It must hurt like hell to put a milking machine on them."

The lesions were varied depending on the duration of the disease. The early ones were hot and firm to the touch. Others had vesicles in their center that had ruptured as a result of milking. When fully developed, they had a raised firm edge and a depressed center containing a scab.

I turned to Mike and said, "Cowpox follows a course and there is only symptomatic treatment. Here's a jar of zinc oxide to dry those weepy spots. Apply this mastitis ointment to those that are pus-like. You'll have to use a teat tube on those cows that fight the milking machine. The only consolation I can offer is that it'll all be gone in two or three weeks. Watch out for mastitis and call me if you need help. Try to isolate the infected cows—certainly milk them last and thoroughly disinfect your milking machine."

It was late afternoon and I drove home slowly. My headache had returned. I reviewed in my mind the day's happenings preparing for my debriefing by Mary. She wanted to know everything. I knew she was baking some angel food cakes for our Saturday night poker game. Friends were coming over to play poker this evening. A couple of medical doctors and their wives were regular visitors, and I had finally learned how to play poker. I was no longer an easy mark for these guys. They all hoped I would get a night call so they could accompany me to a farm. It was always a thrill for them to participate in the delivery of a calf.

Saturday night poker games were a lot of fun. The women joined in and played with surprising gusto, often being the big winners of as much as ten dollars. During the poker game, I became aware of a burning, prickling sensation on the thumb I had scratched during my autopsy of the swine erysipelas pig. As the evening progressed, red streaks formed on my arm and the lymph gland in my armpit became painful. I showed my hand and arm to the doctors and they made an immediate diagnosis—I had contracted erysipelas, or erysipeloid as it is known in man, from the pig I had autopsied. They wanted to give me penicillin, but I refused knowing how allergic I was to that antibiotic. They suggested antiserum, but I was reluctant. In any event, they said I would probably get over it in a few days, so I opted for the hard way. They said I should be sure and call in the event my illness became more severe. Fortunately, I overcame the infection in a few days, but I continued to work in spite of Mary's admonitions to take it easy. I knew there were many diseases lurking out there that were transmissible to man, but I had the immortality syndrome peculiar to the young.

THE FEVER

My head ached. Chills and sweats were my nightly companions. My energy was slowly ebbing. I knew I was feverish and my symptoms were getting worse. Mary had become increasingly concerned, but I assured her that this was just the flu.

"But the flu doesn't last for weeks and weeks," she replied. "You must see a doctor."

Expecting this illness to disappear, I never seemed to find the time to go to one. I found her persistence so irritating that I summoned enough energy to say, "Don't worry about me. Worry about yourself. You're getting fat."

I could be a louse at times, but Mary endured my criticism with silence and tears. She knew I was sick and decided this was not the time to be confrontational.

Some days it was all I could do to make my rounds. Fortunately, George Grenlund, a neighbor and retired farmer, was available to chauffeur me around. I'd slump in my seat beside him trying to husband my strength for the next demand on my energy. George was thrilled to drive me on calls and absolutely refused to accept payment for his services. The calvings, the bloats, foot rots, calf pneumonias, they all fascinated him.

"The only pleasure I get out of this is knowing that they're not my animals," he said. George's interest was extremely clinical and he deluged my fatigued body and mind with questions, questions, questions. I soon began to realize that my answers were to be his fee for driving me. This old guy had a lively, inquisitive mind, and thus began a process of educating George. In his folksy way, he picked my brains clean. He was remarkably strong and of tremendous help in restraining cattle from slamming my weakened body around. He would carry my equipment, hold I.V. bottles high in the air and virtually clean me up after a messy call.

He reported without fail to my home every morning, eager to begin our day. I had never had an assistant before, but to have one like George who was able to anticipate my every move was an unbelievable stroke of luck. I had reached a point where I don't think I could have functioned without him. One morning after a night of sweats and fevers, I just could not drag myself out of bed. This time, in spite of my protests, Mary called a doctor who had recently opened a practice in a nearby town. He looked me over and asked what I thought at the time to be a curious question.

"Have you ever been out of this country?"

"Yes," I replied, "I took a load of horses to Greece about five years ago."

"You know Malaria is endemic in Greece. As an army doctor in the Pacific, I saw lots of Malaria and you fit the clinical picture quite well."

"But that was five years ago," I protested.

"Delayed symptoms are not unusual. Come down to my office for some blood tests. Meanwhile, I'll give you a shot of an antibiotic, as well as a Rx for atabrine. We'll have you shipshape in no time."

In spite of his confidence, I was uncomfortable with his conclusion.

"What about Brucellosis? I see a lot of it in cows and must be exposed to it more times than I imagine. Maybe we ought to check on that as well."

"Most unlikely since I've been practicing in this area have yet to see a case. Come see me in a week."

As far as I was concerned, Brucellosis was an epidemic cattle disease in the United States in the '50s. In this area, using the agglutination blood test, I diagnosed the disease in twenty five percent of the herds. That meant that one out of every four herds tested positive, and overall, five percent of all the cattle in this area were infected. Brucellosis in cattle is primarily an abortion disease, with the abortion mostly occurring in the last trimester of pregnancy. If the abortion occurred in the barn, the fetus and accompanying discharge teeming with the organisms would splatter large areas. Similarly, the expulsion of a fetus in a pasture was equally contagious, often attracting the herd to give the fetus a lick or a sniff. My exposure generally occurred when I was called to assist an aborting cow or to remove a retained afterbirth. No matter how much protective gear I wore, it was almost impossible to avoid exposure. The bull is also a source of infection. He can transmit the disease during breeding or acquire it from an infected cow. Thus, we have all the prerequisites of a bovine venereal disease. However, with the advent of artificial insemination, this type of transmission was minimized.

To further complicate the problem, the Brucella organism is shed in the milk. Since it is customary to drink raw milk on many farms, exposure to this disease was inevitable. The Sears catalogue listed a home pasteurizer for use on a farm. Mary was often successful in persuading farmers to purchase one of these units. In fact, Mary conducted a campaign to educate farmers not to drink milk unless it was pasteurized. She spoke at the Home Bureau, the Grange and even 4-H Clubs. It was indeed fortunate that pasteurization temperature could kill not only the Brucella germ, but the tuberculosis one as well. Yet here was a doctor, practicing in a farm community where Brucellosis in cattle was commonplace, who had never seen a case in a man.

How could he not see a case of this rampant disease? Maybe he was treating them all for Malaria. At any rate, I was resolved to show him his first case. I must say that this doctor left a marked impression on me. No sooner had he left then I began to itch and scratch. My face and chest reddened and granular eruptions developed. If I felt bad before, I was miserable now.

I called the good doctor, and he informed me that I was having an allergic reaction to penicillin.

"Damn, I told you I was allergic to penicillin."

"I don't recall that, but you'll feel better soon. Call me in three days," and with that he hung up.

Meanwhile, I started taking his Rx for malaria. I should have known better because before long, I began to develop the skin color of a banana, and I don't mean a green one. His nurse informed me on the phone that my blood tests for Malaria and Brucellosis were inconclusive, but I must continue to take the atabrine. When my skin developed a lovely mustard color, I decided to return to my Caucasian roots by stopping the medication. I knew that at the present time, there was no treatment for Brucellosis, or Undulant Fever as it is called in man. Mary called our doctor friend in Harvard, but they knew of no treatment. The antibiotic explosion was just starting with sulfa drugs and penicillin, but they had no effect on the Brucella organism. Besides Brucella Bovis, there are two other strains, Brucella Suis, affecting hogs, and Brucella Melitensis, affecting goats. The goat form is the most virulent in man. British soldiers stationed on the Island of Malta were decimated by this disease as a result of drinking goat's milk. Hence the name "Malta Fever" given to this disease in man.

There was a program in place to control Brucellosis in cattle. It involved blood testing and slaughter of reactors, calf vaccination and common sense. How could a farmer buy a cow at auction or from a dealer and then introduce that animal into his herd without having her blood tested? As unbelievable as it may sound, they did it time and time again. It was as if they had never heard of the germ theory of disease. It did not take me long to see why some farmers prospered and others seemed to barely get along. I was always being amazed at how rudimentary their knowledge was of animal husbandry and soil. This heartland of America had a richness and fertility that could forgive abuse and neglect, but those days are numbered. In their defense, I must say that they work enormous hours, often seven days a week, without respite. Some of them are just too ground down by work to take advantage of newer knowledge or technology. Yet, it was rare to have a farmer complain of his workload. Their attitude to the seven-day work week was remarkably dispassionate. They accepted it as one would accept his or her bodily functions. You had to milk your cows twice a day, feed, clean up, plant and harvest. There was no respite. One farmer I knew made an annual trip to Chicago to see the Chicago Cubs play. Although arrangements to get away for the day were very difficult to make, I never heard him bemoan his lot. The only time I knew him to take some time off was when he lost his thumb in a corn-picker accident. His convalescence was a total frustration and he could not endure his idleness. Well before his wound healed, he was back on the job.

It was about 5:00 a.m. when I was awakened by my phone ringing. I reached for the bedside phone, toppling a glass of water over a host of paraphernalia that cluttered my night table. I had taken to smoking a pipe, finding it strangely comforting during my illness, and even that clattered to the floor, spilling its bowl of tobacco ash. When I finally answered the phone, I heard an excited voice saying, "Doc, Doc, are you there? This is Swan Knudsen."

"Yes, I'm here Swan. What's wrong?"

"I just started milking and all the cows are acting crazy. You think they are poisoned? Doc, please come out. Two are down and others are jumping up and down—bellowing. I am going to be wiped out."

This frantic description dissolved my fatigue in seconds. My mind raced with possibilities. Perhaps he was inadvertently feeding them a toxic weed mixed in with hay, or moldy silage, maybe electrical shock, perhaps some encephalitic disease. I've seen cows with rabies do bizarre things. But a whole herd?

"Swan, now listen to me. Listen to me. As quickly as you can, get all your cows out of the barn. And, oh yes, turn off all power. I'm coming right out."

My reputation in town for being a hot-rodder was totally undeserved. When my presence on a farm would mean the difference between life and death, I do confess to a hasty exit. On this occasion I did hustle. If I was sick, I didn't know it. My illness was discarded as if it were something inconsequential. I headed north on a terrible lumpy road, leaving a long plume of dust behind me. As I sat behind the chattering steering wheel, I wondered how I would have handled Swan's call five years ago. I probably would have said "I'll be right out" and would have broken a speed record to get to his farm. It took five years for my response to be, "Swan, turn off all power and get your cows out of the barn. I'll be right out." I know it does not sound like much, but I'm a slow learner.

I was rapidly approaching the turnoff to the farm, and in a minute, I spotted Swan beckoning to me. All the cows out in the barnyard seemed apparently normal. Two cows in the barn were down in their stalls. One cow's head was grotesquely locked in her stanchion, bloody foam oozing from her mouth and nostrils. A tuft of hay looking like a whisk broom emerged from the side of her mouth. She was obviously dead. The other cow had been released from her stanchion and had crawled to the driveway of the barn where she sat chomping on some hay Swan had given her. I examined both cows carefully. Apparently, whatever hit them was severe and sudden. I discarded the possibility of food poisoning or a galloping infection. The cows in the barnyard looked absolutely normal. Undoubtedly their milk yield would be diminished for a few days, but they'd be O. K. I examined the down cow. She continued to eat hay, totally oblivious to the dead cow nearby.

I have seen animals continue to graze unperturbed while one of their kind is devoured by a predator. This remarkable unconcern changes abruptly when their offspring are threatened in any way. Protective instincts are very aroused when it becomes a question of survival of their progeny.

"What's wrong, Doc?" Swan anxiously inquired.

"I think there must be a short circuit somewhere in the barn, probably in the milking machine. We'd better get Roy out here to check things out."

"When I think back, it all started when I switched on the milking machine. Let me get the wife to call the electrician. God, I hope my cows don't dry up. I'd consider it a kindness if you stay on a piece until he gets here."

Anxiety furrowed his face. Apparently he was not entirely convinced my diagnosis of electrical shock was correct.

Swan returned to the barn and said that Roy was on his way. Meanwhile, I decided to get the down cow on her feet. I noisily slapped her haunches and whooped it up while Swan pulled up on her tail. She made a half-hearted effort clawing at the concrete floor. A cow first gets up on her knees, raises her hind end, and with a little heave, she straightens her front legs and she's up on all fours. This cow had no neurological deficits that I could determine and should be able to stand. Swan felt she wasn't trying hard enough and off he went to get his dog, who he claimed was "the best cow git-er-upper in the county." I was agreeable to have Swan's dog give it a try. It was vitally important to get her on her feet as soon as possible. A down cow deteriorates rapidly. Swan returned with Jiggs, a sprightly black and white Fox Terrier, whose paws barely touched the ground as he walked. Jiggs knew his business well. The cow seeing the dog made an ineffectual effort to rise, flinging her head wildly. She was trying to tell Jiggs that she was not as defenseless as she seemed. Her head was indeed a formidable battering ram. Manure began to flow out of her like molten lava and her hysterical bellows echoed in the empty barn.

"Git er up," Swan ordered. Jiggs catapulted at the cow, nipping at her tail, her haunches and her hocks, while at the same time emitting short, sharp barks. The cow was terrorized. God how she wanted to flee this place. She made a tortured effort to stand. I pressed my shoulder into her flank and Swan pressed into the other in an effort to support her, but she finally crumbled to the ground panting, exhausted. I had an electric prod in my car that jolted, amid bellowing and screaming, many a cow to her feet, but it was obvious that no amount of torture was going to get this cow to stand. She had enough shock therapy for the day. I discharged stimulants and vitamins into her body in large amounts. I told Swan to bed her down and to be sure to feed and water her. Maybe her strength would come back. I'll return tomorrow to torture her again. I knew that the longer she lay there, the less chance she had of getting up.

Meanwhile, the electrician had arrived. He headed for the milking machine and in a few minutes confirmed my suspicions. A wire had indeed broken loose and was tickling the steel stanchions, sending an electrical current throughout the barn. Swan was lucky not to have suffered more serious losses.

It was barely 8:00 a.m. and I was overwhelmed with fatigue. I trudged to my car and sagged into the driver's seat. There were a half dozen calls to make this day that I knew of. I prayed that George would be available.

I was very uneasy, having put off a dehorning for weeks. Fly season was approaching and recently dehorned animals are wonderful feeding and egg-laying targets. Maggots spewing out of a heifer's exposed sinus is a disgusting sight. I like to see all animals dehorned. Those that have horns tend to be more rambunctious and have been known to gore farmers as well as other animals. A bull with horns is indeed a menace. Farmers being gored by a bull is not an uncommon news item.

However, I must say a thing in behalf of maggots. They do a good job debriding infected wounds. During World War I, soldiers with maggot-infested wounds often had a more favorable prognosis. In fact, I placed sulfonamide-urea bolets in the uterus of cows to prevent and treat infection, urea being the debriding substance produced by maggots. The trouble with maggots, though, is they don't know when to quit.

Overwhelmed with fatigue, my scheme was to have George and the farmer do the heavy work while I sat back and orchestrated this horrible procedure. As I sat slumped over the wheel, I became increasingly irritated by the thought of why farmers let their animals grow horns in the first place. It is so easy to remove the budding horns of calves—no fuss, no muss, no pain. Oh well, we all procrastinate just as I am doing now. How long can I continue to work before I am completely incapacitated? A tapping on my car door made me look up.

"Are you okay Doc? I appreciate what you done for me."

"Just tired, Swan, I'll come back and check on the down cow tomorrow."

In this state, I drove home. Mary, Mitch, Fang and Nicky were there to greet me, each in their own happy way. A large animal practitioner's life is one of comings and goings and his family is intimately involved in his practice. I prayed that nothing unusual or urgent was awaiting me. Mary had watched me slowly deteriorate in these last months. At every point, I had rebuffed her efforts to help me.

"Get back in the car," she commanded. "I'm driving. Harvey Martin is covering for you. And yes, he'll do the dehorning. I've made an appointment for you to see Dr. Countryman in Rockford. He's done a lot of work with Undulant Fever and has something new. There's nothing urgent and Martin will cover. You covered for him when he was kicked by a horse, remember."

There was no residue of protest left in me.

Dr. Countryman examined me in detail. He drew blood for the Brucella agglutination test and a blood culture. He had me wait while he did the agglutination test in his lab and, of course, the result was positive.

"You're a very sick young man. Your spleen is enlarged and you might be developing an endocarditis. But you're lucky too. There's a new drug out called Chloromycetin. Fortunately, I have it here. It's not generally available. I've had encouraging results with this product. Here's a week's supply, and I want to see you when you have completed this first course of treatment. And you are not to work. You got that?"

I nodded reluctantly.

If this was the good news, I got the bad news during my second visit. My response to the drug was remarkable. In a week, most of my symptoms had subsided and Dr. Countryman was pleased with my progress.

"Did you ever think about practicing with small animals such as dogs and cats?"

"No."

"Well, I think you ought to. You are extremely sensitive to this organism and repeated exposures could bring on serious complications. I strongly suggest you consider some other aspect of veterinary medicine."

"But there are vets all over the place with positive titers to Brucella. They seem to have developed an immunity."

"That may well be, but in your case, you seem to have an allergic response as well. The Chloromycetin will help to a point, but those further exposures could be devastating. You can't keep taking Chloromycetin indefinitely. That drug has had some very disturbing side reactions. Deaths have been reported," Dr. Countryman warned.

He was hitting me straight and hard. My mind was a jumbled mess of thoughts. Here I was doing what I liked doing and had been abruptly told to do something else. How many of us in a lifetime find a life that excites our passion and creativity? How many of us wake in the morning and sally forth, happily anticipating whatever challenges there might be? There were times I felt like a knight galloping off to battle with the forces of evil. I relished the physical hardships and loved those animals I ministered to. Now this physician was telling me to go to the dogs. I knew little about dogs and less about cats. In fact, dogs made me nervous, although I must admit that it was a dog bite as a kid that excited my interest in veterinary medicine.

I needed more than his word before I would pick up and leave. I made arrangements to go to that medical mecca, the Mayo Clinic, in Rochester, Minnesota. After being subjected to a battery of tests, I ended up with a physician who must have been Dr. Countryman's alter ego. He told me essentially the same thing but even more emphatically, if that were possible.

Perhaps I would go into small animal practice. What did I know about dogs and cats and the people who owned them? Not much. Instead of thumbing past all those small animal articles in vet journals, I would now have to carefully read them. My diagnostic and surgical techniques would require a totally different approach. The thought of starting over churned within me and I was uncomfortable.

During my illness, Mary seemed to be increasingly withdrawn. Her concern for me seemed to stifle her outgoing nature. One day her thoughts burst from her in a torrent.

"Our life here has been wonderful, but we've got to get on with it. It will also be better for Mitch and better for me. There's no way I can permit you to stay on with your medical problems."

In her effort to persuade me to leave farm practice, she was resorting to another tactic: it would be good for her and Mitch. I must confess that in our talks together, I perceived a change in her outlook. It all started last Christmas. A sense of isolation and loneliness began to consume her. She discovered that she was not really part of the community in which she lived. Although she was active, involved, she was not included in the camaraderie that existed among the townspeople. It seemed that she still had horns, and everybody was aware of them. The discrimination was subtle, but it was there. God, how she missed her family and friends.

As for me, I was totally immersed in practice, unaware of the loneliness that had rooted within her. If not for my illness, she would never have given me an inkling of how she felt. She knew that I was supremely happy in my work, and would never allow herself to suggest that life here was anything but completely fulfilling. But where in this world was life completely fulfilling? As long as we were together—that was the important thing. Now that my life was threatened, she felt obligated to insist that we move on.

I was feeling pretty good and resumed practice. My impulse was to challenge the advice of Dr. Countryman and the Mayo doctors, but I had to think of Mary and Mitch.

I had taken to parking on a tree-shaded knoll, getting out of my car, and gazing down on the grain and grass carpeted landscape that was so embedded into my life. With the advance of my illness, I developed a morbid interest in where I wanted to be buried. This was the place, this knoll, under these trees—'*Oh bury me on the lone prairie, where the coyotes howl and the wind blows free.*' There are no coyotes and barely any prairie, but the wind still blows free. I wonder who owns my future gravesite?

What about Mary and Mitch? We were expecting a baby in January. Must Mary once again endure the uncertainty of getting to a hospital as she did with Mitch? She adamantly refused having her baby in Chicago as her sister suggested. Mitch was about to enter school. Wouldn't he be happier studying amid diversity rather than this static rural environment? Our school did not have even a minimal library... not even an encyclopedia. As a youngster I had lived in libraries—they were enchanted places.

I placed an ad in the veterinary journal—'Busy large animal practice with home for sale,' and sat back to wait for a response. It was soon forthcoming. A young vet from Iowa was coming with his wife to see the practice. They had the same enthusiasm that we had—loved the house, the town and the countryside, not to mention the busy practice. A deal was struck and they would take over in three months.

I could not believe what had happened. I felt ripped asunder. With the stroke of my pen, I had signed away the life that I loved. The romance was over.

I answered an ad in my veterinary journal for an associate in a small animal practice on Long Island, New York. I flew to New York for an interview and, in spite of my lack of small animal experience, was offered the position. My brother relieved some of my concerns when he offered to find suitable living quarters in the area where I was to be employed.

An afternoon spent with my parents found them delirious with joy at my homecoming. A cloudburst of relatives and friends made the occasion especially poignant. My father had mellowed and my being a pig doctor was not the anathema it once was. I was elevated in his esteem when I told him I was going to be a dog doctor.

I returned to the house that was no longer our home and set about to make the painful preparations for our move. The heartwarming response of the community brought tears to our eyes. Friends were in a state of shock, especially when they heard about the seriousness of my illness. With the arrival of their next milk checks, my clients descended upon Mary *en masse* to pay whatever fees were owed for my services. Of the six thousand dollars outstanding—a considerable sum of money in those days—all but two hundred dollars was paid. The person who owed the two hundred dollars promised to pay his bill at a future date, but I assured him it was not necessary. For him the money might make the difference in the amount of food and clothing he could provide for his four children.

The outpouring of concern and good wishes for our future amazed us. Although my clients and friends indicated their sense of loss about our departure, the loss was more ours than theirs.

Jack and Emma Whitehead came over to express their good wishes and say goodbye. Jack said that in small animal practice I would no longer be dealing with the economic value of an animal to determine treatment... the human bond would now be an ever-present factor. That thought excited me. There was a new set of criteria to be considered, and I began to see a whole array of positive aspects to working with small animals.

The wrenching experience of destroying an animal because it had no economic viability would be over. Only humane considerations would determine treatment... so I naively thought. I was yet to discover that economics would still be a factor, often coupled with cruelty and indifference. Yet, in my small way, I would play a role in determining an animal's life or death... the preservation of its life would always be my goal.

I had loaded the car with our personal effects the day before, and after a sleepless night, Mary and I were ready to leave. The morning mists awaited the sunrise and darkness was once again undergoing its metamorphosis as I carried a sleepy Mitchell to the car. Mary and Faggy followed. Hand in hand we stood under our black walnut tree gazing at the house that held within its silence all those memories.

If there is one thing I will always treasure as a consequence of my years here, it is a reverence for all animals. Hopefully my legacy to the farmers will be an increased gentleness and concern for their animals.

"Let's go dear. It's just too painful standing here," Mary said gently.

That was the nudge I needed to finally get us on our way. Still I dawdled, deciding to drive the long way on my beloved country roads to the highway going east. Morning milking completed, cows were already grazing the dew-moistened pasture.

Perhaps what I shall miss most are the sights and sounds of the very scene I am looking at now. If only I could bottle its essence and sip from it in the insomniac darkness of the night. I shall always hear their voices... their resonant *vibratos*... their *basso profundos*... wafting over the field as if it were a stupendous cathedral.

As the sun was rising, skimming the landscape with its gentle light, my rear view mirror held a portrait of clear, glistening fields, while ahead stretched the glistening possibilities of what our future might be.